"Reading this book, one understands how Ignatius of Loyola's words are true for Pope Francis: 'it is not much knowledge that fills and satisf[...] soul but feeling and tasting inward.' *Discovering Pope Fra[...]* as for Dostoevsky, Bergoglio's logic is not rig[...] elastic, alive. It never loses sight of the h[...] how his way of thinking liberates the ene[...] logos that balances a deep connection and [...] theological and ecclesial traditions of the Cl[...] commitment to reality and all its challenges [...]

— Fr. Antonio Spadaro, SJ, editor-in-chi[...] [...]*la Cattolica*

"Pope Francis has said that ours is not an age of change, but a change of age. In this important collection, we see how the Holy Father is drawing creatively from a range of thinkers and movements—European and Latin American—to bring the people of this age to a new encounter with Jesus Christ and the mercy of God. May these fine essays inspire deeper reflection on the Church's evangelical imperative and the urgency of our calling to be missionary disciples in these times."

— Most Reverend José H. Gomez
Archbishop of Los Angeles

"This work is certainly an excellent interpretation of the 'Theology of the People,' from different people, and for all the people. It is an effective demonstration of a true sign of the times: the catholicity of the theological-pastoral message of Pope Francis. The point of view of each one of the authors is the incarnation of his missionary imprint and a sign of an outgoing Church."

— Emilce Cuda, Argentinian theologian and author of *Para leer a Francisco. Teologia, etica y politica* and *Catolicismo y Democracia en Estados Unidos*

"*Discovering Pope Francis* offers a much-needed panorama of voices necessary to understand the theological roots of a pontificate—roots that are not only in Latin America but also found in 20th-century French (Gaston Fessard and Henri de Lubac) and German-speaking theology (Hans Urs von Balthasar and Romano Guardini). This book provides an appreciation of this pontificate coming from authors who cannot be labeled as 'liberal Catholics.' It is a remarkable contribution because it fills a lacuna in the literature on Pope Francis who is still too often framed, especially in the USA, in purely political and ideological terms."

— Massimo Faggioli, coeditor, *Pope Francis: A Voice for Mercy, Justice, Love, and Care for the Earth*

Discovering Pope Francis

The Roots of Jorge Mario Bergoglio's Thinking

Edited by
Brian Y. Lee and Rev. Thomas L. Knoebel

LITURGICAL PRESS
ACADEMIC

Collegeville, Minnesota
www.litpress.org

1   2   3   4   5   6   7   8   9

Library of Congress Cataloging-in-Publication Data

Names: Lee, Brian Yong, editor.
Title: Discovering Pope Francis : the roots of Jorge Mario Bergoglio's thinking / [edited by] Brian Y. Lee and Rev. Thomas L. Knoebel.
Description: Collegeville : Liturgical Press, 2019. | Includes bibliographical references and index.
Identifiers: LCCN 2019012423 (print) | LCCN 2019017834 (ebook) | ISBN 9780814685280 (eBook) | ISBN 9780814685044 (pbk.)
Subjects: LCSH: Francis, Pope, 1936–
Classification: LCC BX1378.7 (ebook) | LCC BX1378.7 .D57 2019 (print) | DDC 28/2.092—dc23
LC record available at https://lccn.loc.gov/2019012423

This book is dedicated to our Holy Father, Pope Francis. May the Lord Jesus continue to guide your way and grant you the wisdom of his Sacred Heart as you shepherd the holy, faithful people of God.

Contents

PART TWO
European Theology

PART THREE
A North American Theology of the People

Papal Blessing

3339 MASSACHUSETTS AVENUE, N.W.
WASHINGTON, D.C. 20008-3610

Apostolic Nunciature
United States of America

Prot. N. 6878/18   September 27, 2018

Your Excellency,

I have been asked by the Secretariat of State to transmit to you the following papal message on the occasion of an International Symposium entitled *Discovering Pope Francis: Theological, Philosophical, Cultural and Spiritual Perspectives*:

The Most Reverend Jerome E. Listecki
Archbishop of Milwaukee

His Holiness Pope Francis was pleased to learn of the International Symposium entitled Discovering Pope Francis; Theological, Philosophical, Cultural and Spiritual Perspectives *sponsored by Sacred Heart Seminary and School of Theology from 8 to 11 October 2018, and he sends warm greetings to all gathered for this event. As participants reflect on the theme of the Symposium, His Holiness prays that this gathering may contribute to the advancement of a spirit of missionary discipleship, a commitment to serve human dignity and the common good and the zeal to proclaim the joy of the Gospel to local communities and to the global human family. Upon all present Pope Francis invokes Almighty God's blessings of wisdom and strength.*

> *Cardinal Pietro Parolin*
> *Secretary of State*

With cordial regards and prayerful best wishes, I am

Sincerely yours in Christ,

+ Christophe Pierre
Apostolic Nuncio

Most Reverend Jerome E. Listecki
Archbishop of Milwaukee
P.O. Box 70912
Milwaukee WI 53207-0912

Papal Foreword

Presentación

En el ensayo "Teología y Santidad," Hans Urs von Balthasar escribe que "El Cristiano [no] necesita salir de su centro en Cristo con el fin de mediar en el mundo, para comprender su relación con el mundo, para construir un puente entre la revelación y naturaleza, filosofía y teología. . . . En esto los santos son plenamente conscientes. Ellos nunca, en ningún momento abandonan su centro en Cristo. . . . cuando ellos filosofan lo hacen como cristianos, lo que significa como creyentes, como teólogos."

La idea sobre el gran teólogo suizo vino a mi mente al presentar esta colección de documentos, los cuales son el fruto de un simposio internacional de cuatro días organizado por el Seminario y Escuela de Teología Sagrado Corazón de Jesús en Hales Corners, Wisconsin en octubre del 2018. Filósofos y teólogos de tres continentes, unidos en su fe común en Cristo y en la comunión con el Sucesor de San Pedro, vinieron juntos a explorar, como eruditos y creyentes, las formas de llevar la alegría del Evangelio, "que llena los corazones de todos los que se encuentran a Jesús" en el mundo.

Esta colección trae al mundo anglófono la riqueza de las ideas de hombres y mujeres que influyeron mi propio desarrollo espiritual, teológico, y filosófico. Estamos experimentando y viviendo un verdadero cambio de época con cambios culturales y tecnológicos que han marcado este periodo de la historia, haciendo que la transmisión de la fe sea cada vez más difícil. Precisamente en este tiempo, por el bien de la evangelización, los teólogos y filósofos deben comprometerse en investigar, dialogar y sobre todo en orar para desarrollar una síntesis creativa que proponga el atractivo de Cristo para el mundo que necesita desesperadamente de su misericordia. Muchos de los ensayos recogidos aquí resaltan también la síntesis única de fe, políticas y cultura que ha ocurrido en el continente Latinoamericano, el cual en este momento de la historia puede ser un servicio a la misión universal de la Iglesia en obediencia al mandamiento de Cristo de hacer discípulos de todas las naciones.

Ha sido muy apropiado que el mencionado simposio se celebrara en un seminario y escuela de teología, bajo el auspicio de los Sacerdotes del Sagrado Corazón, quienes devotamente se han dedicado a la Eucaristía y dar a conocer la justicia y la misericordia de Dios. Un seminario y escuela de teología es no solo un lugar donde los seminaristas, religiosos, hombres y mujeres pueden venir juntos para conocer a Dios a través del estudio (*ad Deum per scientiam*), sino también es una comunidad de fe reunidos para adorar, produciendo una "teología de rodillas" (*kniende Theologie*), como el santo y fiel pueblo de Dios.

La colección que ahora se publica es entonces el fruto de un encuentro, no solo de teólogos y filósofos, clérigos y laicos, sino también de personas y culturas. En estos ensayos uno no puede dejar de pensar en el encuentro primario, el encuentro con Cristo. Nunca me canso de repetir esas palabras de Benedicto XVI que nos lleva al corazón del Evangelio: "Ser cristiano no es el resultado de una elección ética o una idea noble, sino el encuentro con un acontecimiento, una persona, que le da a la vida un nuevo horizonte y una nueva dirección."

Espero que, a través de estos ensayos, los lectores encuentren a Cristo para que se abran nuevos horizontes.

Vaticano, 15 de marzo de 2019

Translation of Papal Foreword

In his essay "Theology and Sanctity," Hans Urs von Balthasar wrote that "the Christian [does not] need to leave his center in Christ in order to mediate him to the world, to understand his relation to the world, to build a bridge between revelation and nature, philosophy and theology. . . . This is what the saints are fully aware of. They never at any moment leave their center in Christ. . . . When they philosophize, they do so as Christians, which means as believers, as theologians."

This insight of the great Swiss theologian came to mind upon being presented with this collection of papers, the fruit of a four-day international symposium hosted by Sacred Heart Seminary and School of Theology in Hales Corners, Wisconsin in October 2018. Philosophers and theologians from three continents, united in their common faith in Christ and in communion with the Successor of Saint Peter, came together to explore, as scholars and believers, ways of bringing the joy of the Gospel, which "fills the hearts of all who encounter Jesus" to the world.

This collection brings to the English-speaking world the richness of the ideas of the men and women who influenced my own spiritual, theological, and philosophical development. We are living and experiencing a true change of epoch, and the cultural and technological shifts which have marked this period of history have made the transmission of faith increasingly difficult. Precisely at this time, for the sake of evangelization, theologians and philosophers must engage in research, dialogue, and, above all, in prayer to develop a creative synthesis that proposes the attractiveness of Christ to a world that desperately needs his mercy. Many of the essays collected here also

highlight the unique synthesis of faith, politics, and culture that occurred on the Latin American continent, which, at this moment in
history, can be of service to the universal mission of the Church in
obedience to the commandment of Christ to make disciples of all the
nations.

It was quite fitting that such a symposium should be held at a
seminary and school of theology, under the auspices of the Priests of
the Sacred Heart, who devote themselves to the Eucharist and to
making known God's justice and mercy. A seminary and school of
theology is not only a place where seminarians, religious, men and
women can come together to know God through study (*ad Deum per
scientiam*), but it is also a community of faith, which gathers in worship, producing a theology "on its knees" (*kniende Theologie*), as the
holy, faithful, people of God.

Thus, this collection, which is now being published, is the fruit of
an encounter—of theologians and philosophers, of clergy and laity,
and of peoples and cultures. In these essays, one cannot help but
think of the primary encounter—the encounter with Christ. I never
tire of repeating those words of Benedict XVI which takes us to the
heart of the Gospel: "Being a Christian is not the result of an ethical
choice or a lofty idea, but the encounter with an event, a person,
which gives life a new horizon and a decisive direction."

It is my sincere hope that through these essays, readers will encounter Christ and that new horizons will be opened.

Vatican, March 15, 2019
Francis

Foreword

Archbishop Christophe Pierre
Apostolic Nuncio to the United States

My Dear Friends in Christ,

As the Apostolic Nuncio, the Holy Father's representative to the United States, I want to express His Holiness's spiritual closeness and paternal affection for all those who read these pages seeking to deepen your understanding of the theological, philosophical, and spiritual underpinnings of Pope Francis, who has guided the church for more than six years at the time of my writing. I am particularly grateful to Father Tom Knoebel, the President and Rector here at Sacred Heart Seminary and School of Theology, as well as to the outstanding faculty and staff here. This symposium had its origins during my visit here in November 2017 to give the Dehon Lecture. At that time, I began speaking with the faculty about how few people really understood the thought of Pope Francis and how necessary it was for the church in the United States to grasp this for the mission of evangelization. A year later, I was pleased to see the hard work of so many come to fruition in the symposium, *Discovering Pope Francis*,[1] which features many of the world's leading experts in the thought of Pope Francis. Today I am glad to see it made available in book

---

[1] "Discovering Pope Francis: Theological, Philosophical, Cultural, and Spiritual Perspectives," held at Sacred Heart Seminary and School of Theology in Hales Corners, WI, October 8–11, 2018.

form to a wider audience through the editorial work of Fr. Knoebel and Dr. Brian Lee and with the help of Liturgical Press.

As I have traveled around the United States over the last two years, many people have described the pope as one who does not leave us indifferent. By his words and gestures, Pope Francis conveys to many the tenderness and mercy of God. His charisma and his attentiveness, not just to the small things in life but also to people at the margins, have left a lasting impression upon the people of this country and the world.

Nevertheless, many people have asked, "Who is Pope Francis?" Some answers were obvious. He is a Jesuit. He is a Latin American pope, the former archbishop of Buenos Aires. He is a pastor. However, in saying that he is a pastor, there is a temptation to dismiss him as lacking the intellectual sophistication of John Paul II or Benedict XVI. Certainly, critics of the pope have opposed him on these grounds, demanding greater clarity and precision in his thought. Others oppose the Holy Father and his call for pastoral conversion for ideological reasons or simply because they do not understand him.

The symposium that brought forth this book is both timely and necessary, for it allows us to explore the depths of the Holy Father's thought in a scholarly and nonideological way. To date, I have attended or read about different conferences on the Holy Father, but they often remain at a superficial level: "I like Pope Francis, and so I agree with him"; "Pope Francis is a reformer and previous popes were obstructionists"; "Pope Francis is on the side of the poor and those at the margins and agrees with our politics."

These attitudes do not do justice to what the Holy Father offers to the universal church and certainly will not help persuade or convince others of the Holy Father's approach to theology and pastoral activity. Something more is needed; this book provides that something more. Just as Austin Ivereigh's book *The Great Reformer*[2] provided a comprehensive examination of the essential biographical elements to the pope's life and pastoral activity, so, too, last year I began reading the Italian version of the book by Massimo Borghesi, *The Mind of Pope Francis: Jorge Mario Bergoglio's Intellectual Journey*, now translated

---

[2] Austen Ivereigh, *The Great Reformer: Francis and the Making of a Radical Pope* (New York: Henry Holt, 2014).

into English.[3] It opened my eyes to a new world, or, rather, it helped me realize why the Holy Father's words and actions spoke directly to my heart.

In 1969, I arrived at the Catholic University of Paris to begin my Masters in Theology. It was a two-year program that involved studies in theology, philosophy, history, and Scripture. Father Kowalski, my advisor, suggested to me that in theology I should study Hans Urs von Balthasar. At that time, only the first volume of the *Herrlichkeit*[4] had been translated into French. Forty years later, I am still reading von Balthasar; he has helped me throughout my priesthood—theologically, spiritually, and even pastorally.

My philosophy advisor, Claude Bruaire, thought that I should take up the philosophy of Gaston Fessard, who was still alive. I began reading works like *Le Mystère de la Société* and *La dialectique des exercises spirituels de saint Ignace de Loyola*, exploring the philosophy of Fessard but also of Hegel.[5] In the field of history, I was directed toward Maurice Blondel, Paul Ricoeur, and Henri de Lubac. At the time, I did not understand why they were directing me to these authors, but they were obviously preparing me for the future—for life in the church and in the world, a rapidly changing church and world. Later, during my diplomatic missions, I also encountered the movement *Communion and Liberation* and the thought of Luigi Giussani. These authors have been a part of my intellectual formation and have shaped and formed my pastoral activity in my service to the Holy See.

When I arrived in Mexico in 2007 to begin my diplomatic mission, it was the time of Aparecida, when the Latin American bishops had to confront epochal change and the challenges it was posing to the transmission of the faith and evangelization. The approach to evangelization, articulated by the Aparecida document, whose ghostwriter was Cardinal Bergoglio, immediately resonated with me, but I never understood exactly why until I read the work of Massimo Borghesi.

---

[3] Massimo Borghesi, *The Mind of Pope Francis: Jorge Mario Bergoglio's Intellectual Journey* (Collegeville, MN: Liturgical Press, 2018).

[4] Hans Urs von Balthasar, *The Glory of the Lord: A Theological Aesthetics*, vol. 1: *Seeing the Form*, 2nd ed. (San Francisco: Ignatius, 2009).

[5] Gaston Fessard, SJ, *Le mystère de la société. Recherches sur le sens de l'histoire*, ed. Michel Sales (Namur, Belgium: Culture et Vérité, 1997); *La Dialectique des Exercises Spirituels de Saint Ignace de Loyola*, 3 vols. (Paris: Aubier, 1956–84).

His work explores how the Holy Father's pastoral activity, his words, and his gestures have been influenced by the theologians and philosophers whom he has studied and appropriated over the years, including Fessard, Guardini, von Balthasar, de Lubac, and Giussani—the same authors whom I had studied! The pope's ability to synthesize many great thinkers allows him not only to touch the reality of people's concrete situations and circumstances but also provides him with an instrument for dialogue with today's culture. It is my sincere hope that this book will help scholars and pastoral ministers understand these theologians and philosophers who have influenced the Holy Father, so that they too can share in his vision for pastoral ministry and in the work of evangelization.

The scholars who have contributed to this book help us better understand the Holy Father's Latin American background, including the decisive role played by the Holy Father at Aparecida and why Aparecida is so pivotal for evangelization. To understand the Holy Father in that context helps us better understand him now in the post-Aparecida context. This book will also broaden the perspective of English speakers, exposing them to the thinking of men and women like Alberto Methol Ferré and Amelia Podetti, philosophers from Latin America who deeply influenced Pope Francis and his ideas about the holy, faithful, People of God and about listening to those at the peripheries. When Pope Francis is accused of not being a Thomist, one will be able to point to the existential Thomism of Methol Ferré and to see how the Holy Father has appropriated it. When critics unfairly call the Holy Father a Marxist or a Marxist liberation theologian, you will be able to distinguish the elements of liberation theology from the Holy Father's "theology of the people."

In addition to understanding the Holy Father's Latin American background, the book also highlights the fact that Pope Francis was formed thoroughly in the spiritual tradition of the Jesuits, with its emphasis on discernment and engagement with reality. The vision of Pope Francis goes beyond abstract ideas to see the concrete reality of life—of persons, cultures, and the conditions of our world. In his exhortation, *Evangelii Gaudium*, he writes:

> There also exists a constant tension between ideas and realities.
> Realities simply are, whereas ideas are worked out. There has to
> be continuous dialogue between the two, lest ideas become de-

tached from realities. It is dangerous to dwell in the realm of words alone, of images and rhetoric. . . . Realities are greater than ideas.[6]

The vision of the pope requires seeing people and their situations for what they truly are. In considering the vision of Pope Francis, one must remember his Jesuit training. Father Antonio Spadaro, SJ, editor of *La Civiltà Cattolica*, has described the pope as a Jesuit—a man with an "incomplete thought." In academics, when writing an essay, if a thought is incomplete, a professor might count this against a student. However, here by "incomplete" thought is meant an "open thought," one that is in continuous development. This is how the mind of the Jesuit works: to reflect upon reality to discern the will of God. Just as the Holy Father wants to bring Aparecida's approach to evangelization to the whole church with his exhortation *Evangelii Gaudium*, so too we see him bringing the Ignatian approach to spirituality to the universal church, envisioning himself as the "world's spiritual director."

The bulk of the book's essays deal with Pope Francis's intellectual formation, including the influence of von Balthasar, Methol Ferré, and Podetti, and, importantly, Romano Guardini and Gaston Fessard. The idea of polarity in Guardini and Fessard is particularly significant. I think there are many theologians who want everything to be simply black and white. Pope Francis is a man for whom, in many matters, discernment is essential. We must be able to live in tension—between the poles—and from a creative tension, in openness to the Spirit, to find a path forward to many of the world's problems. In a sense, this polarity affords us the opportunity to dialogue and through dialogue to discover the Truth.

While Pope Francis has not elaborated a systematic theology, he has studied and been formed in the Catholic intellectual tradition. He is well aware of the intellectual challenges of our times. He has contemplated ideas and made his own personal synthesis of some of these ideas, applying them to reality in a pastorally effective way. We are the beneficiaries of this synthesis, and this book, I believe, will

---

[6] Pope Francis, apostolic exhortation, *Evangelii Gaudium*, November 24, 2013, par. 231; http://w2.vatican.va/content/francesco/en/apost_exhortations/documents/papa-francesco_esortazione-ap_20131124_evangelii-gaudium.html.

be a major step in equipping the church in the United States to understand, receive, and defend the magisterium of Pope Francis and to
meet the challenges of our day. Once more, I thank Fr. Knoebel and
Dr. Lee and all at Sacred Heart for organizing this conference and
editing this volume, and I thank you for your attention.

Chapter 1

The Story of a Symposium: Why We Need a Theological Understanding of Pope Francis's Thought

Brian Y. Lee and Fr. Thomas L. Knoebel

Sacred Heart Seminary and School of Theology

The Story of a Symposium and a Seminary

The story of the genesis of the important symposium that gave birth to this book is, we believe, one worth telling. Not simply because it helps to contextualize the essays in this book, but also because it reflects the nature, state, needs, and potential of the Roman Catholic Church and its seminaries in the United States today.

Before we can talk about the circumstances, both fortuitous and challenging, surrounding the organization of the symposium, we must start with the scholarship that laid the foundations for such an event to take place. Two of our speakers, in particular, have contributed much to the public understanding of the person and thought of Pope Francis. The first is Austen Ivereigh, through his important research on the early career of Jorge Mario Bergoglio in Argentina in *The Great Reformer: Francis and the Making of a Radical Pope*.[1] The second

---

[1] Austen Ivereigh, *The Great Reformer: Francis and the Making of a Radical Pope* (New York: Henry Holt and Co., 2014).

1

is Massimo Borghesi, for his recent academic study on the intellectual foundations of Bergoglio's theology in *Jorge Mario Bergoglio: Una biografia intellettuale. Dialectica e Mistica* (An Intellectual Biography: Dialectics and Mysticism).[2] As Borghesi's essay in this volume notes, Borghesi's research in many ways expands upon important insights first charted in Ivereigh's book. Together their work represents a game-changing shift in approaching Francis's papacy, highlighting the need for serious study of both the intellectual biography of the pope and the historical development of the magisterium of the Latin American church in order truly to appreciate Pope Francis's Petrine ministry and the emerging direction of Catholicism in the twenty-first century.

But scholarship is one thing, and ecclesial engagement with that research is another. While academic conferences on Francis (happily) are announced with regularity among Catholic universities, it is far less common to see them being organized in Catholic seminaries, whether diocesan or religious. Seminaries generally see themselves as tasked with the day-to-day work of formation of candidates for the priesthood, and rightly so, not with organizing major conferences to promote the development of theological understanding on key ecclesial issues for the wider Catholic Church. Declining numbers of parishioners and priestly vocations in the US Catholic Church in the era of the "nones" and clerical sex-abuse trials, combined with the crippling costs of settlements and payouts, have given seminaries every excuse to maintain a conservative focus on in-house issues. But as Catholic universities and seminaries grow further apart both theologically and politically, it is increasingly clear that the division of labor between the two educational institutions needs rethinking.

Astute voices in the public square have long called for efforts to bridge the gap (particularly in the US) between academic theology on the one hand, and "the church," inclusive of bishops, priests, seminaries, and the laity, on the other.[3] Academic theology, as theo-

---

[2] Massimo Borghesi, *Jorge Mario Bergoglio: Una biografia intellettuale. Dialectica e Mistica* (Milan: Jaca Book, 2017). The book is now available in English translation: *The Mind of Pope Francis: Jorge Mario Bergoglio's Intellectual Journey* (Collegeville, MN: Liturgical Press, 2018).

[3] See, for example, Massimo Faggioli, "A Wake-Up Call to Liberal Theologians: Academic Theology Needs the Church," *Commonweal*, May 18, 2018.

logians in universities themselves often point out,[4] increasingly tends toward the development of methodological standards set by the academy (methodologically secular and interdisciplinary) and specialization of fields of research, under the pressures endemic to university settings. Seminaries, on the other hand, are often left with the task of trying to promote "theological integration" among future pastors of the church, a task increasingly difficult because of the hyperspecialization of academic theology. Seminary education, as a result, too often chooses to default to vague models of theory-praxis, or to ready-made models of theology often out of step with contemporary ecclesial concerns and developments.

When universities fail to provide guidance in how to promote theological integration, theological thinking on the seminary level, we dare say, grows increasingly subjective. In practice, "theological thinking" too often looks more like an education in how new priests should assimilate their preaching to the theological-political opinions of those around them rather than a critical engagement with a breadth of contemporary social and ecclesial concerns on the basis of a deep appropriation of theological method in interpreting revealed tradition—as conversant with contemporary biblical methodologies as with St. Thomas, with the writings of Pope Francis as with those of John Paul II, with an awareness of the pressures of low-income urban settings on minority communities as with natural law ethics. By no means are we confusing priests for theologians: we do not expect every priest to be a theologian. We are simply calling for a theological education strong and honest enough to know that Truth is preserved and glorified (not just for the few but "for the many") by grappling with the hard questions, not by running away from them, an approach that has neither given up on the world nor on Isaiah's hope-filled vision for that world, that "[i]n days to come / the mountain of the LORD's house / shall be established as the highest of the mountains . . . Many peoples shall come and say, / 'Come, let us go up to

---

[4] See, for example, Kathryn Tanner's bold and thoughtful proposal for redefining the practice of theology within academia, "Theology and Cultural Contest in the University," 199–212, in Linell E. Cady and Delwin Brown, eds., *Religious Studies, Theology, and the University: Conflicting Maps, Changing Terrain* (Albany, NY: SUNY Press, 2002). Both Faggioli's article and Tanner's chapter have to do primarily with rethinking academic theology. There is embarrassingly little public attention devoted to rethinking seminary education as a critical element of the gap between theology and church.

the mountain of the LORD, . . . that he may teach us his ways / and that we may walk in his paths'" (Isa 2:2-3).

The seminary is clearly a place acutely important for the future of the church, a truth too often overlooked but one attracting renewed attention in discussions about how to respond to the crisis of sexual abuse in the church. It is a place that welcomes those whose discernment about their vocations from God have led them here, a place that reflects all the personalities and political opinions of the church, a place where theology cannot remain purely academic, but must engage with the values and opinions of the church as a whole as it is actually shaped in the pews and in Catholic homes. It is a place with a profound potential to rediscover in Christ and his church the grace to live a life dedicated to God and his people rooted in something deeper than political ideology and social biases.

What options are there for new priests who want to confront the daunting challenges of preserving a Christian faith in an increasingly secular US society? How does one support their formation, help them nourish the profound gift of their Catholic identity, to cherish the formation of conscience and development of virtue as an integral part of a truly happy personal and communal life without turning back to the supposedly better times before Vatican II confronted the modern world, hoping to find ways to evangelize through cooperation rather than retreat and condemnation, to live up to our vocation to be a universal church rather than a club of the virtuous?

It is in the context of trying to find ways to invite seminarians and priests to these serious theological conversations that we came to the decision to host the symposium that led to this book. It was a decision based on the judgment that promoting a solid theological understanding of the papal magisterium, one everywhere stereotyped and so little appreciated in the US, was a wise way to open the seminary up to the needs of the universal church today and to the action of the Holy Spirit within it.

At a time when our seminary was immersed in the question of the identity and mission of our institution, discerning how to identify the needs of the church and the world and position ourselves to best respond to them, the President-Rector, Fr. Thomas Knoebel, found out about the above-mentioned study of Borghesi from Archbishop Christophe Pierre, Apostolic Nuncio to the United States. The two had become acquainted in March 2017 when Archbishop Pierre came to Milwaukee for the ordination of two auxiliary bishops for Archbishop Jerome Listecki. Accepting Fr. Knoebel's invitation to deliver Sacred Heart's November 2017 Leo John Dehon Lecture, the archbishop delivered a presentation on "The Heart of Christ and the Heart of a Priest" to an audience that included Archbishop Listecki of Milwaukee, Bishop James Schuerman, an auxiliary of Milwaukee, and Bishop Robert Morlino of Madison, Wisconsin, along with two hundred priests and seminarians.

The night before the lecture, Archbishop Pierre expressed his desire that the United States have a better understanding of the theological background of Pope Francis. He expressed the thought that, in his travels across the country, he often encountered the general impression that Pope Francis might be a compassionate shepherd, but that he lacked the intellectual depth and sophistication of his two recent predecessors. On the contrary, the nuncio was convinced that, as Austen Ivereigh states it so well, "I was in the presence of an astonishingly far-reaching intellect, one shaped by a pattern of thinking with deep theological roots."[5] The next day Knoebel and two other members of the administration proposed to the nuncio the idea of a symposium, hosted by Sacred Heart, to help fulfill the archbishop's wish, and the idea was born. Within a matter of weeks, Knoebel met with Borghesi in Rome and received his enthusiastic support. A core group of speakers, including Rodrigo Guerra, Austen Ivereigh, Rocco Buttiglione, and others, all experts on papal magisterium generally and Francis's in particular, were approached and committed themselves to participate, and the general scope of the symposium was set.

During this early stage Fr. Tom brought the idea to the faculty and administration of Sacred Heart, including Dr. Brian Lee. All concerned came to see this symposium as an opportunity to increase appreciation for the role of the papal magisterium and as an opportunity to bridge academic theology and the Catholic Church in the United States—tasks uniquely suited to a seminary in general and Sacred Heart in particular, given the support it enjoys from so many bishops and religious communities across the country. The gathering

---

[5] Review of Massimo Borghesi, *Jorge Mario Bergoglio: Una biografia intellettuale*, *Crux*, November 18, 2017, http://cruxnow.com/book-review/2017/11/18/new-book-looks-intellectual-history-francis-pope-polarity/.

would be an opportunity to bring an emerging European and Latin American conversation about the core of Francis's theology to the North American church and to put on the kind of symposium we wish we saw more of in the United States: one capable of raising the level of US Catholic discourse and understanding of Francis's papal magisterium, in a manner that could potentially bridge conservative and liberal populations, going beyond the political to the theological. All of us at Sacred Heart have a deep-rooted belief and hope that promoting theological understanding is one of the most important ways real unity will come about in the church in the United States today.

The symposium was held over four intense days in early October 2018, in the midst of what now appears to have been the most turbulent section of the turmoil occasioned by the letter of Archbishop Viganò, a turmoil that threatened to divide US Catholic bishops on Francis and further exacerbate divisions among the Catholic faithful. As a seminary that serves both religious and diocesan seminarians from a number of dioceses and religious communities, the release of the letter and the general crisis occasioned by the reports of former Archbishop McCarrick's activities put pressure on Sacred Heart. Given the context, however, and after some discernment, the seminary concluded that the symposium was more necessary than ever. A renewed understanding of the great gift of the papal magisterium is crucially important in such unsettled times with the challenges these events present to the faith.

A related issue always clearly before us during the organization of the symposium is the profound challenge of rethinking the role of seminary education and Catholic understanding vis-à-vis sexuality and sex abuse. While the present book intentionally does not deal with these issues on an explicit level, we are convinced that the universal, papal magisterium has immense gifts and resources to offer to this discussion. We see our symposium and this book as a key preliminary step in addressing these questions, as a means of rooting our response in a renewed capacity for wisdom and discernment of how the church of Jesus Christ should evangelize our deeply fragmented world. While it is very clear to us that we are just at the beginning of developing a more holistic approach to the acute question of sexuality in our culture, a question endemic today to societies globally, we hope you will read enough of the book to see that the present volume has much to say about *what an authentic discernment of the path of human development, and specifically that of the church, might look like*—a path marked by profound respect for justice for all parties, by deep recognition of the need for profound patience and dialogue, by a renewed capacity for appreciating the authentic roots of the culture of peoples (which always includes their lived experience of the mystery of God), by a critique of "spiritual worldliness" in the church, by a profound tenderness for others—*a path that begins with the life-changing and world-transforming encounter with the mercy of God in Jesus Christ.*

Regarding our understanding of Pope Francis in particular, we wish to offer, with this book, a substantial path to understanding his magisterium and ministry in a way that transcends political receptions of the pope, one that goes beyond usual and unhelpful ways of viewing Francis as gentle pastor rather than serious intellectual. Sacred Heart Seminary and School of Theology, its faculty and administration, made the choice to organize this symposium and the publication of its proceedings in this context, a highly politicized context that demanded an articulate and well-considered choice, a choice that touched on the often unexamined question of the role of seminary education in the US. Seminary education can no longer complacently fulfill its traditional role of simply providing priests for parish ministry. Rather, this book represents the ripe fruit of a discernment about what kind of conversation might best contribute to a growth in charity and understanding, and we offer it to Catholics and Christians more broadly as a model for the kinds of theological conversation that seminaries might play a role in fostering. This is a role that Sacred Heart Seminary and School of Theology is committed to furthering.

Outline of the Book

While this book is designed to highlight the theological roots of Francis's magisterium, the order of the book's chapters, starting from his Latin American roots before moving to his appropriation of European theology, is intended to make clear that Bergoglio's engagement with European Catholic theology was by no means an uncritical repetition of the thought of others, but a creative and inspired appropriation grounded in pastoral praxis, spiritual discernment, theological reflection, and an acute awareness of the concrete life of societies and the church.

As for the scope of this collection of essays, we do not pretend to cover exhaustively the thinking and writing of Jorge Mario Bergoglio or to trace every theologian and author that has influenced him. What this book does cover are certain concerns, themes, concepts, and traditions that constitute some of the most important building blocks of his theological thought. Its essays unpack the thinkers and traditions most central to Bergoglio's theological heritage and analyze the way in which Pope Francis has appropriated and transformed that tradition.

While we (here I think I can safely speak for the editors and the authors of this book) are convinced that this appropriation is guided by the Holy Spirit, we offer up our interpretation of the intellectual work of Pope Francis, with great humility, to the judgment of the wider public, with trust that their active engagement with its chapters through critical inquiry, research, reflection, and discussion, will on the whole contribute to the common good and open up a healthy conversation about the theology of evangelization in our times. Our prayer is that divine charity accompanies the reading of this book, so that it might serve as a building block for the renewal of God's church in the United States and beyond.

We opened our book with the gracious contribution of a blessing and short reflection on the significance of our symposium and this volume from the Holy Father, words that we are profoundly happy to share with you, followed by a foreword by the Apostolic Nuncio Archbishop Christophe Pierre, in many ways the catalyst of the symposium. From here on, from chapters 2 through 9, our book follows a simple pattern: we begin with the Latin American roots of Pope Francis's thought, transition to his engagement with European theology, and finally we close by looking to his vision of the church in the United States.

Following this introductory chapter, section one of our book explores "Latin American Roots" in three chapters: an essay by Austen Ivereigh that contextualizes the formation of Bergoglio's early thinking within contemporary Latin American history, and two essays on Bergoglio's indebtedness to the *"teología del pueblo"* (theology of the people) tradition centered around the Río de la Plata basin of Argentina and Uruguay by Guzmán Carriquiry and Rocco Buttiglione, respectively.

From these chapters we move to four essays that explore Bergoglio's reading of European theology. Each of these essays is marked by the acute recognition that Pope Francis's engagement with the important theologians associated with the journal *Communio* (a circle that included Joseph Ratzinger), many of whom shared his Ignatian spirituality, was guided by a deep capacity to recognize the existential ground of their key concepts and concerns and engage them on that level. Two of these essays, by Massimo Borghesi and Robert Barron, highlight the role of Gaston Fessard's thought in Bergoglio's development of the four polar dialectical principles central to his programmatic apostolic exhortation *Evangelii Gaudium*: time is greater than space, unity prevails over conflict, realities are more important than ideas, and the whole is greater than the part.[6] Borghesi's essay, in particular, provides us with a rich genealogical, existential, and historical reflection on the role of polar dialectics in the thought of the pope, based on his groundbreaking research in *Jorge Mario Bergoglio: Una biografia intellettuale*. These are followed by essays by Susan Wood, SCL and Rodrigo Guerra. Wood compares Francis's polar dialectics to the role of paradox in Henri de Lubac's ecclesiology, while Guerra compares the theological aesthetics of Hans Urs von Balthasar and Luigi Giussani with that of Pope Francis.

We close our volume with a contribution by Peter Casarella, who simultaneously brings us back to Francis's Latin American roots and looks forward to Francis's vision for the Americas. Casarella interprets Francis's papacy through the lens of the *teología del pueblo* tradition in order to draw out what he calls Francis's North American theology of the people.

Summaries of Essays

One of the most important lessons our contributors offer us is simply to remind us that we do not really know Pope Francis in the way that we think we do. We are bombarded by media on the pope who interpret his statements and actions through ready-made cultural categories and political positions, but the secular media (and sometimes the Catholic media), to a large extent, still do not realize that their subject has a deep pastoral and episcopal itinerary, a rich and consistent discipline of spiritual discernment, and a robust

---

[6] The four principles are mentioned in chap. 4 of *Evangelii Gaudium*, on "the social dimension of evangelization," in a section on "the common good and peace in society" (EG 217–37).

engagement with Catholic theological tradition, nor do they typically understand the relevance of that personal history for interpreting his actions today. More problematic than the shallowness of media coverage is its increasingly politicized fragmentation. In these days of media flux, where the term "fake news" has become a household term, where the manipulation of our "newsfeed" by foreign governments has become taken for granted as a regular part of international politics, and where social media platforms such as Facebook and YouTube, on which news is filtered by one's circle of acquaintances and one's predetermined interests, more and more become prime sources of news and information for the American population,[7] we are all increasingly aware of how remarkably vulnerable the fabric of our common life is to informational biases in media and media technologies. For this reason, we open the book with a contribution by Austen Ivereigh,[8] whose essay, "Close and Concrete: Bergoglio's Life Evangelizing a World in Flux," provides us with a rich historical framing of the development of Pope Francis's vision of evangelization in the contemporary world that clearly intones some of the most important theological themes that we will explore throughout the book. With a DPhil thesis from the University of Oxford entitled *Catholicism and Politics in Argentina: An Interpretation, with Special Reference to the Period 1930–1960*,[9] and decades of research and journalism on Catholicism and Latin America, his chapter is grounded in remarkable research widely lauded for its insight and accuracy, particularly with regard to Bergoglio's theological education.

Ivereigh's essay highlights the extraordinary insight of Bergoglio's discernment of the "signs of the times": it explores Bergoglio's analysis of the fragmentation of societies in a globalized world and its impact upon people's lives, and his vision of a "close and concrete" mode of evangelization capable of meeting the challenges of today's world head-on—treating not just its symptoms but the roots of its illnesses through missionary discipleship.

[7] Pew Research Center, September, 2017, "News Use Across Social Media Platforms 2017," http://www.journalism.org/wp-content/uploads/sites/8/2017/09/PJ _17.08.23_socialMediaUpdate_FINAL.pdf.

[8] Author of, among other books and articles, *The Great Reformer: Francis and the Making of a Radical Pope*, updated ed. (London: Picador, 2015).

[9] Published as *Catholicism and Politics in Argentina, 1810–1960* (New York: St. Martin's Press, 1995).

Chapters 3 and 4 by Guzmán Carriquiry and Rocco Buttiglione, respectively, continue our study of the Latin American crucible of Bergoglio's early thinking. Ivereigh's research made clear that Bergoglio's sensitivity to the needs of persons and peoples in today's world is rooted in his reflection, influenced by the *teología del pueblo* tradition of theology, on what it means to be a "people." Carriquiry and Buttiglione, both academics of a highly socially engaged type with profound expertise in Latin America and expertise in the papacies of John Paul II, Benedict XVI, and Francis, explore Francis's relationship to his Rioplatense intellectual heritage in distinct ways. Carriquiry, as long-time Secretary of the Pontifical Council for the Laity and Vice President of the Pontifical Commission for Latin America, unpacks the conceptual and theological points of the theology of the people tradition, while Buttiglione, as founding member of the influential Catholic movement *Communion and Liberation* (dear to the past two popes and the current one) and of the Christian Democratic Party in Italy, reflects on the political and cultural insights of the "theology of the people" tradition.

Guzmán Carriquiry's chapter, "The 'Theology of the People' in the Pastoral Theology of Jorge Mario Bergoglio," explores the importance of the theology of Río de la Plata to the thought of Pope Francis and reflects upon the ecclesiological implications of this tradition. Carriquiry explores the rich meaning of *"pueblo"* (people) in the "theology of the people" tradition, making clear that its understanding of the "people" draws on the experience, history, culture, faith, and most central aspirations, meanings, and values of the people, aspects of a people's identity that are often missed in sociological and economic analysis.

Like Borghesi and Buttiglione, Carriquiry discusses some of the bipolar tensions highlighted by Pope Francis's *Evangelii Gaudium*— unity prevails over conflict, reality is greater than ideas—as parts of the authentic, and arduous, path of the development of a "people." This approach to understanding the integral development of a people highlights the need to respect the poor and the marginalized and to privilege the path of dialogue, and is sensitive to the possibilities of the formation of virtues within the social economy. It also warns that forces that would bypass these principles are those that do not speak for the "people" but represent powerful "enlightened" minorities (*anti-pueblo*) that would subvert the common good and manufacture artificial cultures that support their own private interests. Carriquiry demonstrates that central aspects of the papal magisterium about "God's holy and faithful people"—*sensus fidei fidelium*, the evangelization of culture, the appreciation for popular religiosity, the preferential love for the poor and the dignity of their culture, pastoral and missionary conversion, and the "culture of encounter"—are rooted in this rich understanding of what makes for the authentic development of a "people," and thus explains why the pope believes that the people of God is the sacrament of unity for all the world's peoples, the *forma mundi*, witness to the authentic path of full human development.

Chapter 4, "Globalization, Baroque, and the Latin American Pope," by Rocco Buttiglione, helps to situate the four principles outlined by Pope Francis in *Evangelii Gaudium* as they developed in the Latin American experience of the church and reflects on how they might inform our efforts to become missionary disciples of Christ in the United States. Buttiglione, among other things a key interpreter of John Paul II's thought in the 80s and 90s, rightly insists that we need to endeavor to understand Pope Francis and his rich Latin American tradition of theology just as the world did when Karol Wojtyła became pope.

After leading us through the tumultuous history of Argentina in which Francis's thinking on polarities emerged, he meditates on "the Baroque," a cultural paradigm pervasive in Latin America (inherited through colonial-era Spain), capable of taking seriously the historical particularities of diverse peoples with their own distinctive cultural sensitivities while simultaneously intoning their underlying human commonalities.[10] He argues that this paradigm, so important to the theology of the people and to Pope Francis's vision of evangelization in today's globalized world, represents the beginnings of a Catholic modernity distinct from the Protestant and Enlightenment modernities. While each of these modernities represents a new understanding

---

[10] Scholars are beginning to take seriously the cultural complexity of the Baroque as a medium of transatlantic culture. See, for example, Evonne Levy and Kenneth Mills, eds., *Lexicon of the Hispanic Baroque: Transatlantic Exchange and Transformation* (Austin: University of Texas Press, 2014), and Harald E. Braun and Jesús Pérez-Magallón, eds., *The Transatlantic Hispanic Baroque: Complex Identities in the Atlantic World* (Farnham: Ashgate, 2014).

of humanity and the world, the Baroque Catholic rethinking of the human and the world took its starting point from its discovery of the Americas and its indigenous people: it began to rethink our humanity by taking seriously the humanity of the *indio*. Buttiglione argues that this is a vision of modernity in need of rediscovery in today's globalized world, one sensitive to cultures and peoples and capable of discovering one's humanity through the encounter with others.

He concludes with reflections inspired by *teología del pueblo* on ways in which the church can work with peoples to preserve the authentic moral values organically engendered through their histories and help them direct their energies toward the common good, and how US Catholics might "make ourselves disciples of the great experience of faith of the Latin American Church"[11] by reflecting on the four principles of *Evangelii Gaudium*.

Section two of the book explores Bergoglio's engagement with European theology, with a marked focus on theologians of an Ignatian cast.[12] We begin in chapter 5 with Massimo Borghesi's rich examination of a topic broached by all of the preceding chapters, the role of the four dialectical polarities highlighted in Pope Francis's programmatic apostolic exhortation *Evangelii Gaudium*. Borghesi's essay in this volume collects and synthesizes some of the key insights of his 2017 intellectual biography of the pope, *Jorge Mario Bergoglio: Una biografia intellettuale*, a book that dismantled the commonly held impression that Pope Francis is a compassionate shepherd but lacks the intellectual depth of his recent predecessors.

Borghesi's essay traces the conceptual genealogy of Bergoglio's understanding of "polarity," a theme so central to and characteristic of the thinking of the pope, with more clarity and precision than we have yet seen in scholarship on the subject. Trained in the Jesuit school, especially that of the French Jesuits, Bergoglio assimilated the message of St. Ignatius through the dialectical and mystical reading of one of the most acute philosophers of the 1900s: Gaston Fessard, SJ. Fessard's understanding of Catholicism as *coincidentia oppositorum*,

---

[11] Buttiglione, "Globalization, Baroque, and the Latin American Pope" (chap. 4, p. 86, in this volume).

[12] Gaston Fessard (the subject of chaps. 5 and 6) and Henri de Lubac (the subject of chap. 7) were French Jesuits, as was, at one point, Hans Urs von Balthasar (the subject of chap. 8).

a synthesis of the antinomies that divide humanity and history, would deeply impress itself on Bergoglio's understanding of how the church must relate to the world. It is this model, which has deep roots in nineteenth- and twentieth-century Catholic thought, that eventually led him to study the polar anthropology of Romano Guardini.

For Bergoglio, the polar dialectical principles teach us to respect those aspects of the human experience that must be held in tension in order to cultivate real development. To do so is to transcend the human temptations that have ripped apart peoples throughout history, and to cultivate an authenticity of the human spirit through wise and honest discernment. Borghesi's reconstruction of Pope Francis's intellectual journey is the story of how an original and fruitful engagement with some of the most important European Catholic theologians raised academic theology to a higher level—one capable of meeting the great challenges to the church in the era of globalization.

Borghesi's chapter, however, goes beyond a genealogy of Bergoglio's ideas. It unpacks the way in which Francis develops the notion of polarity into a robust spirituality and theology of tenderness and discernment throughout his vocation as priest, provincial, bishop, and pope. Borghesi tells the story of how Francis roots the notion of polarity in Ignatian spirituality and in the scriptural revelation of the incarnation of Christ to create a distinctive method of discernment: one both profoundly sensitive and open to the dynamics of the human heart and to the dynamics of the Holy Spirit as it moves through human history. The polarities, he makes clear, are rooted in the polar tensions of revelation itself: the cross as true triumph, the paradoxical bridge between heaven and earth, humanity, and God.

Borghesi also surveys the origins of Francis's Petrine discernment of how missionary disciples are called to evangelize in the context of the fragmentation of the contemporary world, starting from his remarkable ability to combine spiritual discernment and historical awareness in his pastoral reflections upon the Latin American experience, from the role of colonial-era Jesuits in shaping the encounter between the church and native cultures in Latin America to the tumultuous contemporary history of Argentina.

Chapter 6, Bishop Robert Barron's essay on "Gaston Fessard and Pope Francis," fills out our understanding of the role of polarity in the thought of the French Jesuit Gaston Fessard and the broad ways in which Fessard's thought may be seen to coincide with that of the pope. While other speakers primarily touch on Fessard's reading of St. Ignatius's *Spiritual Exercises*, Barron helpfully articulates the broader structure of Fessard's philosophy of history, and the relationship between human history and God in it, that runs throughout his writings.[13]

Barron not only makes analytic distinctions between, for example, Fessardian dialectics and that of Hegel (while for Fessard the resolution of the various dialectical tensions always happens through free choices, resolution of tensions are always somewhat deterministic in Hegel), he also surveys the way in which the dialectical structure of Fessard's thought functions in his analysis of contemporary history, particularly his critiques of National Socialism and communism: as totalitarian ideologies, tantamount to pseudoreligions in their claims to identify the supreme good in the temporal goods that serve humanity, they react to the overemphasis on the rights and privileges of the individual in enlightenment rationalism by positing an equally extreme overemphasis on the state and the proletariat, respectively, as the criterion of the good. For Fessard, in contrast, "it is only in the mutual surrender to the will and purposes of God"[14] that the manifold dimensions of human life, often in tension with one another, can find their equilibrium.

With chapter 7, "Pope Francis and the Ecclesiology of Henri de Lubac," by Susan Wood, SCL, we leave behind Fessardian dialectics only to compare the dialectical polarities of Bergoglio's thought with the role of paradox in the ecclesiology of another Jesuit, Henri de Lubac. Both de Lubac and Bergoglio make use of similar forms of paradox or dialectic to characterize aspects of the church. As was true with Fessardian dialectics, theirs are also distinguished from Hegelian dialectic, in which two opposing principles are resolved in a synthesis that somehow combines both poles in a new reality. For the two Jesuits de Lubac and Bergoglio, whose shared "intuition of the profoundly paradoxical and dialectical nature of the church and of the spiritual life"[15] goes back to the dialectical character of the thought

---

[13] On Fessardian dialectics, see especially Ana Petrache, *Gaston Fessard, un chrétien de rite dialectique?* (Paris: Les Éditions du Cerf, 2017).

[14] Barron, "Gaston Fessard and Pope Francis" (chap. 6, p. 121, in this volume).

[15] Wood, "Pope Francis and the Ecclesiology of Henri de Lubac" (chap. 7, p. 149, in this volume).

and spirituality of St. Ignatius, the poles of dialectic are to be held in tension, resolved not by human effort or concepts but by divine mystery, into a unity that, as Wood explains, does "not erase the polarities but encompass[es] diversity and difference within a higher plane."[16]

Wood's comparative essay highlights the way in which fidelity to the paradoxes of divine mystery guides the two thinkers beyond pragmatic and worldly approaches to the church. Both of these men share a wisdom rooted in the paradox of the cross expressed in profoundly countercultural pastoral sensibilities. Wood explores the ways in which Pope Francis draws on dialectical thinking in discerning principles for guiding the authentic development of human life in general and the church in particular: from privileging the organic development of communities of faith over the maintenance of institutional structures for their own sake, to building communion amid disagreements, to appreciating the lived experience of mystery in the faithful even when not elevated to the level of speculative theological reflection on mystery, to developing the principle of subsidiarity in ecclesial governance, to critique of "spiritual worldliness" in the church—careerism, self-referentiality, and clericalism—and establishing the spiritual and institutional building blocks of curial, pastoral, and episcopal reform necessary to bring about a truly missionary church.

The deep pattern Wood helps us see through her insightful analysis is the way in which Pope Francis's reform finds a resolution to a dialectical tension between doctrines and pastoral presence to sinners in his "proclamation in a missionary style" that focuses on the essentials.[17] The notion of missionary discipleship reminds us that dogmas are not meant to be merely repeated for oneself. The beauty of the revealed truths must be lived out with love for others, the love that animates them, in order to awaken the moral consequences of that encounter in others. Wood makes clear that Francis's approach seeks to help us to rediscover in the faith of the church a path to encountering Christ in the world. Quoting Pope Francis, she concludes: "The solution he seeks is for the Gospel's proposal to be 'simpler, profound or, more radiant,' for 'it is from this proposition that moral consequences then flow.' Holding the dialectic in tension means not

---

[16] Wood, 140.
[17] Wood, 147.

choosing one pole over the other, so critics that suggest that his pastoral approach is a denial of doctrine miss the entire structure of his thought."[18]

Chapter 8, Rodrigo Guerra's essay "An Encounter That Becomes Method: The Influence of Hans Urs von Balthasar and Luigi Giussani in the Theology of the Post–Vatican II Popes," opens with a reflection on recent controversies over *Amoris Laetitia* 8, surmising that underlying the objections of many of Pope Francis's critics is a certain dissatisfaction with Vatican II and the tradition of *nouvelle théologie* that shaped much of it. Against those who would pit Francis against his immediate predecessors John Paul II and Benedict XVI, Guerra explores an important line of continuity between the popes: the appreciation for theological aesthetics, a field that richly demonstrates how deeply the popes drew inspiration from theological *ressourcement* and the commitment to incorporating the spiritual life into theological method characteristic of *nouvelle théologie*.

Guerra reminds us that in order to appreciate the thought of Pope Francis, we really need to appreciate two other thinkers whose thought profoundly influenced the Second Vatican Council, Pope Francis, and his papal predecessors: Hans Urs von Balthasar and Luigi Giussani. He offers an insightful diagnosis of the present and invites us, as a remedy to our ills and as a means of better appreciating Pope Francis's vision of evangelization, to reflect deeply on three central and influential themes in the thought of von Balthasar and Giussani: theological aesthetics, Christianity as event, and Mary as a figure of the church. All three, Guerra shows us, help us understand better what Papa Francisco means by situating "encounter" at the beginning of faith. Guerra's essay helps us to understand that the beauty of Francis's simple witness to the Gospel, often superficially interpreted as a savvy "P.R." campaign, has profound roots in a deep theological appropriation of the aesthetic dimension of the incarnation as the revelation of the glory of the Lord.

We bring our book to a close with our final section and chapter of the book, Peter Casarella's essay "Pope Francis, Theology of the People, and the Church in the United States." Casarella's chapter at once revisits our discussion of Pope Francis and the theology of the

---

[18] Wood, 147.

people, but, bringing his expertise in Latino/a theology in the United States to bear, he does so in order to interpret Francis's apostolic visits to the Americas, lifting out of them the outline of Pope Francis's ecclesial vision for the church in the US.

Casarella begins by noting the way Francis's apostolic visits to the Americas have looked to the suffering of the countries of the Americas and how they hold together "tears and dreams" in standing in solidarity with their peoples: "the shedding of tears is a cry for the establishment of new structures that stand in solidarity with God's tears."[19] His visits have always sought to find ways to walk with the people of God and are always designed to bring concrete hope to them, from supporting the political integration of popular movements for justice for the marginalized in Bolivia, to working to reopen relations between the US and Cuba, to supporting peace talks in Colombia. Casarella also looks to the way the pope's historic speech to the joint session of Congress weaves together figures of faith in the American heritage (Abraham Lincoln, Martin Luther King, Jr., Dorothy Day, and Thomas Merton), noting how he embodies the political intuitions of the theology of the people in seeking "to forge a new discourse for political inclusion and participation that is grounded in the Christian doctrine of hope. . . . Past, present, and future need to be brought together anew into a creative synthesis. Political ideologies by themselves cannot create such a hope."[20]

Casarella's essay then turns to unpack the theological implications of Francis's understanding of the "people," a concept underlying his apostolic visits. He defuses fears about the prominence of the intellectual category "people" in Francis's thought, distinguishing it from exclusionary forms of nationalist populism or socialist notions of the proletariat. The core of Casarella's reflection here is his explanation of the notion of unity inherent in Francis's model of the "polyhedron": it reflects the way in which God establishes a complex mysterious unity in his people that transcends our comprehension, the *gratia preveniens* of the Spirit that brings about unity in the midst of diversity before we are even aware of it. The polyhedron is meant as a representation of a complex harmony wrought by God through the work

---

[19] Casarella, "Pope Francis, Theology of the People, and the Church in the United States" (chap. 9, p. 182, in this volume).

[20] Casarella, 187.

of his people to transform society. It is a model of the common good that preserves an appreciation of cultural particularity: not detracting from unity but enhancing it. It is "a faith-filled vision of reality and history that seeks greater inclusion of those at the margins and the promotion of the common good in the midst of real strife and individualizing fragmentation."[21] The "people" chosen by God to bring about a new polyhedral unity in the church and in society is called to challenge the individualism and consumerism of the US, forces that act against the fostering of peoplehood, and witness to "what it means to accompany those who are most in need."[22]

Casarella then reflects on how Pope Francis's vision of the church in the US overlaps in important ways with that of Latino/a theology. He notes the similarities between their understandings of *pueblo* and its sense of belonging to a people, their communitarian ethos that contrasts with the rampant individualism of US culture, and the culture of encounter. While he sounds a warning about the departure of US Hispanic Catholics to Pentecostal groups and the "nones," he sees hope in a growing presence of young adult Hispanic Catholics that might be viewed as evidence of the possibility that a North American *teología del pueblo* "is transforming and can continue to transform the Catholic Church in the U.S."[23]

Finally, Casarella draws his essay, and our volume, to a close by wisely noting, in the wake of scandals surrounding the letter published by Archbishop Carlo Maria Viganò, that Francis's multipolar catholicity is not intended to resolve every conflict in the church: "It is," rather, "the starting point for advocating a culture of encounter" that makes a fruitful dialogue about these issues possible.

We would like to invite our readers to reimagine our society and church through this vision of a culture of encounter, a culture not without its conflicts, but one shot through and united powerfully by a common awareness of the divine love working through it, and a common hope in the full reconciliation of the one Body with God, starting with those most in need. We hope that discovering Pope Francis through our contributors' essays will help our readers to discover this profoundly rich vision of catholicity, more challenging

[21] Casarella, 194.
[22] Casarella, 200.
[23] Casarella, 204.

but more authentic, and ultimately to rediscover Jesus Christ and his mission in our lives with a startling freshness and a more profound faith, one deep enough to honestly confront the big problems that our church faces today.

We end our introduction with the prayer that closed each of the four days of our symposium in October 2018. As you read this volume, we invite you to ask God's Holy Spirit to stay with you and guide your reading, reflection, and discussion of the book with others:

Come Holy Spirit,
fill the hearts of your faithful and kindle in them the fire of your love.
Send forth your Spirit and they shall be created.
And you shall renew the face of the earth.

March 13, 2019
Sixth Anniversary of the
Election of Pope Francis

PART ONE

Latin American Roots

Chapter 2

Close and Concrete: Bergoglio's Life Evangelizing a World in Flux

Austen Ivereigh

*Fellow in Contemporary Church History,
Campion Hall, Oxford University*

With the turmoil in American Catholicism following further revelations of past abuse and its cover-up within the church, our task of
unpacking the mission and thinking of Pope Francis has been made
even more urgent and necessary. Strange as it may first seem, the two
are closely related. His vision for evangelizing the contemporary
world speaks very directly to this time of tribulation, which he sees
as a chance for change, for a new humility through humiliation, which
will lead to a renewal of evangelizing fervor and closeness to the
poor. It is the transformation that lies at the heart of his program as
pope, captured in the phrase used by the Latin American church in
2007: "a pastoral and missionary conversion."

As with any conversion, it is not automatic, because our freedom
and will are in play; just when the need for it is greatest, the resistance
to it is at its most intense. True reform requires patience, gradually
overcoming the temptations attendant on any apostolic body in desolation and tribulation, temptations to which the church has often

succumbed in response to secularization—which is why it needs that conversion.

It also requires humility, a capacity to admit and embrace failure as an opportunity for a humble and joyful dependence on God's mercy. As Francis put it in October 2018 to some French priests in Rome, describing "a context in which the boat of the church faces violent headwinds as a result of the serious failings of some of its members," the pastors were called "to witness to the strength of the Resurrection in the wounds of this world." The wounds are part of the witness. Do not fear, he told them, to look on the wounds of our church, not in order to lament them but to be led to where Christ is.[1]

This is never easy to do, for it means renouncing our own illusion of power and leaning on the power of God's mercy, precisely at the moment when the fear of turmoil leads us to trust more firmly in our own methods. At times of crisis, Pope Francis observed in 2017, discernment does not work; we prefer to seek out saviors who we think will restore our identity and protect us with barbed wire fences.[2] There are not a few of those saviors offering themselves in the wake of the revelations of the torrid summer of 2018: people of wealth and power who are calling for a "cleansing" by self-proclaimed "faithful Catholics" who speak as if the pope's path of reform either did not exist or needs replacing with punitive, purgative methods.

Theirs is the way of accusation of others; Francis's way, based on ancient spiritual wisdom, is the way of *self*-accusation: being willing to suffer as a body, as Pope Francis urged in his remarkable letter to the people of God the week before his Dublin visit in August 2018. The first way (accusation) blames, divides, and slows reform; the second creates the unity of purpose and humility required for authentic reform.[3]

---

[1] Pope Francis, "Discours du Pape François aux prêtres du diocèse de Créteil (France)," October 1, 2018, http://w2.vatican.va/content/francesco/fr/speeches/2018/october/documents/papa-francesco_20181001_sacerdoti-creteil.html.

[2] Pope Francis, "El peligro en tiempos de crisis es buscar un salvador que nos devuelva la identidad y nos defienda con muros," interview by Antonio Caño and Pablo Ordaz, *El País* (Madrid), January 22, 2017, http://elpais.com/internacional/2017/01/21/actualidad/1485022162_846725.html.

[3] Pope Francis, "Letter of His Holiness to the People of God," August 20, 2018, http://w2.vatican.va/content/francesco/en/letters/2018/documents/papa-francesco_20180820_lettera-popolo-didio.html. See Christopher White, "Wealthy Catholics to Target Cardinals with 'Red Hat Report,'" *Crux*, October 1, 2018, http://cruxnow.com

Francis's experience of spiritual leadership of apostolic bodies facing precisely such tribulations, combined with his mastery of the discernment in St. Ignatius's *Spiritual Exercises* as well as his own life experience of desolation and being accused, have left him uniquely equipped to guide the church at times like these. His insights of the late 1980s—when he experienced such tribulations at first hand— have been deployed to great effect in his guidance of the universal church this year, and in particular cases such as Chile.[4]

He knows that tribulation always brings with it mimetic phenomena: polarization and mutual recrimination, blame and scapegoating, false accusations and crusades. Like St. Peter leaving the boat, we too easily focus on the high waves rather than on Christ calling us out. In falling silent, we allow the truth to emerge, and the spirits involved to be exposed. This is not passivity, or evasion, but the wisdom of one who has faith in God's methods of change, not ours. As he wrote in 1990: "The meekness of silence will show us to be even weaker, and so it will be the devil who, emboldened, comes into the light, and shows us his true intentions, no longer disguised as an angel, but unmasked."[5]

Francis sees this current crisis as part of a broader tribulation that the church has been undergoing in the Western world, triggered by its response to technological change, and the rapid expulsion of Christianity from Western culture and law. Describing in a 1987 text the apostles' dismay following Christ's crucifixion, he observed how, "at such times, when the tempest of persecutions, tribulations, doubts and so forth, is raised by events, it is not easy to find the path to follow. These times have their own temptations: to debate ideas, to avoid the matter at hand, to be too concerned with our enemies. . . . And

---

/church-in-the-usa/2018/10/01/wealthy-catholics-to-target-cardinals-with-red-hat -report/; Heidi Schlumpf, "At 'Authentic Reform,' Conservative Catholics Rally to 'Fix' Church Failures," *National Catholic Reporter*, October 5, 2018, http://www .ncronline.org/news/accountability/authentic-reform-conservative-catholics-rally -fix-church-failures.

[4] Austen Ivereigh, "A Time to Keep Silence," *Thinking Faith*, August 30, 2018, https: //www.thinkingfaith.org/articles/time-keep-silence. See also Diego Fares, SJ, "Contro lo spirito del 'Accanimento,'" *La Civiltà Cattolica* 4029 (2018), 216–30, http://www .laciviltacattolica.it/articolo/contro-lo-spirito-di-accanimento/.

[5] "Silencio y Palabra," in Jorge Mario Bergoglio, *Reflexiones en esperanza* (1992; repr., Madrid: Romana Editorial, 2013), 115–53.

I believe that the worst temptation of all is to keep dwelling on our discouragement."[6]

This is essentially his explanation of the contemporary church's inability to evangelize. Rather than discern the spiritual forces at work in our time, we have blamed secularization. Rather than offer the person of Jesus Christ, we have focused on ethics and ideas and so end up offering truth at the expense of charity, or charity at the expense of truth. Rather than a body of joyful believers offering the transforming experience of Jesus's relationship with the Father of Love and Mercy, we become defensive dogmatists, or peddlers of banalities. At the origin of our failure is our refusal humbly to ask: *How is the Holy Spirit asking us to change that we might evangelize in this new context?*

His call to the church to a "pastoral and missionary conversion" in order to evangelize our contemporary age of liquidity is Francis's response to this crisis. It is not his alone, but the product of a deep and far-ranging discernment of our age by the Latin American church at the turn of the century. Bergoglio was very involved in this process, which culminated in the great meeting of the Latin American bishops at Aparecida, Brazil in May 2007.

Nor is Francis's vision some theory or hypothesis drawn up on a desk, but the fruit of decades of pastoral and missionary experience—above all in three places where he has developed his evangelizing vision.

The first is the Colegio Máximo in San Miguel, Buenos Aires, where Jorge Mario Bergoglio spent most of his Jesuit life: first in the 1960s as a student or scholastic, then, in the 1970s and 1980s, as novice master, provincial, and finally rector of the College. It was in this last phase that he created a vast new parish, Patriarca San José, and missioned the hundred or so Jesuits training in the college at the time to evangelize and minister to the area.

The second place was, of course, the city of Buenos Aires, where in the 1990s he was auxiliary bishop and regional vicar of Flores, a lower middle-class area of the city where there are a number of sanctuaries and shrines. From 1998, he was head of the archdiocese of the original city of Buenos Aires, with close to 3 million people, but his canvas was in reality much broader, for his was one of eleven dioceses

---

[6] Jorge Mario Bergoglio, prologue to *Las Cartas de la Tribulación* (Buenos Aires: Diego de Torres, 1988).

of the so-called Buenos Aires region, essentially an urban sprawl of around 13 million, of whom perhaps 85 percent are Catholics. Under Bergoglio's leadership, these eleven dioceses worked closely together in a common urban pastoral mission, especially after the gathering of the Latin American church at Aparecida.

Aparecida is the third locus in our story. In May 2007 the bishops of Latin America met collectively there for the first time in twenty-five years to define their continental mission. Bergoglio was not just a key contributor to the discernment process, but redactor-in-chief of the concluding document. His experience of mission in Buenos Aires is reflected above all in those sections on the *pastoral urbana* that ended with a series of concrete proposals for what it called a new urban ministry, as well as in the mindsets and attitudes for which such a ministry call.[7]

Francis has often compared Aparecida to *Evangelii Nuntiandi*, Paul VI's great 1975 document on evangelization. *Evangelii Gaudium* is, in turn, the fruit of both, drawing on the five years from 2007 to 2012 in which Bergoglio and the other bishops of the Buenos Aires region sought to implement Aparecida. It was this experience that flowed into Cardinal Bergoglio's famous brief speech to the cardinals prior to the conclave, in which he imagined Jesus not on the outside knocking to be let in, but on the inside, asking to be let out; and in which he portrayed the church as paralyzed by introversion, reflecting its own light rather than Christ's.

He used the powerful image from Luke 13:10-17 of the bent-over woman who can see little beyond the ground she is standing on. He contrasted that woman with the image of a fruitful, outgoing mother, who lives out the joy of evangelizing. He suggested that the next pope was the one to lead the church from one to the other. That has been his mission.

My task in this essay is to fill out this picture, in two parts. The first, longer part is about Francis's discernment of the era in which we are now living; where he sees that the church has been tempted to withdraw when faced with the invitation of the Holy Spirit to evangelize. The second, shorter part flows from this: on the nature

---

[7] CELAM, Aparecida: Concluding Document, sec. 509–18, https://www.celam.org/aparecida/Ingles.pdf.

of the pastoral and missionary conversion he is calling for—and why we need now to be, as he puts it, "close and concrete."[8]

Mission in Response to Epochal Change

The Colegio Máximo was founded in the early 1930s in an area an hour or two outside the city of Buenos Aires, in what was then mostly *pampa*, fertile agricultural plains. In the following decades the local area of San Miguel came to be occupied by hundreds and thousands of migrants from the interior of the country and neighboring nations who came in search of a better life. The people who arrived were generally Catholic, but unchurched, poorly catechized, with strong popular devotions but little formal practice.

At the end of his time as provincial, Bergoglio founded a huge parish, Patriarca San José, to minister to the new arrivals, sending out the Jesuit students each weekend to organize and evangelize by visiting house by house, blessing homes, saying prayers with those inside, inviting children to catechesis, discovering where there was suffering and need and connecting these with others who had time and resources to give. For the migrants of San Miguel, it was the experience of becoming a "people of God"; for the Jesuits, it was an encounter with God in the lives of ordinary people.

Today, the parish is run by Fr. Rafael Velasco, SJ. It covers a large area: some forty thousand people across seven *barrios*, five of which have churches with Sunday Mass and other liturgies, social projects, and catechesis. In Bergoglio's day "Rafa" was among the Jesuit students sent out by their rector each weekend; these days the missions are carried out by the young people in his parish. I sat down in July 2018 with eight of them following their four-day mission. I saw how moved they had been at discovering God's presence in people's lives as they went from house to house, praying with people, learning about their lives and their challenges. One of the leaders, filled with emotion, said: *misionando, fuimos misionados,* "in going out on mission, we were missioned to."

---

[8] On Pope Francis's fondness for this language, see, for example, Pope Francis, "El peligro en tiempos de crisis"; Austen Ivereigh, "The Papal Obsession with Getting Close and Concrete," *Crux*, January 23, 2017, http://cruxnow.com/analysis/2017/01/23/papal-obsession-getting-close-concrete/.

That sums up what Francis means by the *Iglesia en salida*, the "Church that goes out," and what he said to his catechists after Aparecida, when he spoke of the church that "evangelizes and is evangelized constantly through the proclamation of the *Kerygma*." It is what the first Christians discovered: that, as Cardinal Bergoglio put it in 2008, "God is present in, encourages, and is an active protagonist in the life of his people."[9] The insight of Aparecida was to recall that the church was born precisely in a context of urban pluralism, which it made use of to grow. Further, that which now prevents the church from growing was an attitude of fear and defensiveness that caused its leaders and the institution to withdraw from God's people.

Aparecida was by far the most sophisticated signs-of-the-times discernment happening in the church anywhere in the world at that time. What it grasped were the implications for evangelization in this "change of era," this *cambio de época*.[10] It understood that beyond the losers and winners, our globalized technocracy brings a new anguish, because of the erosion of the bonds of belonging, a way of being described in terms of "liquidity," to use Zygmunt Bauman's famous metaphor.[11]

The anguish was *affective*, in the sense of suffering the loss of the ties of love and trust we need for a healthy life; but also *existential*, in that the impermanence of contemporary life made it hard to dream a future. It was also *spiritual*, in that the geography and architecture of modern existence was increasingly empty of signs of the transcendent.[12] Noting how the old transmission belts of faith were now

---

[9] Jorge Mario Bergoglio, "Volver a las raíces de la fe: la misión como propuesta y desafío," in *En tus ojos está mi palabra: Homilías y discursos de Buenos Aires, 1999–2013*, ed. Antonio Spadaro (Madrid: Claretianas, 2018), 753. Jorge Mario Bergoglio, prologue to *Dios en la ciudad* (Buenos Aires: San Pablo, 2011), 5.

[10] This phrase can be traced back first to the work of the Mexican Bishops' conference and then to CELAM: see, for example, Conference of Mexican Bishops, *Carta pastoral del encuentro con Jesucristo a la solidaridad con todos: El encuentro con Jesucristo, camino de conversión, comunión, solidaridad y misión en México en el umbral del tercer milenio* (Mexico: Conferencia del Episcopado Mexicano, 2000), sec. 246; CELAM, *Globalización y nueva evangelización en América Latina y el Caribe. Reflexiones del CELAM 1999–2003*, no. 165 (Bogotá: CELAM, 2003), sec. 16. See Rodrigo Guerra López, "Cristianismo y cambio de época: Transformaciones educativas y culturales de la sociedad y de la Iglesia en América Latina" (forthcoming).

[11] See Zygmunt Bauman, *Liquid Modernity* (Cambridge, UK: Polity Press, 2000).

[12] CELAM, *Globalización y nueva evangelización en América Latina.*

largely broken, Aparecida saw that the church had to go out to the people and facilitate the personal encounter with Christ.[13] What was needed now, as Bergoglio put it to his priests after Aparecida, was a return to the "attitude that planted the faith in the beginnings of the Church," when faith was the product of a personal encounter with Jesus Christ and the experience of his transforming mercy.[14] The challenge to the church now was how to enable this encounter in the context of technocracy and liquidity. Bergoglio called this *el encuentro fundante de nuestra fe*, the "foundational experience of faith," which it described as "a personal and communal encounter with Jesus Christ which will raise up missionary disciples."[15]

The most important thing about this discernment was not its analysis of the changes of contemporary society, but the way it believed the church should respond to them. Aparecida's response was not to lament and condemn, but to discern and reform. Rather than asking, "How can we defend ourselves against this?" or "How can we go back to how things were?" the question was, "What is the Holy Spirit calling us to do? What changes must we make?" This humble, discerning response was in itself part of the conversion it called for.

A key insight was that mission had to become a way of being, both "permanent" and "paradigmatic." Not just *ad extra*, but *ad intra* at the same time. In going out on mission, the church is itself evangelized; in missioning, the church is itself converted. If the church is not missionary in a context of liquidity, it cannot evangelize; and if it does not evangelize, it shrinks. Hence the necessary spiritual, pastoral, and also institutional reforms "to make the Church visibly present as a mother who reaches out, a welcoming home, a constant school of missionary communion."[16] Hence, too, Francis's famous

---

[13] CELAM, Aparecida: Concluding Document, sec. 243–57, 258–65.

[14] Jorge Mario Bergoglio, "La misión de los discípulos al servicio de la Vida Plena," in Spadaro, ed., *En tus ojos*, 852–59.

[15] Jorge Mario Bergoglio, "Propuesta de Aparecida para la Pastoral de la Iglesia en Argentina," message to the meeting of the Sociedad Argentina de Liturgia, June 15, 2009, http://www.arzbaires.org.ar/inicio/homilias/homilias2009.htm#Propuesta _de_Aparecida_para_la_Pastoral_de_la_Iglesia_en_Argentina. "La memoria del encuentro fundante de nuestra fe aparece desde el comienzo y llega hasta el final del Documento." Cf. CELAM, Aparecida: Concluding Document, sec. 13.

[16] See Pope Francis's addresses in Spadaro, ed., *En tus ojos*, esp. "Volver a las raíces de la fe," 745–54, "El mensaje de Aparecida a los presbíteros," 797–806, and "La misión de los discípulos al servicio de la Vida Plena," 852–59.

dream in *Evangelii Gaudium* of a "missionary option," that is, "a missionary impulse capable of transforming everything, so that the Church's customs, ways of doing things, times and schedules, language and structures can be suitably channeled for the evangelization of today's world rather than for her self-preservation" (EG 27).

It is easy to miss the sting at the end there. As Bergoglio put it after Aparecida, the purpose of evangelization is not to recruit adherents, but to raise up disciples. If the aim is to fill pews and restore market share, that is spiritual worldliness; it is to put the institution in the center, rather than Christ, and to leave it untouched and unconverted, and so to compound the problem. The aim is the encounter with Christ in his people, and the institution must adapt to that end. Evangelization is to make possible the encounter with the God of mercy and to raise up missionary disciples who can communicate that experience.[17] It is not to restore the success or prestige of the institution, but to open the gates of God's grace.

In Asunción, Paraguay, in July 2015 Francis noted: "How many times do we see evangelization as involving any number of strategies, tactics, maneuvers, techniques, as if we could convert people on the basis of our own arguments. Today the Lord says to us quite clearly: in the mindset of the Gospel, you do not convince people with arguments, strategies or tactics. You convince them by learning how to welcome them."[18]

This Pelagianism of methods—evinced in a certain triumphalism in some apologetics—is one obstacle to evangelizing. But the greater obstacle in the past decades has been a Gnostic temptation to present Catholicism as a kind of ethical system or a moral code. In the final chapter of *The Mind of Pope Francis*, Massimo Borghesi calls this "the moralistic drift that characterizes Catholicism in the era of globalization,"[19] although I think his original Italian, *desviazione etica*, is easier to connect to Francis's critique in the Spanish version of *Evangelii*

---

[17] Jorge Mario Bergoglio, "La misión de los discípulos al servicio de la Vida Plena," sec. 1, in Spadaro, ed., *En tus ojos*, 852–59.

[18] Pope Francis, Homily, Campo grande, Ñu Guazú, Asunción (Paraguay), July 12, 2015, http://m.vatican.va/content/francesco/en/homilies/2015/documents/papa-francesco_20150712_paraguay-omelia-nu-guazu.html.

[19] Massimo Borghesi, *The Mind of Pope Francis: Jorge Mario Bergoglio's Intellectual Journey*, trans. Barry Hudock (Collegeville, MN: Liturgical Press, 2018), 228–29.

Gaudium of *eticismo sin bondad*, or "heartless moralism" (EG 8).[20] "It is not enough for our truth to be orthodox and our pastoral action to be efficient," Cardinal Bergoglio said in 2011; "without the joy of beauty, truth turns cold and even pitiless and arrogant."[21]

Borghesi points out that Benedict XVI shared this discernment of where contemporary Catholicism had gone wrong, which is why right at the start of his first encyclical, *Deus Caritas Est*, he said that "being Christian is not the result of an ethical choice or a lofty idea, but the encounter with an event, a person, which gives life a new horizon and a decisive direction." The quote appears in the Aparecida document and again in *Evangelii Gaudium*, where Francis says he never tires of repeating these words, "which take us to the very heart of the Gospel" (EG 7).[22] The beauty of God is his mercy, which, because it is relationship, is experience, not knowledge.

What gets lost in this "ethicist deviation," in other words, is the primary truth about our faith: the love of God for us in Jesus Christ. When we evangelize, we communicate Jesus's "Abba" relationship with the Father.[23] So "mission starts precisely from that divine enchantment, the amazement of the encounter," as Francis told the Brazilian bishops, recalling Aparecida. The church loses people, he

[20] See also CELAM, Aparecida: Concluding Document, sec. 12; Congregation for the Doctrine of the Faith, "Letter *Placuit Deo* to the Bishops of the Catholic Church on Certain Aspects of Christian Salvation," February 22, 2018, 8, http://www.vatican .va/roman_curia/congregations/cfaith/documents/rc_con_cfaith_doc_20180222 _placuit-deo_en.html. *"Eticismo sin bondad"* is badly rendered in the official English translation of *Evangelii Gaudium* as "ethical systems bereft of kindness." He is not referring to "systems" but to the reduction of the Christian offer to an ethical idea.

[21] Jorge Mario Bergoglio, "La verdad que más brilla es la verdad de la misericordia," in Spadaro, ed., *En tus ojos*, 1013–16. His Communications Day message in 2016 says something similar: "Only words spoken with love and accompanied by meekness and mercy can touch our sinful hearts. Harsh and moralistic words and actions risk further alienating those whom we wish to lead to conversion and freedom, reinforcing their sense of rejection and defensiveness" (Pope Francis, "Communication and Mercy: A Fruitful Encounter," January 24, 2016, http://w2.vatican.va/content/francesco /en/messages/communications/documents/papa-francesco_20160124_messaggio -comunicazioni-sociali.html).

[22] CELAM, Aparecida: Concluding Document, sec. 12, 243.

[23] Pope Francis, "Lettera a chi non crede. Papa Francesco risponde al giornalista Eugenio Scalfari," *La Repubblica* (Rome), September 4, 2013; the English translation of the article archived on the Vatican website is more accurate, http://w2.vatican .va/content/francesco/en/letters/2013/documents/papa-francesco_20130911 _eugenio-scalfari.html.

warned, when it imports a rationality that is alien to people, forgetting the "grammar of simplicity."[24]

The two greatest evangelizers of our age, arguably, are Mother Teresa and Pope Francis, famous for their gestures as much as their words. Their graciousness, attentiveness, and compassion perform the God they proclaim.

As Francis puts it in his letter to Chile's Catholics, "the salvation offered by Christ is always an invitation, a gift which calls for and demands freedom."[25] That is why the attempt to reduce the Christian offer to some kind of moral code or dazzling ethical system leads quickly to the Gnosticism of which Francis warns in the second chapter of *Gaudete et Exsultate*. As Thomas Merton says in *Conjectures of a Guilty Bystander*, "an exclusively ethical emphasis on right and wrong, good and evil, in Christian education, breeds doubt and not faith."[26]

In a 2004 talk he gave in praise of *Veritatis Splendor*, St. John Paul II's great defense of objective truth against the threat of relativism, Cardinal Bergoglio made a similar point to Merton's, that the reduction of Christianity to a series of precepts had in effect produced relativism. When we seek to evangelize through the state and its laws, we turn morality into a judicial code or a dazzling ethical system imposed from the outside, to which the only response can be resistance or surrender rather than a free response of the heart to the experience of God's mercy. Faith becomes ideology, and ideology is an instrument of power.[27]

As St. Augustine famously insisted, it is not the keeping of the commandments that earns God's love but the other way around: we are offered God's mercy and love unconditionally, and in receiving it, we are morally transformed.[28] Bergoglio made this point with

[24] Pope Francis, "Meeting with the Bishops of Brazil, Archbishop's House, Rio de Janeiro (Brazil)," July 27, 2013, http://w2.vatican.va/content/francesco/en/speeches/2013/july/documents/papa-francesco_20130727_gmg-episcopato-brasile.html.

[25] Pope Francis, "Al Pueblo de Dios que peregrina en Chile," Letter to Chilean Church, May 31, 2018, http://w2.vatican.va/content/francesco/es/letters/2018/documents/papa-francesco_20180531_lettera-popolodidio-cile.html.

[26] Thomas Merton, *Conjectures of a Guilty Bystander* (New York: Image, 2014), 164.

[27] See Bergoglio's essays in *La verdad los hará libres: Congreso internacional sobre la Encíclica* Veritatis splendor, ed. Carlos Alberto Scarponi (Buenos Aires: Paulinas, 2005), 19–36.

[28] For example, Augustine, *On Rebuke and Grace*, 3; *Sermons on John*, 17:6; *Against Two Letters of the Pelagians*, 1:37; 4:11, 13–15; *On the Spirit and the Letter*, 5; *On Nature and Grace*, 4–5; *On the Grace of Christ and Original Sin*, 1:27, 34.

wonderful directness in a retreat he gave just months before his election. The Gospel does not tell us if the adulterous woman whom Jesus forgave in John 8:1-11 returned to her sinful, promiscuous life, he said, but you could be sure that she did not, "because whoever encounters such great mercy cannot depart from the law, it's the result."[29]

In suggesting the opposite, that we are loved by God because we are good, we eliminate grace and turn the moral journey into a human achievement rather than a response to God's mercy. Such Pharisaism or Pelagianism is paralyzing, and deadly for evangelization. Because it is easier for the prosperous and well educated to be moral, the church soon becomes intolerable to the poor and those most in need of mercy. In withdrawing from the people of God and making itself, rather than Christ, the object of worship, the church becomes decadent, finally collapsing into the abusive, cover-up, clericalist culture of which we have been made brutally aware in news reports: a church famous for the sins of its institution, rather than for the love and beauty of Christ's mercy.

All this helps explain why, in *Evangelii Gaudium*, Francis is so fierce in deploring "doctrines that are at times more philosophical than evangelical" (EG 165), of people who speak more of law than grace, or who imply that Christianity is a form of stoicism or self-denial. The Gospel invites us to respond to the God of love who saves us, to see God in others and to go forth from ourselves to seek the good of others. "If this invitation does not radiate forcefully and attractively," Francis says in *Evangelii Gaudium*, "the edifice of the Church's moral teaching risks becoming a house of cards, and this is our greatest risk" (EG 39). The paradox that many of Francis's critics find hard to grasp is that his bid to restore grace and mercy is not about diluting the church's moral teaching, but restoring its foundations. In the absence of a culture and law permeated with Christian moral and ethical wisdom, that wisdom must be the result of a response to God's grace, or else it will be built on sand.

For Francis, evangelizing means to reconnect the church with God's presence in his holy faithful people, with those whom Francis

---

[29] The quote is from a Caritas retreat he gave in November 2012, mentioned in Austen Ivereigh, *The Great Reformer: Francis and the Making of a Radical Pope* (New York: Picador, 2015), 210. Cf. Luke 7:36-50.

called in a leaked letter to the bishops of Chile "the Church's immune system," those who "know themselves to be sinners but never cease asking forgiveness because they believe in the Father's mercy."[30] *Evangelii Gaudium* notes how "in all the baptized, from first to last, the sanctifying power of the Spirit is at work, impelling us to evangelization" (EG 119). As Francis said to the Jesuits in Colombia, "sadly we are often tempted to evangelize *for* the people, *toward* the people, but *without* the People of God. Everything for the people, but nothing with the people."[31] Yet "the People of God does not have first, second or third-class Christians," Francis tells Chile's faithful, "their participation is not a question of goodwill, concessions, rather it is constitutive of the nature of the Church."[32]

Aparecida's great insight, Bergoglio told his clergy in 2008, was to see that the greatest danger to the church came not from outside but from within, "from the eternal and subtle temptation of enclosing ourselves and putting on armor in order to be protected and secure." He used this same word for putting on armor, *abroquelamiento*, in his 1984 writing on self-accusation in which he shows how the devil sows division and confusion with a series of "reasons"—which may be true, false, or most often half-truths—that create confusion. The result is to *abroquelar el corazón*, to "armor-plate our hearts," in "egotistical convictions that lead to a world closed off from all objectivity."[33] Over time, this leads to a distorted hermeneutic which colors the way we view the world: a sense of persecution, a sense of victimhood, a tendency to divide the world into good and bad, becoming anxious, controlling and accusatory. In other words, a state of spiritual sickness that eventually separates a person or people from the body as well as from reality.

---

[30] Private letter of Pope Francis to Chile's bishops, May 15, 2018, leaked to Chilean news outlet Tele 13, http://www.t13.cl/noticia/nacional/la-transcripcion-completa -del-documento-reservado-papa-entrego-obispos-chilenos.

[31] Antonio Spadaro, SJ, "Grace Is Not an Ideology: Pope Francis' Private Conversation with Some Colombian Jesuits," *La Civiltà Cattolica*, September 28, 2017, http: //laciviltacattolica.com/grace-is-not-an-ideology-a-private-conversation-with-some -colombian-jesuits/.

[32] Pope Francis, "Al Pueblo de Dios que peregrina en Chile."

[33] Jorge Mario Bergoglio, "La Acusación de sí mismo," in *Reflexiones espirituales sobre la vida apostólica* (1987; repr., Bilbao: Mensajero, 2013), 118–25.

In his April 2018 letter to Chile's bishops calling them to Rome to discuss the clerical sex abuse crisis there, he used the word *abroquelar* again. He wrote of how, at times of tribulation, when we are "frightened and armor-plated in our comfortable 'winter palaces,' the love of God comes out to meet us and purifies our intentions so we can love as free, mature and critical men."[34] As the pope told Chile's bishops when they arrived in Rome in sackcloth and ashes following Archbishop Charles Scicluna's devastating report, this was "a time of grace" in which, "under the impulse of the Holy Spirit and in a climate of collegiality, we can take the necessary steps to generate the conversion to which the Holy Spirit is calling us." Later in the letter he spelled out what he meant by the climate of collegiality: avoiding the temptation to scapegoat, or to save ourselves by accusing others. Of course, there must be punishment and personnel changes.[35] But he warned against believing that by such punitive measures conversion would come about.[36]

This is important, because in so many indignant, angry responses to this summer's crisis, we hear what can only be described as juridical or corporate remedies: a desire for the Catholic equivalent of the FBI that will identify the guilty and calls to renew the leadership of the church from people who sound like shareholders at a corporate annual general meeting. But in his essay on Luther, the great novelist Georges Bernanos reminds us that "anyone who tries to reform the Church . . . by the same means by which one reforms a temporal society not only fails in his attempt but inevitably ends up outside the Church. . . . One reforms the visible Church only by suffering for the invisible Church."[37] Bergoglio made the same point in a 1991 reflection on the Third Week of the *Spiritual Exercises*: the church's true reforms "are born from within the entrails of the Church itself,

[34] Pope Francis, "Letter Sent by the Holy Father to the Bishops of Chile Following the Report of Archbishop Charles J. Scicluna," April 11, 2018, https://w2.vatican.va /content/francesco/en/letters/2018/documents/papa-francesco_20180408_lettera -vescovi-cile.html.

[35] At the time of writing, November 2018, seven Chilean bishops have so far been removed.

[36] Private letter of Pope Francis to Chile's bishops, May 15, 2018.

[37] Georges Bernanos, "Frère Martin," *Esprit* 19, no. 183 (October 1951): 433–45.

and not from outside." God's reform, almost by definition, occurs "where there is no alternative but to hope against hope."[38]

In his addresses to the church in Chile in 2018, Francis used the transformation of Peter after Christ's resurrection to show that conversion taking place, with the apostle standing in for the church as a whole. Jesus's forgiveness of Peter following his betrayal transforms Peter from an inward focus, ruminating on his desolation and on his persecutors, and turns him outward, to mission and evangelization—the bold, evangelizing Peter we encounter at the start of the Acts of the Apostles.

In accepting failure, and allowing God's mercy to change us, our focus shifts: in becoming Christ-centered, we become de-centered. "A wounded church does not make herself the center of things, does not believe that she is perfect, but puts at the center the one who can heal those wounds, whose name is Jesus Christ," Francis told Chile's bishops. "To know both Peter disheartened and Peter transfigured is an invitation to pass from being a Church of the unhappy and disheartened to a Church that serves all those people who are unhappy and disheartened in our midst."[39] This is, in a nutshell, what pastoral conversion means.

A Missionary Evangelization is Close and Concrete

What does a church look like that embraces God's invitation to leave its winter palaces and evangelize? After Aparecida Bergoglio drew up a list for his priests and catechists based on its section on the urban pastoral mission, which he would later develop in *Evangelii Gaudium*. "A Church in a missionary key lives a constant pastoral

[38] Jorge Mario Bergoglio, "En él sólo poner la esperanza," in *Reflexiones en esperanza* (1992; repr., Madrid: Romana, 2013), 254.

[39] Pope Francis, "Meeting with Priests, Consecrated Men and Women and Seminarians, Address of his Holiness Pope Francis," Santiago Cathedral, January 16, 2018, http://w2.vatican.va/content/francesco/en/speeches/2018/january/documents/papa-francesco_20180116_cile-santiago-religiosi.html. More or less the same words are repeated in each of his three subsequent "Chile missives," suggesting that this is indeed the pattern of conversion he is leading. See Austen Ivereigh, "Discernment in a Time of Tribulation: Pope Francis and the Church in Chile," *Thinking Faith*, May 8, 2018, https://www.thinkingfaith.org/articles/discernment-time-tribulation-pope-francis-and-church-chile.

conversion which produces new attitudes and forms of evangelization," he said, before going on to list them. They included a church
of open doors; of mission as the living expression of faith; of a deep
(not merely formal) relationship with Jesus; of the parish as a school
of communion; and evangelization as making disciples, not adherents. The path from here to *Evangelii Gaudium* is easy to see.[40]

One of the attitudes was "pastoral action with a Samaritan heart."
Like the Holy Trinity in the *Exercises* responding with love to a suffering and sinful world, the church looked now upon the city with
the "gaze of faith" as the Good Shepherd, noticing especially the
descartados, those "thrown away" in what Aparecida called "the new
peripheries." Christ is there, in his flesh. What prevents our seeing
them, and him, is our myopia: our Pharasaism, our intellectualism,
our seeking to apply "what has been said in some document or other,"
rather than looking at concrete realities with the gaze of faith.[41] As
ever with Francis, evangelization is really a hermeneutic question.
Once we see with the eyes of faith, with the merciful gaze of the Good
Shepherd, what follows is mission.[42]

This shift had a concrete expression in the pastoral experiences of
the eleven dioceses of Buenos Aires in the wake of Aparecida. Each
year there was a joint congress, known as PUBA (Pastoral Urbana de
la Región Buenos Aires), to develop new methods and visions to
evangelize this new context of plurality and liquidity. A key principle
was to "take life as it comes": to allow realities to determine pastoral
responses, learning how to open the church to people where they are
and to fit in with their timetables. That meant a church that was less
bureaucratic, more dynamic and flexible, in order to become attentive
to the presence of God in people's lives in the city, especially in the
peripheries.

PUBA came to understand the parish not just as a collection of
church buildings, but as the life of the people of God also lived in
houses, on the street, in celebrations, liturgies, and fiestas. There was

---

[40] Appendix to Bergoglio, "Volver a las raíces de la fe: la misión como propuesta y
desafío," in Spadaro, ed., *En tus ojos*, 753–54.

[41] Jorge Mario Bergoglio, "Dios vive en la ciudad: Palabras iniciales del cardenal
Jorge Mario Bergoglio, arzobispo de Buenos Aires, en el Primer Congreso Regional
de Pastoral Urbana," Buenos Aires, August 25, 2011, http://es.catholic.net/op
/articulos/43353/dios-vive-en-la-ciudad.html#modal.

[42] CELAM, Aparecida: Concluding Document, sec. 513.

talk of *santuarizar las parroquias*: parishes learning from the popular shrines, making it easy for people to offer petitions, and to take part in liturgies and to access the sacraments. A particular emphasis was placed on the apostolate of the ear, what the Jesuit theologian Christoph Théobald calls *le charisme des sourciers*, the gift of water divining, meaning those with a gift for listening to the presence of God in those who are passing by.[43]

The Good Samaritan church—Francis's by now iconic "field-hospital" church—is attentive to wounds, which nowadays means those caused by secularizing, globalized technocracy: wounds of separation from creation, from God and our fellow creatures; of the anguish of the loss of bonds, and of place; of the stress and distraction of the idolatrous cult of technology and power. His priorities as pope are the priorities of evangelization at this time: to rebuild and restore our environments—natural, ecclesial, familial—so that they reflect the hospitality and mercy of God. Francis is an ecological pope in this broader sense of *oikos*, our shared home, from which we get the word "ecology." He is concerned to rebuild our world, to offer not just a refuge from technocracy but a real alternative to it, starting with church and family and our relationship with the natural world.

The *how* matters. If we do not rebuild from below and from the edges, in poverty and service, to drink from what PUBA called "the wells of grace: the poor and their religiosity," we make the church complicit in the idolatry of power we are rejecting.[44] Francis's call is for us to imitate *synkatabasis*, God's self-abasement: to show—in what we are, how we speak, and what we do—a God who attends to the particular, to the person, to realities rather than ideas. Faced with a lack of hope, the Lord is moved, comes down, and gets close; the church's task, Francis believes, is to rediscover the Lord's way of coming near in order to evangelize.

At a time when technocracy has rendered our institutions abstract and remote and inhuman, Francis calls the church to go in the opposite direction: to be "close and concrete." Without this closeness, this mercy, this helping people open to the workings of grace in their

---

[43] Christoph Theobald, SJ, *Urgences pastorales: comprendre, partager, réformer* (Paris: Bayard, 2017), 315–16. PUBA, "Aportes para una reflexión pastoral de las parroquias urbanas," Buenos Aires, 2013.

[44] PUBA, "Aportes," par. 45.

lives, the church's ethical proclamation will become, like so many narratives today, remote and rigid, and the institution cold and distant. It is a closeness that Francis is seeking to introduce at every level of the church: through reforms in governance furthering synodality and collegiality, by making accompaniment and discernment part of church life, in urging bishops to be close to their pastors and pastors to their people.

The pastoral reforms are designed to facilitate that proximity. "We have long thought that simply by stressing doctrinal, bioethical and moral issues, *without encouraging openness to grace*, we were providing sufficient support to families, strengthening the marriage bond and giving meaning to marital life," Francis notes in *Amoris Laetitia* 37.[45] But in a liquid, postmodern world, it is not enough to oppose divorce laws or defend the principle of indissolubility as a precept. People must be helped so that permanency is their hope and their desire, and supported to stay together. That is why *Amoris Laetitia* does not simply teach the truth about marriage—although it reaffirms it on every page—but focuses on how better to enable God's grace to help people actually live it (AL 37–38).

This is what Francis means by "close and concrete," the quality of mercy that is not strained. Mercy never stands outside, shaking fingers or lecturing; it gets in with you. As James Keenan, SJ puts it, mercy is the "willingness to enter into the chaos of another."[46] That is what the incarnation does. It is what God does. It is what the church has to do. Which is why, as Francis points out in both *Evangelii Gaudium* and *Gaudete et Exsultate*, nothing better expresses the Gospel than Matthew 25 and the Beatitudes.

Mercy has a threefold evangelizing dynamic, captured in the title of *Amoris Laetitia* 8: "Discernment, accompaniment, integration." It begins with sensing need (seeing with the eyes of faith, attentive to suffering and anguish, whether physical or existential), moves to a concrete response (through the works of mercy, both corporal and

---

[45] Pope Francis, *Amoris Laetitia*, post-synodal apostolic exhortation, March 19, 2016, http://w2.vatican.va/content/dam/francesco/pdf/apost_exhortations/documents/papa-francesco_esortazione-ap_20160319_amoris-laetitia_en.pdf.

[46] James Keenan, SJ, "The Scandal of Mercy Excludes No One," *Thinking Faith*, December 4, 2015, https://www.thinkingfaith.org/articles/scandal-mercy-excludes-no-one.

spiritual), and culminates in conversion and integration, through patient and careful attention to the operation of God's grace in people's lives. To the extent that it reflects this threefold dynamic of mercy, our evangelization performs the concrete experience of God that it proclaims.

When Francis means that this is a privileged time, a *kairos* of mercy, he refers to God's own response to our time of secularization, of technocracy, of institutional failure. The summons to the church is to renew its dependence on God's power, which is his mercy. It is as if everything is now geared to revisit the birth of the church itself, to return to the "founding encounter" with the mercy of God. Our task is to respond with humility and openness and not take refuge in nostalgia, or worldly solutions, or the lure of prestige and power. Our humility, the fruit perhaps of an institutional humiliation that we are living now, will in time produce greater holiness. The very act of surrendering our illusions and idols will in time lead to a new joy, the joy that Francis has never lost since the night of his election.

He told the Jesuits in 2016—but it applies to all those who evangelize—that their "true work" was "to console the faithful people and through discernment help them so that the enemy of human nature does not rob us of our joy: the joy of evangelizing, the joy of the family, the joy of the Church, the joy of creation."[47]

Joy runs through the titles of Francis's three apostolic exhortations, *Evangelii Gaudium*, *Amoris Laetitia*, and *Gaudete et Exsultate*. It is the joy that comes from trusting God to guide us through the storm, the sweet joy of evangelizing, in a time of tribulation, a world in flux.

---

[47] Pope Francis, "Address of his Holiness Pope Francis to the 36th General Congregation of the Society of Jesus," October 24, 2016, http://w2.vatican.va/content/francesco/en/speeches/2016/october/documents/papa-francesco_20161024_visita-compagnia-gesu.html.

Chapter 3

The "Theology of the People" in the Pastoral Theology of Jorge Mario Bergoglio

Guzmán Carriquiry Lecour

Vice President, Pontifical Commission for Latin America

Toward a Better Understanding of His Pontificate

If we set out to examine the intellectual and pastoral biography of Jorge Mario Bergoglio, a matter of great importance for a deeper understanding of Pope Francis's pontificate, we must bear in mind, among many other influences, the current of thought that has been called the "theology of the people." As Juan Carlos Scannone explains, this theological current was born out of the Episcopal Pastoral Commission established in 1966 by the Argentine Bishops' Conference to welcome and contextualize the spirit and teachings of the Second Vatican Council into Argentina. Members of this commission included bishops—such as Vicente Zazpe and Enrique Angelelli—and theologians and pastoral theologians—among them Lucio Gera, Rafael Tello, Justino O'Farrell, Gerardo Farrell, Fernando Boasso, and others.[1] It was within this atmosphere that the theology of the people

---

[1] See Juan Carlos Scannone, SJ, "Pope Francis and the Theology of the People," *Theological Studies* 77 (2016): 118–35; Scannone, *La teología del pueblo: Raíces teológicas*

began to incubate, as is visible in the Argentine bishops' declaration in 1969, known as the "Document of San Miguel," which stated that "the Church's action must not only be directed towards the people but also, and principally, derive from the people itself," especially from "the poor, the sacrament of Christ."[2]

Father Lucio Gera, its greatest exponent, taught generations of young priests, above all in Buenos Aires, with his strong theological and spiritual heritage. Founder of the Argentinian Theological Society and Dean of the Faculty of Theology in Buenos Aires, he was part of the CELAM Theological and Pastoral Reflection Team and the first International Theological Commission called by Pope St. Paul VI. He was also invited to be an adviser to the Latin American Bishops' Conferences in Medellín and Puebla. Cardinal Bergoglio had great esteem for Fr. Gera and, upon his death in 2012, expressed his desire that Fr. Gera's body be buried in the cathedral of his archdiocese.[3]

---

del papa Francisco (Maliaño: Sal Terrae, 2017); Rafael Luciani, *Pope Francis and the Theology of the People*, trans. Phillip Berryman (Maryknoll, NY: Orbis, 2017); Josep-Ignasi Saranyana, *Teología en América Latina*, vol. 3, *El siglo de las teologías latinoamericanistas (1899–2001)* (Madrid: Iberoamericana-Vervuert, 2002). Fernando Boasso, *¿Qué es la Pastoral Popular?* (Buenos Aires: Patria Grande, 1974), writes that the book expresses the commission's thinking. Those widely recognized as the most significant authors of the theology of the people include Lucio Gera, Rafael Tello, Fernando Boasso, and Justino O'Farrell, to name but a few. They all studied between 1948 and 1956 in Europe, receiving doctorates from German universities or from the Angelicum in Rome, and thereby came into contact with the currents of *nouvelle théologie*. Gera completed his Licentiate in 1956 in Bonn, along with the dogmatic theologian Johannes Auer, who later became Joseph Ratzinger's colleague in Regensburg, wherein prevailed a spiritual climate influenced by the works of Romano Guardini and Max Scheler. Their Catholic formation in Europe was later "Latin Americanized," based on the hermeneutics of those who reflect on the Americas from a Latin American outlook.

[2] Conference of Bishops of Argentina, *San Miguel Document* (Conferencia Episcopal Argentina, Documento de San Miguel, *Declaración del Episcopado Argentino sobre la adaptación a la realidad actual del país de las Conclusiones de la II Conferencia General del Episcopado Latinoamericano [Medellín]*), 1969, http://www.familiasecnacional.org.ar/wp-content/uploads/2017/08/1969-ConclusionesMedellin.pdf.

[3] Virginia R. Azcuy, Carlos M. Galli, and Marcelo González, as members of the Editorial Theological Committee, published substantial tomes compiling the numerous and varied texts authored by Lucio Gera: *Escritos Teológicos Pastorales de Lucio Gera*, vol. 1, *Del Preconcilio a la Conferencia de Puebla (1956–1981)* (Buenos Aires: Agapé-Facultad de Teología, 2006), and vol. 2, *De la Conferencia de Puebla a nuestros días* (Buenos Aires: Agapé-Facultad de Teología, 2007). See also Juan Carlos Scannone, SJ, "Lucio Gera: un teólogo 'dal' popolo," *Civiltà Cattolica* 3954 (March 2015), 539–50.

Another friend and collaborator of Fr. Gera was Fr. Rafael Tello, who helped found the popular yearly pilgrimages from Buenos Aires to the Sanctuary in Lujan, and who received Pope Francis's gratitude and affection.[4] It is important, moreover, to mention Alberto Methol Ferré from Uruguay, who can also be considered part of this intellectual movement. Pope Francis referred to him as "that great thinker from Río de la Plata" who "helped us to think."[5] The theology of the people heavily influenced the document produced by the Third General Conference of the Latin American Bishops in Puebla de los Angeles (January 1979), and its legacy proved important for the Fifth General Conference of the Latin American Bishops in Aparecida (May 2007).[6]

Numerous studies and doctoral theses are being published in Argentina on the writings of Lucio Gera.

[4] In the presentation of Enrique Ciro Bianchi's book, *Pobres en este mundo, ricos en la fe (Sant 2,5): La fe de los pobres en América Latina, según Rafael Tello* (Buenos Aires: Agape libros, 2012), Cardinal Bergoglio expressed his affection and gratitude for Tello, writing in the prologue: "An admirable person, a man of God, sent to open new paths . . . Like every prophet, he was misunderstood by many of his time. Under suspicion, slandered, chastised . . . he did not escape the destiny of the cross with which God marks the great men of the Church. . . . He therefore opened many roads that we travel today in our pastoral work, and he knew how to join prophetic impetus with adhesion to the Church's sound doctrine." "Tello faithfully sought paths for the integral liberation of our people by striving ahead with evangelical newness, without falling into ideological reductionisms . . .": these are the words pronounced on May 10, 2012 by the then archbishop of Buenos Aires to the Faculty of Theology at the Catholic University of Argentina. Recently, Father Tello's body was transferred to the Shrine and Basilica of Our Lady of Luján, Patroness of Argentina.

[5] The Methol Ferré Association has collected the numerous, scattered writings of Alberto Methol Ferré on its website. A summary of some of his most significant texts was published in Italian by CSEO-Incontri, Bologna, 1983. Of particular interest is the book by Alver Metalli, *El Papa y el filósofo* (Siena: Cantagalli, 2014). The similar lines of thought shared by Bergoglio and Methol Ferré are well illustrated by Massimo Borghesi, *The Mind of Pope Francis*. Numerous studies and doctoral theses in Latin America have been written and are being written on Methol Ferré's thought.

[6] Cardinal Bergoglio was present and very active at the Fifth General Conference of Latin American Bishops in Aparecida (2006) as part of the drafting team of its Concluding Document, along with younger proponents of this current of thought, such as the theologian Carlos M. Galli—a prominent figure at the Faculty of Theology of Buenos Aires, whose doctoral thesis on "The People of God in the Peoples of the World" was directed by Father Lucio Gera, Father Victor Eduardo Fernandez, then rector of the Pontifical Catholic University of Argentina and currently archbishop of La Plata, and the author of this text, Dr. Guzmán Carriquiry Lecour, then undersecretary of the Pontifical Council for the Laity and currently vice-president of the

Nevertheless, for decades these authors were almost completely unknown in academic institutions and in American and European publications. In the 1970s and '80s, however, due to the ideological influence of secularizing progressivism and radical Marxism, the books of Gustavo Gutiérrez, Hugo Assman, Leonardo Boff, and other proponents of liberation theology received much attention. Perhaps it had to do with the fact that the prolific literary output of authors such as Gera, Tello, and Methol Ferré touched on so many diverse topics. But it was above all because they were subjected to the suspicion of coming from "conservative" churches, of being critical of Marxist-inspired ideological and political currents, and of falling into a cultural and populist romanticism.

Today, after the fall of communist regimes and revolutionary messianism, we should recognize that while the theology of the people should be understood as a variant of liberation theology, it goes beyond it and yet is no less prophetic in its criticism of "social sin." Neither is it inferior regarding the "preferential love for the poor" or the struggle to liberate people from oppressive and dominating structures. It is, however, distinct from secularist theologies and the attraction to Marxism, which many authors of Liberation Theology, including Gustavo Gutiérrez—perhaps the best of them—have now abandoned. Some of the prophetic intuitions and major themes coming from liberation theology have resisted the flow of time. After undergoing the discernment of the church's magisterium,[7] they have been assimilated by the Latin American church through the framework provided by "theologians of the people" from the Río de la Plata school and today find global influence in Pope Francis.

A line of continuity emerges between the Third General Conference of the Latin American Bishops in Puebla de los Angeles (January 1979), the Fifth General Conference of the Latin American Bishops in Aparecida (May 2007), and the apostolic exhortation *Evangelii Gaudium*—the most important programmatic document of the current

Pontifical Commission for Latin America. Father Diego Fares, SJ, one of the many Jesuit disciples of Bergoglio, was also present.

[7] Important documents related to this discernment included the following produced by the Congregation for the Doctrine of the Faith, whose prefect was Cardinal Joseph Ratzinger: *Libertatis Nuntius* (1984) and *Libertatis Conscientia* (1986), as well as the dialogues and reflections carried out by CELAM. In the encyclical *Centesimus Annus* (1991), John Paul II promoted the positive aspects of an "integral liberation theology."

pontificate. Each of these documents is heavily influenced by the theology of the people.

Once the initial impact and surprise of Pope Francis's pontificate was overcome, an awareness emerged of the need to dedicate serious and systematic study to the writings of Jorge Mario Bergoglio as well as to those of his favorite authors, such as Lucio Gera, Juan Carlos Scannone, and Methol Ferré. Likewise, a more in-depth study of the magisterium of the Latin American bishops is needed, especially of Puebla and Aparecida.

Several theological and pastoral concerns present in Pope Francis's writings can only be understood when placed in the context of the theology of the people and the writings surrounding it. This raises the question: How do we define the Theology of the People?

Who Are the "People"? Echoes and Implications

For those who follow Pope Francis's teachings, one word resonates deeply and strongly: *"pueblo"* (people). It has been said that Pope Francis has a certain sparkle in his eyes every time he says the word. The term "people" has been a part of the pope's vocabulary ever since his first papal greeting, when he said, "the people and their Bishop together." "People" is the most frequently used noun in the most important programmatic document of his pontificate, the apostolic exhortation *Evangelii Gaudium*, appearing there 164 times. Do not the people of the United States feel the same profound echoes and implications when they declare in the Preface to the Constitution: "We, the people of the United States of America . . ."?

The "people" cannot be reduced to a simple sum total of individuals, nor to the body of citizens who compose a society, nor to the gray and impersonal term "population." "The term 'citizens' is a logical category," writes Jorge Mario Bergoglio. "People is an historical and mythical category. We live in a society, and together we understand it and explain it logically. 'People' cannot be explained in a merely logical way. It contains a wealth of meaning that eludes us if we don't resort to other modes of comprehension and other hermeneutics. . . . To be in a society and to belong to it as citizens, in the sense of order, is a great step forward in functionality. But the social person acquires their fullest identity as a citizen in belonging to a 'people.'" This is key, Bergoglio affirms, because identity is founded on "belonging." "There is no identity without belonging. A person's identity as a citizen is directly proportional to the extent that he or she lives their belonging. To whom? To the people in which he or she was born and lives. . . . Being a faithful citizen is a virtue, and participation in political life is a moral obligation. But to become a people is something greater, and requires a constant process in which each generation is involved."[8] Just as "the fatherland" evokes the notion of paternity—where the traditions of past generations are passed on as a patrimony that must be made fruitful in the present, and just as "the nation" comes from the Latin for "born" (*natus*)—evoking a notion of maternity that always welcomes new generations, so also does "people" relate to a form of solidarity, of fraternity, that goes beyond lineage.

Thus the theology of the people has resisted the tendency to think that the "people" can be fully explained through sociological and economic analysis. It is acutely aware that a people's reality is wrought in the awareness of its origins and historical vicissitudes, in the heritage of its tradition, in its cultural and religious background, in its social ethos, in its capacity to integrate diverse components into an ethnic and cultural fusion, in the social framework of family and work, and in its shared destiny with the goal of a worthy and good life for all members. It is enriched by a historical-cultural method that is vastly more capable of penetrating into the deepest fibers of the identity of a people.[9] Bergoglio defined the "people-nation" as "a shared experience of life centered on values and principles, on history, customs, language, faith, causes, and collective dreams."[10] Within the concept of "people" that derives from this theological current, a current embraced by Pope Francis, there exists an understanding of the social and cultural experience of the people—a substantial, daily experience of solidarity—that is not to be confused with the mass-produced commercialized culture of its people. It is permeated by deep, rich, and fruitful roots, by an awareness of whole-hearted citizenship that exercises its rights and expresses its collective aspirations, by an inclusive participation in a common project of nation building that is united by a passion that is in itself liberating. The experience of "we as a people"—that is, of this unique form of

---

[8] Jorge Mario Bergoglio, *Nosotros como ciudadanos, nosotros como pueblo: Hacia un bicentenario en justicia y solidaridad 2010–2016* (Buenos Aires: Claretiana, 2013).

[9] See Scannone, *La teología del pueblo.*

[10] Bergoglio, *Nosotros como ciudadanos.*

a "communion of persons" involved in an intrinsic search for good-ness, truth, and beauty, joined by a common fight for peace, justice, and solidarity—is what gives flesh and blood to participatory de-mocracies, dynamic realities that cannot be reduced to the vacuous rules of procedural systems.[11] In this sense, "the people" is a collective subject aimed at the construction of a nation and driven by a *telos*—a historical project, a utopian horizon, a "way toward" (or "final cause" in scholastic terms) that draws a person and leads them toward their goal: in other words, the "common good."[12]

It is not surprising, then, that Pope Francis writes about the joy of belonging to a people and of living the experience of the people. He entrusts the peoples with a mission of the "globalization of hope"—including the poor, whom he recognizes as the backbone of grassroots organizing efforts—in contrast to a "globalization of exclu-sion and indifference."[13] Fr. Lucio Gera spoke of the "anti-people" when referring to the oligarchies that abandon the interest of the common good of the people and nation and think only of defending their own privileges, those responsible for situations of exploitation and exclusion.

Tendencies to Fracture the Awareness and Experience of Being a People

This is no romanticized, idealized vision. Pope Francis makes it clear that the tides of hedonistic and asocial neo-individualism—widespread in our time—erode the experience and awareness of being a people. The pope calls these tides the "globalization of indif-ference." Their effects are manifested in the rupture of familial and

[11] See Mario Toso and José Paradiso, prefaces to Jorge Mario Bergoglio, *Noi come cittadini, noi come popolo* (Milan: Jaca, 2013), 7–17, the Italian translation of Bergoglio, *Nosotros como ciudadanos*.

[12] Bergoglio, *Noi come cittadini*. Elsewhere, Bergoglio speaks of the "soul" of a people as "a hermeneutic, a way of viewing reality, an awareness . . . of one's own dignity," in Jorge Mario Bergoglio, "Una istituzione che vive il suo charisma: Discorso di ap-ertura della Congregazione provincial" (San Miguel, Buenos Aires, February 18, 1974), in Jorge Mario Bergoglio, *Pastorale sociale*, ed. Marco Gallo, trans. A. Taroni (Milan: Jaca Book, 2015).

[13] Pope Francis, "Address to the Second World Meeting of Popular Movements," Santa Cruz de la Sierra (Bolivia), July 9, 2015, http://w2.vatican.va/content/francesco /en/speeches/2015/july/documents/papa-francesco_20150709_bolivia-movimenti -popolari.html.

social bonds. They create "liquid societies": fragmented realms of conflicting individual interests that augment polarized oppositions and make dialogue and social cohesion impossible. This process of erosion is manifested and quickened by the takeover of genuine politics by the power games and media shows put on by corporations that make up an "establishment," falling short of the needs and hopes of the people. It is also manifested in the colonization of culture by ideologies that militate against the shared ethos. The end result is the absence of collective passions and ideals—a hostile environment, without communal memory, where cohesion depends more on an ephemeral succession of images and perceptions transmitted by the media for social control rather than on the awareness of a common destiny lived over time. Individuals are reduced to passive spectators of television and electronic devices. In the global village built by the communications revolution, what is most lacking are authentic human relationships, friendship, and communion. On the one hand, separation and indifference prevail; on the other, manipulation and exploitation triumph.

In this way, the fragmentation of the experience of being a "people" reduces society to a chaotic and confused group of individuals, oscillating between narcissism and depressed loneliness. Vulnerable to the influence of a powerful and persuasive cultural assimilation determined by the dominant powers, peoples are reduced to masses ruled by the dictates of political, economic, technocratic, and ideological elites. These "enlightened" minorities, warns the pope, try to appropriate collective identities and pretend to be teachers and guides policing the masses, whom they consider uncultured and easily manipulated. The devil works among the elites, through the idolatries of money, power, and ideologies.

Bipolar Tensions Along the Path toward Becoming a People

Pope Francis makes it clear that to belong to a people—to be part of a common identity—is the fruit of a process, a journey of "becoming a people." It requires individuals to grow in the awareness and experience of being a people in which every generation must take part, throughout the important stages of its history. Pope Francis sees this long path of the creation of a people through history as marked by a series of bipolar tensions, tensions that characterize any form of human society (EG 217–37).[14] "It is an arduous and slow effort," he writes in *Evangelii Gaudium*, "calling for a desire for integration and a willingness to achieve this through the growth of a peaceful and multifaceted culture of encounter" (EG 220).

One of these bipolar tensions is that between unity and conflict. The unity of the people must prevail over the conflicts that threaten to tear it apart, and yet conflicts are often intrinsic to the healthy development of a people. These insights are forged and tested by history: the Argentine people, and certainly the former Jesuit Provincial of Río de la Plata, suffered a great deal from civil war and the unparalleled violence caused by the tragically blinding passions of guerrilla violence and the murderous repression of armed forces. The "unity" in question is not "a consensus on paper or a transient peace for a contented minority" (EG 218). It is not brought about by fleeing conflict, ignoring it, or silencing dissent. Many conflicts are legitimate and necessary. One must know how to suffer conflict—working through it with respect and authenticity—in order that it might be resolved in a greater fusion of the people's unity and prevented from tearing the nation apart and rendering it impotent. Unity in diversity is required. Such are the insights conceptually represented by the image of the "polyhedron" that Bergoglio proposes for national societies and the international community. It is neither a global, stateless, technocratic, and managerial "sphere" that nullifies the richness of plurality, nor is it the impoverishment of an "isolated, sterilizing partiality" born of localisms and petty xenophobic tendencies (EG 234–35).

Another of these bipolar tensions is that between reality and ideas. An awareness that reality is always greater than ideas must prevail over those who want to impose the narrow molds of ideology on the people. Oligarchs and liberal technocrats on the one hand and Marxist-Leninists on the other both despise the theology of the people; they cling to their ideological programs in order to impose them by force on a reality that transcends them. For them, people, and especially the poor, are merely electoral clients, mass labor, or the uninformed recipients of the politics of the "enlightened"—in no way protagonists of their own lives and destinies, capable of living

---

[14] In *The Mind of Pope Francis*, Massimo Borghesi delves into Bergoglio's unique thought on bipolar tensions and the intellectual influences related to it.

according to their own wisdom and preferences, and capable of forming new, life-giving paths inspired by their own cultural resources.

Growing as a people, therefore, means being able to generate consensus and convergence in pursuit of a project of integral and mutually supportive development. It means attacking the causes of inequality and discrimination while privileging dialogue and affirming what unites more than what divides and opposes. An authentic people is an inclusive, egalitarian reality where everyone can be integrated within an enriching diversity, where the poor are not excluded but are protagonists who share in the common project of society, where there are no second-class, discarded, or excluded citizens, where there is movement along paths of peace, justice, and solidarity.

Neither can the autocratic hierarchy of the state nor the utopia of market self-regulation pretend to replace democratic participation wrought through a people's varied forms of association. When everything revolves around power plays, the bureaucratic management of the state, or confidence in the "invisible hand" of the market, without taking into consideration the dignity and centrality of real subjects—persons, families, communities, associations, companies, popular movements, and social initiatives—a people's agency is obfuscated, the democratic fabric of the state comes unraveled, and the possibilities of the formation of virtues within the social economy are blocked.

"People" and "Populism"

Some commentators have identified certain literary roots in Bergoglio's hermeneutics on the "people," especially Fyodor Dostoevsky, one of the pope's beloved authors, for whom the concept of "people" (particularly as interpreted by Romano Guardini) defines and summarizes what is most genuine, profound, and substantial in society. Even more important are the author's political roots, which greatly influenced the proponents of the theology of the people. Bergoglio also experienced a certain political and cultural affinity with the vast national and popular movement of Peronism in Argentina. His interaction with it was influenced by the social doctrine of the church, which expresses the needs and rights of a nation's laborers and seeks a "third way" beyond capitalism and communism. Jorge

Mario Bergoglio was part of an entire generation that was outraged by the violent repression against Peronism and the ban imposed by the armed forces on the political and electoral participation of its representatives. At the same time, Bergoglio neither professed adherence to the messianic ideology of Peronism nor participated in its political activities. He has never declared himself a Peronist.

Still less was he ever a "populist," "a word so overused and worn out lately, due to intellectual laziness, that it has already lost all meaning."[15] No one is more removed from irresponsible demagoguery, from superficial responses to the problems of people, and from "bread and circus" handouts to the needy as political clients than Jorge Mario Bergoglio. He makes clear that welfare subsidies should only be provisional and supplementary; they cannot substitute for striving for sustainable and meaningful work for all members of an inclusive society.[16] Workers and their popular movements are fundamental protagonists of a people on a journey. These organizations seek to organize the labor of those excluded from the job market in the struggle for an inclusive society in which full employment is achieved.

[15] Víctor Manuel Fernández, ed., *Hacia una cultura del encuentro: La propuesta del papa Francisco* (Buenos Aires: EDUCA, 2017), 12. Pope Francis makes many clear statements against the evils of "populism." In *Evangelii Gaudium* 204 he affirms his interest in "the creation of sources of employment . . . which goes beyond a simple welfare mentality," and he also maintains that "welfare projects, which meet certain urgent needs, should be considered merely temporary responses" (EG 202). In his encyclical *Laudato Si'* (May 24, 2015, http://w2.vatican.va/content/francesco/en /encyclicals/documents/papa-francesco_20150524_enciclica-laudato-si.html), he repeats the need "to prioritize the goal of access to steady employment for everyone" and affirms that "helping the poor financially must always be a provisional solution in the face of pressing needs" (LS 127–28). In response to a question on the same subject posed by Hernan Reyes Alcaide in his book-interview *Papa Francisco: Latinoamérica* (Buenos Aires: Planeta, 2017), 58–59, Pope Francis affirms the following: "Today the word 'populism' is abused and used without nuance to refer to an excess of different situations. In the first place, I would distinguish 'populist' from 'popular.' The term 'popular' is used to refer to someone who manages to interpret the feelings, tendencies, and culture of a people. There is nothing wrong with this in itself. It could even form the basis for a transforming and lasting project." The Pope here explicitly criticizes "populism" "when it expresses someone's ability to politically manipulate a people's culture to serve their own ends." "The problem is that today," the Pope concludes, "this word has been turned into the 'battle horse' of ultra-liberal programs to serve selfish interests, (such that) anyone who tries to defend the rights of society's weakest members will be presented as a 'populist' with a markedly derogatory tone."

[16] Cf. Alcaide, *Papa Francisco*, 58–59.

How can a laudable polyhedral society be built if everyone's capabilities, sense of freedom and responsibility, gift of sacrifice and solidarity, and culture of work and creativity are not encouraged to flourish? "To be popular," Pope Francis has said, "is so different from being populist."[17]

The Holy, Faithful People of God

"It is evident in our usage," wrote Jorge Mario Bergoglio many years ago, "that 'people' has become an ambiguous term due to the influence of ideological presuppositions with which this reality is affirmed and perceived."[18] Bergoglio prefers the expression "faithful people," which captures what is essential to an authentic people. The pope assumes the major themes presented in the ecclesiology born out of the biblical and conciliar notion of the "people of God." This concept, found 184 times in the documents of the Second Vatican Council, was developed in chapter 2 of the Dogmatic Constitution on the Church, *Lumen Gentium*, under the title: "The People of God." For this reason, Bergoglio has always presented the church as God's holy and faithful people (EG 95, 130). In an interview granted to Father Spadaro, he states it very simply: "The image of the Church that I like most is that of the holy, faithful people of God. This is the definition I use most often . . . from paragraph 12 of *Lumen Gentium*. Belonging to a people has a strong theological value. God, in the history of salvation, has saved a people. There is no full identity without belonging to a people. . . . The people itself constitutes a subject. The Church is the People of God who journey through history, with their joys and sorrows."[19]

The Faculty of Theology in Buenos Aires, under the guidance of Lucio Gera, led the way in commenting on *Lumen Gentium* in 1965, emphasizing the unity of its two chapters on "Mystery" and "People." *Evangelii Gaudium* reflects this understanding when it affirms that

---

[17] Alcaide, *Papa Francisco*, 58–59.

[18] Bergoglio, "Una istituzione che vive il suo charisma."

[19] Antonio Spadaro, SJ, "Intervista a Papa Francesco," *La Civiltà Cattolica* 3918 (September 19, 2013), 449–77; English translation published as "A Big Heart Open to God," *America*, September 19, 2013, https://www.americamagazine.org/faith/2013/09/30/big-heart-open-god-interview-pope-francis.

the church "is certainly a mystery rooted in the Trinity, yet she exists concretely in history as a people of pilgrims and evangelizers, transcending any institutional expression, however necessary" (EG 111). The church is "the mystery of the pilgrim People of God in communion." "We" are the social and historical subject of the mystery.[20] "Everything the first chapter of the Constitution says about the church as sacrament, or as mystery, or as the Body of Christ, or as *Ecclesia de Trinitate . . .* has as its historical subject the People of God. In other words, it indicates the people of the Covenant, a pilgrim people, with a deep eschatological connotation, a people historically walking along the path towards the Kingdom of God."[21] Bergoglio evokes the fundamental teachings of *Lumen Gentium*: "Therefore, the chosen People of God is one: 'one Lord, one faith, one baptism' (Eph 4:5); sharing a common dignity as members from their regeneration in Christ, having the same filial grace and the same vocation to perfection; possessing in common one salvation, one hope and one undivided charity" (LG 32).

I would now like to highlight several fundamental aspects of the people of God according to the Argentine theological tradition that is so present in Pope Francis's teaching.

The *Sensus Fidei Fidelium*

In 1974 Jorge Mario Bergoglio began reflecting on the conciliar doctrine of the *sensus fidei fidelium* and the infallibility *in credendo* of God's holy and faithful people, continuing the teachings of *Lumen Gentium* 8 and 12. These same teachings were explicitly echoed in the

[20] See Carlos M. Galli, *Cristo, Maria, la Chiesa e i popoli: La mariologia di papa Francesco* (Rome: Libreria Editrice Vaticana, 2017), 92. See also Carlos M. Galli, "El 'retorno' del pueblo de Dios. Un concepto-símbolo de la eclesiología del Concilio a Francisco," in Virginia R. Azcui, Jose C. Caamaño, and Carlos M. Galli, *La eclesiología del Concilio Vaticano II: Memoria, reforma y profecía* (Buenos Aires: Agape-Faculty of Theology, 2015), 405–72. See Joseph Ratzinger, "The Ecclesiology of the Second Vatican Council," in *Church, Ecumenism, and Politics: New Endeavors in Ecclesiology*, trans. Michael J. Miller et al. (San Francisco: Ignatius Press, 2008).

[21] Fr. Dario Vitale, "Il Papa sottolinea il ruolo dei laici per superare il clericalismo," interview by Andrea Tornielli, *Vatican Insider*, April 29, 2016, http://www.lastampa .it/2016/04/29/vaticaninsider/il-papa-sottolinea-il-ruolo-dei-laici-per-superare-il -clericalismo-yHbS2KESAr93tsC8ChYGGL/pagina.html.

Concluding Document of Aparecida. Father Bergoglio has pointed out on several occasions how magisterial teaching and theology faithfully illustrate the content of what we believe, but that both must attentively observe the people in order to appreciate how the church lives the faith. "If you want to know *what* the Church believes, go to the magisterium—because it is charged with teaching it infallibly—but if you want to know *how* the Church believes, go to the faithful people." Bergoglio repeats himself in a more specific manner: "The magisterium teaches you who Mary is, but the faithful people will teach you how to love Mary."[22]

Pope Francis always emphasizes that the people of God, to which one belongs by baptism—the first and fundamental consecration, the indelible seal of our Christian identity—"is anointed with the grace of the Holy Spirit."[23] He comes down so harshly against both old and new forms of clericalism within the church because "it has a tendency to diminish and devalue the baptismal grace that the Holy Spirit placed in the hearts of the people."[24] This is at the root of the neo-Gnostic and Pelagian heresies that Pope Francis denounces as still present among us.[25]

Inculturation of the Gospel and the Evangelization of Culture

The Catholic Church is clearly undergoing a rapid inclusion of the ecclesiastical peripheries and their various forms of inculturation. Latin America is home to more than 40 percent of the world's Catholics, to which must be added the vast majority of the 60 million Hispanics in the United States. More than half of the world's Catholics live in the Americas. Brazil, Mexico, the Philippines, and the United States are the countries with the greatest number of Catholics, which

[22] Jorge Mario Bergoglio, *Meditaciones para religiosos* (Buenos Aires: Diego de Torres, 1982), 47.

[23] See Pope Francis, "Letter to Cardinal Marc Ouellet," March 19, 2016, http://w2 .vatican.va/content/francesco/en/letters/2016/documents/papa-francesco _20160319_pont-comm-america-latina.html.

[24] Pope Francis, "Letter to Cardinal Marc Ouellet."

[25] See Pope Francis, apostolic exhortation, *Gaudete et Exsultate*, March 19, 2018, par. 36–65, http://w2.vatican.va/content/francesco/en/apost_exhortations/documents /papa-francesco_esortazione-ap_20180319_gaudete-et-exsultate.html.

in about fifteen years will be followed by Argentina, Colombia, the Democratic Republic of Congo, and Nigeria, while only in Italy and in Poland do Catholics remain prevalent in Europe. Catholicity unfolds, in fact, in "the beauty of her varied face."[26]

It is not surprising, then, that the perspective of the evangelization of culture and cultures forms a central theme of what we call the theology of the people. It acts as a counterbalance to the risks of generic abstraction when speaking of "world" or "people," and it avoids all Eurocentrism. It translates the broad relationship between "the Church and the world," of which, for example, *Gaudium et Spes* speaks, into the more historically specific terms of the incarnation or inculturation of the faith of the people of God within their cultural, political, and historical contexts. As Pope Francis wrote in *Evangelii Gaudium*, "The People of God is incarnate in the peoples of the earth, each of which has its own culture"; for this reason, he speaks of the church as "a people of many faces" (EG 115–18).

Father Lucio Gera was largely responsible for writing the remarkable chapter on the "evangelization of culture" in the Puebla document. He contextualized for Latin America the precious references in the apostolic exhortation *Evangelii Nuntiandi* of recently canonized Pope St. Paul VI that speak of the divorce between the Gospel and culture as "the drama of our time."[27] Many have pointed out that, when Bergoglio was Provincial and participated in the 32nd General Chapter of the Society of Jesus (1975–1976), he frequently stressed that what seemed to him most important in Decree 4 of the General Chapter—"Our mission today"—was not so much the question of faith and justice as the perspective of inculturation. Later, in 1985, Father Bergoglio, then Rector of the Faculty of San Miguel in Buenos Aires, organized the first International Congress on the Evangelization of Culture and the Inculturation of the Gospel, which was held in Latin America.

---

[26] Pope John Paul II, apostolic letter, *Novo Millennio Ineunte*, January 6, 2001, sec. 295, http://w2.vatican.va/content/john-paul-ii/en/apost_letters/2001/documents/hf_jp-ii_apl_20010106_novo-millennio-ineunte.html; cited by Pope Francis in *Evangelii Gaudium* 116.

[27] Pope Paul VI, apostolic exhortation, *Evangelii Nuntiandi*, December 8, 1975, sec. 20, http://w2.vatican.va/content/paul-vi/en/apost_exhortations/documents/hf_p-vi_exh_19751208_evangelii-nuntiandi.html.

The greatest exponents of the theology of the people have spilled much ink regarding the inculturation of the faith of the people of God in the throes of history, in the cultural substratum, and in the religiosity of the new *mestizo* American peoples. Embracing the reality of the people has led them to recover a historical awareness, leading them to recognize how God has acted in the birth and life of the people through his "founding evangelization" and how God's promise of liberation was realized in the history of the people. The fruits of the theology of the people are clearly present in the Puebla document: "When incarnated in our peoples, the Gospel gathers them together in the historical and cultural uniqueness that we call Latin America." The luminous symbol of Latin American identity is "the mestizo face of Our Lady of Guadalupe," a founding event that occurred at the beginning of the evangelization of the New World.[28] The introduction to the Aparecida document—which boasted Cardinal Bergoglio as its editor-in-chief—affirms that "the gift of Catholic tradition is an indispensable foundation of the identity, unity, and originality of Latin America and the Caribbean. It is a historical-cultural reality sealed by the Gospel of Christ, a reality in which sin abounds— neglect of God, vicious conduct, oppression, violence, ingratitude, and misery—but where the grace of Easter victory abounds even more."[29] The Catholic faith thus characterizes the essential historical identity and cultural matrix of the new peoples. This is evident in the baptism of the vast majority of Latin Americans, in the mature faith of many baptized persons, and in popular piety, which is manifested in the "love for the suffering Christ, the God of compassion, pardon, and reconciliation . . . the love of the Lord present in the Eucharist . . . the God who is close to the poor and to those who suffer, and the profound devotion to the most holy Virgin of Guadalupe, the *Aparecida*, the Virgin invoked under various national and local titles."[30]

---

[28] CELAM, Puebla: Concluding Document, sec. 446. English translation, *Puebla and Beyond: Documentation and Commentary*, ed. John Eagleson and Philip J. Scharper (Maryknoll, NY: Orbis, 1979).

[29] CELAM, Aparecida: Concluding Document 8.

[30] Pope Benedict XVI, "Opening Address to the Fifth General Conference of the Bishops of Latin America," Shrine of Aparecida, May 13, 2007, sec. 1, http://w2 .vatican.va/content/benedict-xvi/en/speeches/2007/may/documents/hf_ben-xvi _spe_20070513_conference-aparecida.html.

Revaluing Popular Religiosity

The theme of the inculturation of faith and the evangelization of culture is intimately linked to that of a renewed appreciation of popular religiosity as a hermeneutic key to understanding the profound reality of our peoples.

Immediately following Vatican II—an extremely rich and fruitful period, but also contradictory and tumultuous, something of an "existential crisis" of ecclesial renewal, "popular religiosity experienced its most serious eclipse within the Catholic Church in centuries, at least within the church's priestly and intellectual strata. During this period, popular religiosity was scorned, and at best treated as an inevitable evil on its way towards disappearing, a fetish or magical holdover which had to be purified in the best of cases or temporarily suffered in condescension. This is one of the most extraordinary paradoxes of this period, which was so fruitful under other aspects," especially given that the ecclesiology of the people of God was then at its height.[31] A combination of cultural forces converged to create this paradox: secularizing theologies of Protestant origin provoked rampant iconoclasm, resulting from the separation and even opposition between faith and religion; a fascination with Marxism and its obsession with the "opium of the people"; and the spread of North American functionalist sociologies and their emphasis on the conflict between "tradition" and "modernity." All this took place during a period in which there was a serious crisis of priestly identity and even of the identity of the church itself. On the other hand, this crisis helped to "strip popular religiosity of a kind of worldly rigidity, and to surrender it to one of its most creative and radiant moments. Innovative positivity cannot be achieved without a stormy passage through negativity."[32]

Pope Francis, not surprisingly, recalls the admiration he felt for Paul VI's apostolic exhortation *Evangelii Nuntiandi* (1975), which he still considers to be among the most successful and important documents of the postconciliar pontifical magisterium, and which certainly inspired elements of *Evangelii Gaudium*. This admiration is concen-

---

[31] Alberto Methol Ferré, "Marco histórico de la religiosidad popular," in CELAM, *Iglesia y religiosidad popular en América Latina: Ponencias y documento final* (Bogotá: CELAM, 1977), 47.

[32] Methol Ferré, "Marco histórico de la religiosidad popular," 48.

trated in a very special way in paragraph 48 in reference to "popular piety": "If it is well oriented, above all by a pedagogy of evangelization, [popular piety] is rich in values," wrote Paul VI. "It manifests a thirst for God which only the simple and poor can know. It makes people capable of generosity and sacrifice even to the point of heroism, when it is a question of manifesting belief. It involves an acute awareness of profound attributes of God: fatherhood, providence, loving, and constant presence. It engenders interior attitudes rarely observed to the same degree elsewhere: patience, the sense of the cross in daily life, detachment, openness to others, devotion." Paul VI also recognized its limits, but stressed: "When it is well oriented, this popular religiosity can be more and more for multitudes of our people a true encounter with God in Jesus Christ" (EN 48).[33]

Evangelii Nuntiandi was heavily influenced by the contributions of the Latin American synod fathers during the Third General Assembly of the Synod of Bishops on "Evangelization in the Modern World." It proved a turning point that had profound consequences for the church's postconciliar journey. Paul VI recognized this when he affirmed: "These expressions were for a long time regarded as less pure and were sometimes despised, but today they are almost everywhere being rediscovered" (EN 48). Around the same time, Father Lucio Gera periodically gathered a group of friends and collaborators to expound on the theme of "popular religiosity." An extraordinary meeting was organized by CELAM in 1976 that proved a decisive moment in this cultural, pastoral, and theological turning point in Latin America. The contributions of Fr. Lucio Gera, Alberto Methol Ferré, and the Chilean Fr. Joaquin Alliende, among others, stood out

---

[33] At the Third General Assembly of the Synod of Bishops, on "Evangelization in the Modern World," the fathers of Latin American origin, though with differing styles, let their common experience, converging concerns, and pastoral requests be thoroughly known. Noteworthy in this respect was the speech made by the president of CELAM, the Argentine Cardinal Eduardo Pironio. It could be said that this synod marked one of the highest contributions of the Latin American church to the universal church. The fundamental themes pointed out from a Latin American perspective, including popular religiosity (highlighted in Pironio's speech), provided important input for the apostolic exhortation *Evangelii Nuntiandi* (1975). The churches in Latin America—with their pastors at the forefront—felt that their experiences, concerns, and needs were very much reflected in this document. It could be said that it was a synod heavily influenced by Latin America.

in the meeting's deliberations. A book published by CELAM in 1977, along with the notes and debates of that meeting, entitled *The Church and Popular Religiosity in Latin America*, was frequently consulted and well appreciated by Fr. Jorge Mario Bergoglio and continues to hold great validity and richness even today.[34]

In its revaluation of popular piety, with its vast implications and repercussions for the church and Latin America, the apostolic exhortation *Evangelii Nuntiandi* formed the base document for the preparation of the Third General Conference of Latin American Bishops in Puebla de los Angeles (1979), convened by John Paul II during the first apostolic journey of his pontificate to Mexico. The meeting was a mature expression of the second phase following Vatican II and proved an important step forward in ecclesial and Latin American self-awareness. "The religion of the Latin American people, in its most characteristic cultural form, is an expression of the Catholic faith. It is a popular Catholicism," observes the final Puebla document. It points out that "this religion of the people is lived primarily by the 'poor and simple,' but it encompasses all social sectors, and is sometimes one of the few bonds that unite the people of our politically divided nations." This document defines popular religiosity "at its core" as "a collection of values that respond with Christian wisdom to the great questions of existence. Popular Catholic wisdom has a capacity for providing a living synthesis. Thus it creatively joins the divine and the human; Christ and Mary; spirit and body; communion and institution; person and community; faith and country; intelligence and affection."[35] It gathers multitudes in shrines for religious feasts, fulfilling the universal imperative to transmit a message that "is not reserved for a small group of privileged or chosen initiates, but is destined for all."[36] The document also warned: "If the Church

---

[34] CELAM, *Iglesia y religiosidad popular en América Latina: Ponencias y documento final* (Bogotá: CELAM, 1977). This book contains important writings by Alberto Methol Ferré, Lucio Gera, the Chilean Joaquín Alliende, and other scholars writing on popular religiosity in Latin America. The book became a "classic" on the subject and was later cited by the *Catechism of the Catholic Church* (1674–76) and by the *Directory on Popular Piety and the Liturgy: Principles and Guidelines* (2002) produced by the Congregation for Divine Worship and the Discipline of the Sacraments, http://www.vatican.va /roman_curia/congregations/ccdds/documents/rc_con_ccdds_doc_20020513_vers -direttorio_en.html.

[35] CELAM, Puebla: Concluding Document, sec. 448.

[36] Puebla: Concluding Document, sec. 449.

does not reintegrate the religiosity practiced by the Latin American people, a vacuum will be created that will be filled by sects, secularized political messianisms, bone-numbing consumerism, and either indifference or pagan pansexualism."[37]

Jorge Mario Bergoglio, first as a priest and later as a bishop, considered these chapters on popular culture and religiosity as the most original and important results of the Third General Conference of Latin American Bishops and a precious contribution of the Latin American church to the whole Catholic Church. Its reflections were like a pastoral "summa" of his role as archbishop of Buenos Aires. His affection for the people acquired its most expressive manifestation in his participation in celebrations at shrines (Our Lady of Luján, of St. Cajetan, and so forth) and in patronal feasts. He even proposed making parishes more like "sanctuaries," especially those that welcomed many people passing through, so as to make visitors feel at home. He envisioned them with their doors always open and with a priest constantly on hand, in order to facilitate participation in the sacraments of reconciliation, the Eucharist, and matrimony.

It is also well known that as president of the drafting committee for the concluding document of Aparecida, Cardinal Bergoglio dedicated special attention to the paragraphs on popular religiosity and even helped to write them. Following the conference, Cardinal Bergoglio set about expressing his explicit appreciation for these sections, pointing out that in a way they expressed the reality of the multitudes of pilgrims—the "poor and simple of heart"—who filled the beautiful Marian shrine of Aparecida, accompanying the eucharistic celebrations and prayers of the bishops during each of the nearly twenty days of the conference. The "success" of this event, according to Bergoglio, could not be dissociated from having worked for almost a month inside a Marian shrine.

"Popular piety" is presented in the Aparecida document "as a place of encounter with Christ." The bishops of Latin America are recognized in the conference's opening speech by Pope Benedict XVI, which affirms that "in the rich and profound popular religiosity . . . we see the soul of the Latin American peoples . . . a precious treasure of the Catholic Church in Latin America."[38] It is expressed in "patronal feasts, novenas, rosaries and *via crucis*, processions, dances and

---

[37] Puebla: Concluding Document, sec. 469.
[38] Pope Benedict XVI, Opening Address, sec. 1.

songs filled with religious folklore, devotion to the saints and angels, promises to God, and family prayers."[39] Pilgrimages, which Pope Francis particularly appreciates, are especially noteworthy, "in which one can recognize the People of God on their journey." "In shrines, many pilgrims make decisions that mark their lives. These walls contain many stories of conversion, of forgiveness, and of gifts received, which millions of people could tell," reads the Aparecida document.[40] The document seeks to affirm forcefully that "popular spirituality is a legitimate way of living the faith, a way of feeling like part of the Church, and a way of being missionaries,"[41] so that in no way "can we deprecate popular spirituality, or consider it a secondary mode of Christian life."[42] This would be "to forget the primacy of the Spirit's action and the gratuitous initiative of God's love."[43] "It is also an expression of supernatural wisdom, because the wisdom of love does not depend directly on the enlightenment of the mind but on the inner action of grace."[44] For this reason it is called "popular spirituality." The people "evangelize themselves" through their popular piety, under the inspiration of the Holy Spirit.[45]

There is a perfect continuity in this regard between Aparecida and *Evangelii Gaudium*, in which the "active evangelizing power" of popular piety is emphasized (EG 126). Pope Francis exclaims: "Let us not stifle or presume to control this missionary power!" (EG 122–26), which develops spontaneously under the influence of the Holy Spirit.

A Poor Church and a Church for the Poor

It is important to remember that while the church in Latin America felt urged by the conciliar renewal to open its windows to the world, especially to the world of its peoples, it could not but notice that the great majority of the baptized lived in poverty and that they undergo many discriminations and injustices. They were, however, rooted in

[39] CELAM, Aparecida: Concluding Document, sec. 259.
[40] Aparecida: Concluding Document, sec. 260.
[41] Aparecida: Concluding Document, sec. 264.
[42] Aparecida: Concluding Document, sec. 263.
[43] Aparecida: Concluding Document, sec. 263.
[44] Aparecida: Concluding Document, sec. 263.
[45] Aparecida: Concluding Document, sec. 264.

the faith they received, which gave them an awareness of their own dignity, an experience of solidarity, a joy even in the midst of suffering, and a living hope against all hope. The poor are those who best guard and express a people's culture as they pursue their goal of solidarity. At the same time, it is the Catholic faithful who best guard and express this popular piety. This is so because it is to the poor, the little ones, and the suffering—and not to the wise or those who are slaves to power, money, and ephemeral pleasure—to whom the mysteries of God are revealed. For this reason, ever since the Second General Conference of the Bishops in Medellín fifty-one years ago, the Latin American church proclaimed its preferential love for the poor, thereby recovering its profoundly essential, evangelical, and christological mission. Already in 1966, the Argentine bishops' document of San Miguel developed the perspective of the poor as the "sacrament of Christ," marking the beginning of the theology of the people.

However, during times of high ideological tides and hyperpoliticization, there lies the risk of reducing the poor to a political instrument. This was one of the most serious criticisms that the theology of the people, including Bergoglio himself, raised against liberation theology. The theology of the people always starts from the living reality of a people, from their thirst for God, and from their faith-filled culture. Their wisdom about life, their styles, their language, and their way of facing reality deserves respect. We must certainly also fight for their rights, dignity, and liberation, but only from within the journey of those who suffer poverty and violence.

The poor are like the "second Eucharist of the Lord." It was the incarnate Son of God in his abasement in poverty and self-identification in a mysterious but very real way with the poor and the little ones, which, according to Matthew chapters 5 and 25, forms the criteria according to which we will be judged by God. For this reason, the concluding document of Aparecida and *Evangelii Gaudium* dedicate a great deal of space to the theology and spirituality of the option for the poor, affirming that "we must all allow ourselves to be evangelized by them" and gather the "mysterious wisdom that God wants to communicate to us through them" (EG 198).[46] Pope Francis's actions and words bring us closer and make us "neighbors" to the faces

---

[46] Cf. Aparecida: Concluding Document, sec. 391–98.

of the poor, which the enormous global bubble of indifference tends to hide or reject. He shows us the living Gospel, charity's embrace, and the compassionate gift of self. He shows us what he expects of Christian communities, of their witness, of their priorities and efforts: a "Church which is poor and for the poor!"[47]

Pastoral and Missionary Conversion

The theology of the people also places heavy accent on the shared responsibility of the baptized to become disciples and missionaries of the Lord. The entirety of the baptized forms the people of God. How can we not remember what was said, with high-flown rhetoric, about the "Copernican revolution" that led to the placement of the chapter on the people of God in *Lumen Gentium* before those referring to the hierarchy, the laity, and consecrated persons? It led to the overturning of the image of the church as a stratified pyramid with the hierarchy at its apex and the faithful as simple executors at its base. For this reason, chapter 3, section 1, of *Evangelii Gaudium* bears the heading: "The Entire People of God Proclaims the Gospel" (EG 111). The people of God acts as the protagonist of the evangelizing community. The pope no longer addresses "pastoral agents," "enlightened" ecclesiastical minorities, or self-styled "committed adults"—which can represent a pharisaic tendency—but rather all the baptized faithful. Every Christian is called to share responsibility for the church's communion and mission and to grow as "missionary disciples" of God's people on the journey. Herein resides the dynamic of mutual support that Pope Francis proposes for the church. The pyramid has now been inverted, and the summit, which consists in the Apostolic College and has Peter as its "rock," now forms its base. For this reason, those who exercise authority are called "ministers," since they are the least of all, as seen in the word's etymological meaning. They must recognize themselves as servants of the people of God, to whom they belong and whose feet they wash, as Jesus did.

Pope Francis's insistence on a "pastoral conversion" derives *naturaliter* from love for the people and the shared missionary responsibil-

[47] Pope Francis, "Meeting with the International Press," Paul VI Audience Hall, March 16, 2013, http://w2.vatican.va/content/francesco/en/speeches/2013/march/documents/papa-francesco_20130316_rappresentanti-media.html.

ity of all God's people. It was already present at Aparecida and was experienced by Archbishop Bergoglio while in Buenos Aires. *Evangelii Gaudium* states it clearly: "To evangelize souls, we must develop a spiritual enjoyment from being close to the life of the people, even to the point of discovering that this is the source of a superior joy. Mission is a passion for Jesus, but at the same time a passion for his people" (EG 268). Jesus's life was based on many encounters. Therefore, "captivated by this model, we want to integrate ourselves more deeply into society, to share the life of all, to listen to their concerns, to collaborate materially and spiritually with them in their needs, to rejoice with those who are happy, and to weep with those who weep. So we commit ourselves to creating a new world, working side by side with everyone" (EG 269). We must not allow ourselves to be enclosed by bureaucratic, functional, or ideological zeal. A church enclosed in self-referentiality becomes ill. We must overcome every type of remoteness. Above all, we must be merciful, supportive, and missionary in the midst of the people.

Pastoral conversion is the conversion of pastors. "The pastor is the shepherd of a people, so that the people are served from within. . . . Gazing upon the Holy People of God, and feeling like an integral part of it, shows us our place in life,"[48] and saves us from abstractions, from mere theoretical speculations, and from self-enclosed, functionalist ecclesiastical structures. The pope says even more: "When we uproot ourselves from shepherding our own people, we get lost."[49] We lose ourselves in ecclesial walled gardens and clerical refuges, while remaining distant from our people. This leaves pastors without the joy of spending time in the midst of their own people; without the knowledge of the concrete realities of their lives, a knowledge born from the affective closeness that love provides; without that all-embracing, merciful love which avoids discrimination and prejudice; without a feel for the flesh of the poor and the wounds of those who suffer in body and soul; and without a nearness to those who are far from the church. Pope Francis has often reminded pastors that they have "to walk with the People of God." They must walk ahead, indicating the path; walk in the midst of the people to strengthen

---

[48] Pope Francis, "Letter to Cardinal Marc Ouellet."
[49] Francis, "Letter to Cardinal Marc Ouellet."

their unity; walk at the rear so that no one is left behind;[50] but above all they must follow the scent of the people of God in order to discover new paths.[51] "Pastoral conversion" requires shepherds to love the people entrusted to them, to live in their midst with the closeness proper to "faith-filled wanderers," to embrace them with a merciful tenderness that excludes no one—because God's love excludes no one—in solidarity with their sufferings and hopes, especially those of the weakest, the sick, the poor, and the excluded.

For this reason, Pope Francis condemns the "spiritual worldliness" of bishops who become "princes" and look down contemptuously on their people from afar, who at times are obsessed with privileges and recognitions, and at other times are reduced to administrators of a religious organization.

We must go out and meet them! Do not wait in churches for the faithful to enter. Pastoral conversion requires a missionary conversion toward all ambits of the common life, to all existential and social peripheries, and to all human-made borders.[52] Pope Francis's pontificate has a missionary heart at its core, especially toward those who are distant from the church. We must go out to look for the many lost sheep, rather than tending the few that remain within the enclosure. The proportions of that parable have been enormously inverted. We must not remain hemmed in, waiting within an ecclesial walled garden. We need to be centered in Christ and well-rooted in his Body, which is the church, but in diaspora for the mission. It is a question of fearlessly going out to meet others, without in any way jeopardizing our own belonging. The mission is nothing other than communicating the gift of the encounter with Christ, who has changed our lives, despite our resistance and misery. The mission is carried out

[50] Pope Francis, "Profession of Faith with the Bishops of the Italian Episcopal Conference," Vatican Basilica, May 23, 2013, http://w2.vatican.va/content/francesco/en/homilies/2013/documents/papa-francesco_20130523_omelia-professio-fidei-cei.html; cf. *Evangelii Gaudium* 31.

[51] Pope Francis, "Address of Holy Father Francis to a Group of Recently Appointed Bishops," Clementine Hall, September 19, 2013, sec. 2b, http://w2.vatican.va/content/francesco/en/speeches/2013/september/documents/papa-francesco_20130919_convegno-nuovi-vescovi.html.

[52] Jorge Mario Bergoglio, "Message to the Cardinals in the General Congregations prior to the Conclave," March 9, 2013: "La Iglesia está llamada a salir de sí misma e ir hacia las periferias, no solo las geográficas, sino también las periferias existenciales: las del misterio del pecado, las del dolor, las de la injusticia, las de la ignorancia y prescindencia religiosa, las del pensamiento, las de toda miseria."

with "overflowing gratitude and joy." It must fundamentally attract others through the beautiful witness of newness of life, one which is more human, full, and happy.

The mission of transmitting the Gospel of Jesus Christ is a task requiring holy patience, because we are aware that the Spirit of God always "precedes" us. The Spirit is the true protagonist in evangelization. The Spirit goes ahead of us in the hearts of individuals and in the culture of peoples. As St. Augustine said: "You made us for yourself, Lord, and our hearts are restless until they rest in you."[53]

Toward a Culture of Encounter

The last, but by no means least important, aspect regarding the interpenetration of God's holy and faithful people and secular peoples is the "culture of encounter," a pillar of the theology of the people and something that Bergoglio has developed in an innovative way both before and after becoming Pope Francis.

The concept is no desk-born fantasy. One of his disciples described him as the "man of encounters" of which Romano Guardini speaks. "Faith is an encounter with Jesus, and we must do just as Jesus does: encounter others."[54] We live in a culture of disassociation, disagreement, and waste. Our culture is so mediated by abstract, virtual relationships that a deep thirst for true encounters pervades it. Pope Francis came to fill this hope through warm, gratuitous, and all-embracing encounters.[55] Pope Francis never tires of proposing a culture of encounter and of friendship, where we find solidarity, where we can speak even with those who do not think as we do, and where we can "learn to receive from all, especially from the poorest and most insignificant, and from those who for the world 'do not count' and are overlooked."[56]

---

[53] St. Augustine, *Confessions*, trans. Henry Chadwick (Oxford: Oxford University Press, 2009), I.i.1.

[54] Pope Francis, "Address of the Holy Father Francis on the Vigil of Pentecost with the Ecclesial Movements," Saint Peter's Square, May 18, 2013, http://w2.vatican.va/content/francesco/en/speeches/2013/may/documents/papa-francesco_20130518_veglia-pentecoste.html. See Diego Fares, SJ, *Papa Francisco. La cultura del encuentro* (Buenos Aires: Edhasa, 2014), 15–20; Andrea Riccardi, *La sorpresa di papa Francesco* (Milan: Mondadori, 2013), 45–83.

[55] Fares, *Papa Francisco*, 16.

[56] Fares, 16.

"Between selfish indifference and violent protest," Cardinal Bergoglio affirmed, "there is always another option: that of dialogue. Dialogue between generations, dialogue within the people . . . constructive dialogue . . . between [the nation's] many rich cultural components,"[57] the democratic dialogue of politics when rehabilitated to its proper dignity. Dialogue cannot exist unless its interlocutors' identities are well founded. Shouted slogans, ideas thrown as stones, visceral outbursts, reciprocal delegitimization, and the raising of walls do not constitute dialogue.

God's holy and faithful people are called to play a decisive role and provide a fundamental contribution to the creation, promotion, and development of a culture of encounter capable of rebuilding the unique form of solidarity that constitutes a people. Communal coexistence needs to be regenerated through friendship and the reconstitution of the family, education, work, and the social fabric. The goal is an organized community in which technocratic coldness, utilitarianism, social inequalities, and exclusions do not prevail, and where all people, throughout life's various stages from conception to natural death, are welcomed and respected. All must be considered important for the life of a community! In his reflections on urban pastoral care in Buenos Aires, Archbishop Bergoglio proposed "making the city a sanctuary," making the shared existence of citizens a slice of heaven and a sanctuary for all people. He also sought to form a group of "shanty-town" priests. Their presence as shepherds among those excluded from city life was an important pastoral and social experience.

The people of God is the sacrament of unity among the peoples of the world. The church is the *mysterium tremendum* that tears down the walls of iniquity that separate and divide persons and peoples, and that makes them recognize one another, through baptism, as "members of the Body" (1 Cor 12:12), all made "one in Christ" (Gal 3:28; Col 3:11), in the "sign of unity" and "bond of charity" that is the Eucharist.[58] Truly participating in this sacrament of communion

---

[57] Pope Francis, "Address of Pope Francis to Meeting with Brazil's Leaders of Society," Municipal Theatre, Rio de Janeiro, July 27, 2013, sec. 3, http://w2.vatican.va/content/francesco/en/speeches/2013/july/documents/papa-francesco_20130727_gmg-classe-dirigente-rio.html.

[58] St. Augustine, *Homilies on the Gospel of John*, 26.13.

generates an infinitely more radical and powerful bond of unity than any form of social, political, ideological, or even family solidarity. Thus the church is presented as *forma mundi*, a community of forgiven sinners reconciled by the merciful love of God, whose relationships with one another are characterized more by who they are than by power or what they have. They are united in a surprising solidarity and are the seed, sign, and influx of a new society within the world. Though all human efforts to build the perfect, utopian community end in "towers of Babel"—if not in the creation of new forms of hell—the human "heart" and all cultures yearn for communion, to which all are called and destined. The ecclesial witness of the first Christians aroused that type of amazement: "See how they love each other!"[59] It is like something from another world, right here in our own! Everyone can live in this manner, even though we possess this communion in earthen vessels (cf. 2 Cor 4:7) and are called to continual conversion.

In societies weighed down by flagrant inequalities, conflicts, and fragmentation, the dynamic impulse toward friendship that seeks to create a community should be founded and nourished by the gratuity of charity. Only a love that exceeds our human capacities can provide the energy required to rebuild the bonds of participation, coexistence, and solidarity among people. For this reason, the church constantly generates and regenerates communities and peoples. St. John Paul II pointed out in his post-synodal apostolic exhortation *Christifideles Laici* that, in order to reconstitute the fabric of human society, the very fabric of Christian communities must first be rebuilt so that they reflect and transmit, as clearly as possible, the mystery of communion that is the church.[60]

The church's unique contribution is indeed decisive for the formation and destiny of the "people-nation," because she is the sacrament of unity. The people of God is the fulfillment of the filiation, fraternity, and solidarity to which all people are called.

---

[59] Tertullian, *Apology*, 39.

[60] Pope John Paul II, post-synodal apostolic exhortation, *Christifideles Laici*, December 30, 1988, sec. 34, http://w2.vatican.va/content/john-paul-ii/en/apost_exhortations/documents/hf_jp-ii_exh_30121988_christifideles-laici.html.

Chapter 4

Globalization, Baroque, and the Latin American Pope

Rocco Buttiglione

Pontifical Lateran University, Rome, Italy

An Epoch of Change

Pope Francis insists on the fact that we do not live in an epoch of change but rather in an epochal change.[1] What are the characteristics of the new epoch that is waiting for us in the coming future? The future is known only to God and it is largely dependent upon our free decisions and actions. There are, however, some facts that are changing the face of the earth that can already be clearly detected.

In Europe (and to a lesser extent in the United States) the influence of religion and of the Catholic Church in public life is declining. The dominant culture is centered on new and purely individualistic rights while the duties that constitute communities are decaying. The only objective laws seem to be those of the market.

The influence of Europe (and, to a lesser extent, of the United States) in the world is declining, demographically, economically,

[1] Pope Francis, "Meeting with the Participants in the 5th Convention of the Italian Church," Florence, November 10, 2015, http://w2.vatican.va/content/francesco/en/speeches/2015/november/documents/papa-francesco_20151110_firenze-convegno-chiesa-italiana.html.

culturally. Not only are our population numbers declining but our participation in global output is steadily decreasing, and the other continents no longer recognize our cultural hegemony. They do not think that they will follow the trend that we have set.

Globally, the role of religion is on the increase and the Catholic Church is growing, slowly, but with a remarkable continuity.[2] In Latin America the Catholic Church is growing for demographic reasons and because great efforts at the re-evangelization of the masses contain the advance of Baptist churches and dechristianization. In Africa and in Asia the church grows because of extraordinary missionary work and mass conversions. Sub-Saharan Africa has become largely Christian and not Islamic, as many had forecast. In Asia there is an unexpected growth of flourishing communities and an incredible abundance of priestly vocations. In China the old atheistic communist state ideology is in shambles and more than one billion people are seeking a new spiritual orientation. Many look with interest and hope to the Catholic churches. Today scarcely one-third of Catholics live in Europe and the United States, a little less than one-half live in Latin America, and the rest live in Asia and Africa.[3]

One could say that globalization has globalized the Catholic Church too, but, of course, the church has been global since the beginning. The term "catholic" comes from the Greek phrase *katholou*, meaning "according to the totality." It is the totality of the *oikoumene* ("the inhabited world") as well as the totality of the dimensions constituting the human being. Thus, while the church was already global, in this time of globalization the Spirit has called the church to become more global, more "catholic." It is in this context that we must understand the election of the first non-European pope since the eighth century.

It may be interesting to dwell for a while on the history of the last non-European pope, St. Gregory III. He was a Syrian from "the East," but he soon came into conflict with the emperor of the East over sacred images. The emperor wanted to have those images destroyed

---

[2] "The Future of World Religions: Population Growth Projections 2010–2050," Pew Research Center, Washington, DC (April 2, 2015), http://www.pewforum.org/2015/04/02/religious-projections-2010-2050/.

[3] Data derived from Vatican Secretary of State, *Annuario Pontificio (2017)* (Vatican City: Libreria Editrice Vaticana, 2017).

in order to defend the purity of monotheism and the absolute transcendence of the one God (the same position that we find in Islam). The pope defended iconography in incarnational terms: God has assumed human flesh in Jesus, is present in the life of his saints who constitute the people of God, and humanity is the image of God on earth, therefore the use of sacred icons should not be confused with the pagan cult of idols. The confrontation between the two took place during an epochal change coinciding with the beginning of the split between the Eastern and the Western churches. Gregory III was the first pope to demand the assistance of Charles Martel, Mayor of the Palace of the King of France, against his enemies the Lombards and the Emperor of Constantinople. The barbarians had been converted to Christianity, and the pope, welcoming the (baptized) barbarians, gave them a place within Christianity that the Greeks were not willing to accept. This is also the reason why there were, after Gregory III, no more Eastern popes. A few decades later, Photius caused the first schism. It was a time of globalization and epochal change, full of opportunities (the conversion of the barbarians) but also of dangers (the schism of the Eastern churches).[4]

In our epochal change we have seen the first non-Italian pope, after many centuries of a well-established tradition of Italian popes, and now the first non-European pope. I recall the words of St. John Paul II on the occasion of his first pilgrimage to Poland in his homily in Victory Square (now Pilsudsky Square) of Warsaw. He said: "Leaving myself aside at this point, I must nonetheless with all of you ask myself why, precisely in 1978, after so many centuries of a well-established tradition in this field, a son of the Polish nation, of the land of Poland, was called to the chair of St. Peter. Christ demanded of Peter and of the other apostles that they should be his 'witnesses in Jerusalem and in all Judaea and Samaria and to the end of the earth' (Acts 1:8). Have we not the right to say, with reference to these words of Christ, that Poland has become nowadays the land of a particularly responsible witness? . . . The right to think that one must come to this very place, to this land, on this route, to read again the witness of his Cross and his Resurrection?"[5]

---

[4] See Aidan Nichols, *Rome and the Eastern Churches: A Study in Schism*, 2nd ed. (San Francisco: Ignatius Press, 2010).

[5] Pope St. John Paul II, "Homily in Victory Square," Warsaw, June 2, 1979, sec. 1, http://w2.vatican.va/content/john-paul-ii/en/homilies/1979/documents/hf_jp-ii _hom_19790602_polonia-varsavia.html.

In our epochal change we have seen what tremendous effect these words have carried with themselves: one global empire was shaken, and for a while God put his finger into history, beginning with Poland, "God's Playground."[6] For a while we were all confirmed in our faith by the witness of the faith of the Polish church. Now we can repeat these words in a different context. Shall we not say that today there is something that we all have to learn from the history of the Latin American church, that we all, so to speak, must become pilgrims along a route that travels through Rio, Medellín, Puebla, Santo Domingo, and Aparecida? Why did the Holy Spirit choose in our time a Latin American pope, and what does the Spirit want us to learn from this pope?

The Argentina of Jorge Mario Bergoglio

In 1979, when John Paul II came to Latin America for the first time for the Third General Conference of Latin American and Caribbean Bishops in Puebla, Jorge Mario Bergoglio was rector of the Faculty of Philosophy and Theology of the College of San Miguel, after having been the Provincial Superior of the Argentinian Jesuits for six years. These were difficult years for Argentina.

In 1973 Juan Domingo Perón had been reelected President of the Republic of Argentina after having been president in 1946–1955. When Perón first came to power, Argentina was a rich country with a tremendously unequal distribution of national wealth. Perón introduced many social reforms, giving to the working masses for the first time the sense that they constituted an integral part of the national community. A military coup, however, sent him into exile, and for eighteen years the Peronists were outlawed, yet they succeeded in retaining the support of the vast majority of the Argentinian people.[7]

Under the military regimes supported by Great Britain and by the United States there was a growing political radicalization, especially of the youth. The Peronist youth movement (*Joventud Peronista*) split:

---

[6] See Norman Davies, *God's Playground: A History of Poland*, 2 vols. (Oxford: Oxford University Press, 1981–83). See also Rocco Buttiglione, *Karol Wojtyła: The Thought of the Man Who Became John Paul II*, trans. Paolo Guietti and Francesca Murphy (Grand Rapids, MI: Eerdmans, 1997).

[7] See Austen Ivereigh, *Catholicism and Politics in Argentina: 1810–1960* (New York: St. Martin's Press, 1995).

the *montoneros* felt the fascination of Castro and Che Guevara and entered the path of armed struggle and terrorism, while other groups answered with an equally cruel anti-communist terrorism, supported by the military. In the hopes of putting an end to the march toward full-fledged civil war, democratic elections were held and Perón won and became president again.[8] In 1974, however, Perón died, followed by yet another military takeover and the dramatic growth of the armed struggle between the *montoneros* and other similar groups. The colonels claimed they were defending a Christian and Western civilization while the *montoneros* wanted a world revolution, and their war made many victims of civilians who refused to take sides. Both the right and the left wanted to split the nation in two parts: each resolving to destroy the other, each treating as enemies those who did not identify with their own political goals.

Bergoglio was the spiritual and cultural point of reference of one part of the *Joventud Peronista* (mainly the so-called *Guardia de Hierro*, the "Iron Guard")[9] that refused armed struggle and sought the promotion of human rights, the restoration of democracy, and an Argentinian revolution of social justice according to Christian social doctrine. They wanted a nonviolent struggle and were targeted by both the *montoneros* (who considered them traitors of the revolution) and the military (who considered them traitors of Christianity and the West). They said that before being a communist or a fascist or whatever else, a human being is a human being and as such deserves respect and has rights. They said "no hay cosa mejor para un argentino que otro argentino" (there is no more precious thing for an Argentinian than another Argentinian).[10] It was not easy to utter these words in a time in which the most cherished sport of Argentinians seemed to be the slaughtering of other Argentinians. Many lost their lives defending this cultural and ecclesiastical position, most of them as victims of the colonels but some also murdered by the *montoneros*. I wish here to remember in particular a great friend of Jorge Mario Bergoglio,

[8] Oscar Anzorena, *Tiempo de Violencia y Utopía: 1966–1976* (Buenos Aires: Editorial Contrapunto, 1988).

[9] Alejandro C. Tarruella, *Guardia de Hierro: De Perón a Bergoglio* (Buenos Aires: Punto de Encuentro, 2016).

[10] These words originate from Perón when he returned in 1973, but I learned them from my friends in *Guardia de Hierro*. It was a kind of summary of their position. Before 1973 the motto of the Peronistas was "*no hay cosa mejor para un peronista que otro peronista*" (there is no more precious thing for a Peronist than another Peronist).

Msgr. Enrique Angelelli, bishop of La Rioja, killed by the military who camouflaged the murder as a car accident on August 4, 1976.[11]

The Four Principles

It is in this context that Bergoglio comes to appreciate a principle that would become fundamental to his thought: unity is more important than division (EG 226–30). He found this principle in the works of Romano Guardini[12] but it acquired an existential confirmation in the terrible years of the struggle to keep the Argentinian nation united (as well as the Argentinian church, the Argentinian Jesuits . . .).

At the same time, he also became aware of the fact that large parts of Argentinian society were only superficially evangelized. While Christian values were officially respected and even socially enforced through legal sanctions, they were severed from their origin, the living experience of the presence of Jesus Christ, and had therefore lost their power of attraction—they did not fascinate the hearts of the youth. What should be done? Should the church devote her energy to trying to preserve an official public observance of those values, or should it attempt to rekindle the source of all values, the presence of the love of Jesus, in missionary communities? Whether despite their small beginnings or because of them, these communities, with time, often have the capacity to conquer many and reawaken the sleepy Christian heart of the nation.[13] Here we find another of the four fundamental principles of *Evangelii Gaudium*: "time is greater than space" (EG 222–25). Activating living processes is more important than protecting spaces of social influence that are no longer animated by a living spirit.

[11] Luis Miguel Baronetto, *Vida y Martirio de Mons. Angelelli, Obispo de la Iglesia Católica* (Córdoba: Ediciones Tiempo Latinoamericano, 1996). I wish here to remember also the names of Carlos De Dios Murias, Gabriel Longueville, and Wenceslao Pedernera, who suffered the same fate.

[12] Romano Guardini, *Der Gegensatz: Versuche zu einer Philosophie des Lebendig-Konkreten*, 4th ed. (Mainz: Matthias-Grünewald, 1998). First published 1925 by Matthias-Grünewald (Mainz).

[13] These reflections were perhaps strengthened through the reading of some of the writings of Luigi Giussani; see, for example, Giussani, *Il Movimento di Comunione e Liberazione (1954–1986): Conversazioni con Robi Ronza* (Milan: BUR Rizzoli, 2014).

This principle finds its roots in the small community animated by the presence of the Spirit and growing through obedience to this presence. This growth is led through occasions that the Spirit puts along its path. We grow through encounters. The universal in history grows (and occupies spaces) together with the growth of the community that carries it in itself. This is the real universal in opposition to the abstract universal. The community, of course, needs abstract knowledge to orient itself in the world, but in action the abstract idea acquires new determinations, intelligibility, meaning. As the creator of all things God knows things perfectly "from within" through the same act by which he creates them. We know things "from without"; we try to move from the effects to their causes, from the surface to the depth. This is the reason why the real is always fuller than the concepts through which we try to understand it.[14] This should not be confused with an unprincipled pragmatism. We need concepts to articulate our understanding of the real, and we must hold firmly to the conceptual expressions of our true judgments about reality. We must, however, recognize that what we have seen of the truth is not the totality of the truth; our concepts and our insights can always be enriched through new events and new encounters (cf. EG 231–33).

This third principle, that "realities are more important than ideas," stands in close relationship with the principle that unity is more important than division. My opponent may have seen a side of the truth that I have not seen, and I shall never convince him to abandon his error until I have incorporated his insights into my account of the truth.

The fourth principle of Bergoglio says that "the whole is greater than the part," and is greater even than the sum of the parts, because only in the whole do the parts acquire the fullness of their meaning (EG 234–37).

The Baroque

Pope Francis has reformulated these principles in the apostolic exhortation *Evangelii Gaudium* and on one occasion he said that he took them from his (unfinished) doctoral thesis on Romano Guardini.

---

[14] St. Thomas Aquinas, *Summa Theologica*, trans. Fathers of the English Dominican Province (New York: Benziger Brothers, 1911–25), I-II, q. 91, a. 3.

They correspond clearly to the method of Guardini. Some friends of Bergoglio, however, remember having listened to him explaining these principles already in the 1970s, when he was the provincial of the Jesuits, and at the beginning of the 1980s, when he was Rector of San Miguel, before he went to Germany to write his thesis on Guardini. It seems that Guardini helped Bergoglio to systematize what he had already lived in the struggles of the '70s in Argentina.

To understand the way in which this happened we must look to the peculiar connection between theory and praxis that Bergoglio developed in those years. Nothing is more foreign to the mentality of Bergoglio then a naive pastoralism and anti-intellectualism. In order to act we must have a vision of the history in which our initiative is situated, a hypothesis of the intention of the Spirit who sets history in motion. Bergoglio was a friend of some of the greatest thinkers of the Argentina of his time. These thinkers were not pure academics. Their intellectual efforts were aimed at understanding history in order to educate a new generation of leaders capable of moving their nation toward a better future.[15] They tried to develop a theological and philosophical vision of the political struggles of their time in Argentina, in Latin America, and in the world. I wish here to mention only a few of them: Amelia Podetti, Alberto Methol Ferré, Lucio Gera, Juan Carlos Scannone, and Geraldo Farrell—most of them connected to *Guardia de Hierro*. They read the classics in order to understand the problems of the day-to-day struggles in which they were involved. They were keenly interested in European philosophy (Amelia Podetti translated Hegel into Spanish[16]) and at the same time convinced that they had the task of understanding Latin America in its historical specificity; this task gave them a thoroughly different perspective on world history. Their purpose, really, was not so much to understand Latin America per se as to rethink the world from the perspective of Latin America.[17]

---

[15] Juan Pedro Denaday, "Amelia Podetti: una trayectoria olvidada de las Cátedras Nacionales," *Nuevo Mundo, Mundos Nuevos*, August 29, 2013, http://journals.open edition.org/nuevomundo/65663.

[16] Amelia Podetti, *Comentario a la Introducción a la Fenomenología del Espíritu* (Buenos Aires: Editorial Biblos, 2007), with an introduction by Jorge Mario Bergoglio.

[17] Amelia Podetti, *La irrupción de América en la historia* (Buenos Aires: Centro de Investigaciones Culturales, 1981).

Amelia Podetti read Hegel from the point of view of what is missing in Hegel: the category of possibility. Possibility is the result of a
discrepancy between divine and human intellect. The categories
through which we try to understand reality always fall short of the
target because the human intellect is finite and the kind of totality
that we are capable of grasping is always incomplete. The lack of the
category of possibility in Hegel is strictly correlated with the principle
of immanence and with the identification of God's intellect with the
human intellect. It is an effect of the loss of the transcendence of God.

Another consequence of the same position is the impossibility of
understanding Latin America within the boundaries of the "closure
of history" and the "already given," the eurocentric worldview that
confuses itself for an objective historical perspective. The discovery
of America, on the contrary, is an event that goes beyond the "already
given": in order to be understood it demands that we break our
horizon, our transcendental categories, and become open to an absolute novelty. There is a collection of poems of Borges with the title
"El otro, el mismo" that expresses well this reality.[18] We see (and must
see) reality through transcendental categories, but now and then
reality breaks our transcendental categories and obliges us to refor-
mulate them. When America is discovered the *indio* is the other, the
absolutely different. Is he human? The dispute between Sepúlveda
and Las Casas is a clash over the humanity of the *indio*.[19] If he is
human like us, then we must change the measure of our humanity;
we must recognize dimensions of our humanity that we had covered
up and obliterated. We must become foreign to ourselves in order to
reappropriate our common humanity with our new *indio* brother. We
must return to the center from the periphery, and the center must
discover itself anew in order to be able to integrate the periphery.

This reminds me of the words of Jesus that Wojtyła quoted in
Warsaw: the disciples are invited to be "witnesses in Jerusalem and
in all Judaea and Samaria and to the end of the earth" (Acts 1:18).
The "missionary disciple" will become the fundamental category of
the pastoral renewal that, many years later, Bergoglio will propose

---

[18] Jorge Luis Borges, "El otro, el mismo," in *Obras Completas* (Barcelona: Círculo de
Lectores/Emecé, 1995), 5.

[19] Daniel R. Brunstetter, "Sepúlveda, Las Casas and the Other: Exploring the Tension
between Moral Universalism and Alterity," *Review of Politics* 72, no. 3 (2010): 409–35.

in the Conference of Latin American Bishops in Aparecida.[20] The missionary disciple is faithful to what he has seen and heard and he is, nevertheless, open to what the Lord has in store for him. He knows that God's design is broader than his human vision and full of surprises: the reality is greater than the (human) idea. What is already known has to be discovered again in the encounter with new peoples and new cultures. The missionary disciple does not protect spaces but activates organic processes. He does not want to begin by imposing a rule that comes from without; he wants to change hearts so that they can rediscover for themselves the rule as the fulfillment of their longing for perfect justice. He knows that the totality is greater than his work and that his work will find its true fulfillment and its true meaning only in the unity of the church, under whose judgment he ultimately stands.

Alberto Methol Ferré, whom we already quoted among the friends of Bergoglio, has said that modernity begins with the discovery of America.[21] This discovery breaks the closed horizon of medieval Christianity. For Methol Ferré, the first modernity is Catholic and takes the form of the Baroque.[22] The Baroque is marked by a complexity in which things are, and at the same time are not, what they seem to be. When we think that we have thoroughly penetrated a problem, we discover that it has deeper layers we have not yet

---

[20] CELAM, Aparecida: Concluding Document.

[21] See, for example, Alberto Methol-Ferré, "El resurgimiento católico latinoamericano," in *CELAM, Religión y cultura: Perspectivas de la evangelización de la cultura desde Puebla* (Bogotá: CELAM, 1981), 63–124.

[22] Rocco Buttiglione, "Elementos para interpretar el Papado latinoamericano: A partir de algunas reflexiones de Alberto Methol-Ferré," in *Humanitas* 22, no. 86 (Spring 2017): 66–79, http://www.humanitasreview.com/16-anthropology-culture/20-elements-for-interpreting-the-latin-american-papacy. The notion of the Baroque as the cultural medium *par excellence* of the expression of Latin American identity can be seen in other Latin American intellectuals as well. For example: Ángel Guido, *Fusión Hispano-indígena en la arquitectura colonial* (Rosario: La Casa del Libro, 1925); José Lezama Lima, *La curiosidad barroca: La expresión Americana* (Mexico: Fondo de Cultura Económica, 1993); Pedro Morandé, *Cultura y modernización en América Latina: Ensayo sociológico acerca de la crisis del desarrollismo y de su superación* (Santiago: Pontificia Universidad Católica de Chile, 1984), *Iglesia y cultura en América Latina* (Lima: Paulinas, 1989); Carlos Cullen, *Reflexiones desde América* (Rosario: Fundación Ross, 1986); Lucio Gera, in *Escritos teológico-pastorales de Lucio Gera*, ed. Virginia R. Azcuy, José C. Caamaño, Carlos M. Galli, and Marcelo González, vol. 1, *Del Preconcilio a la Conferencia de Puebla (1956–1981)* (Buenos Aires: Agape-Facultad de Teología, 2006).

recognized. This rule is even more apparent when the problem we are considering is the human person; this is the reason why the person, properly, is not a problem, but a mystery. You will never understand a person if he does not choose to let himself be understood by you, and this may only happen in an act of love.

Compare a paleo-Christian basilica or a Romanesque cathedral to a Baroque church. In the Romanesque (and, with some minor differences, in the Gothic) cathedral your eye embraces the whole space with one glance. The space is filled with the one people of God that moves toward the altar, where Jesus, the center of cosmos and history, is present. In the Baroque church the space is not unidimensional and straight but rather curvilinear. There is not just one altar but many. Many chapels aggregate different communities that converge toward the main altar in the unity of the one church. Each of the different chapels houses a people with its history of glories and of defeats, of love and of hatred. Jesus is present in all these histories and only through him do they become histories of hope and of salvation. Only in him and through him, through participation in his cross, can they be reconciled with one another and with the Father. Only the Baroque church is large enough to contain both conquerors and vanquished, Spaniards and *indios*, blacks and whites, all sorts of people and all kinds of sinners.

The Baroque world is a world of complexity and of contradictions.[23] One might say it is a world of (creative) disorder, but Henri Bergson once argued that disorder is only an order that is not understood.[24] The Baroque is therefore a permanent challenge to broaden our spirit to keep pace with this order.[25]

Baroque art encompasses not only architecture but also rhetoric, something that suffered a devaluation in the Protestant and Enlightenment forms of modernity. In these latter traditions the complexity of rhetorical argumentation was often unfavorably contrasted with

---

[23] Pedro Morandé, *La formación del ethos barroco como núcleo de la identidad cultural iberoamericana*, in *América Latina y la Doctrina Social de la Iglesia: Diálogo latinoamericano-alemán*, ed. Carlos M. Galli and Luis Scherz, vol. 2, *Identidad cultural y modernización* (Buenos Aires: Paulinas, 1992).

[24] Henri Bergson, *Creative Evolution*, trans. Arthur Mitchell (1911; repr., New York: Dover, 1998), 186–271.

[25] For a similar perspective on the Baroque see Walter Benjamin, *The Origin of German Tragic Drama* (London: Verso, 1998).

the simplicity of scientific demonstration—a simplistic opposition that underappreciates the intrinsic complexity involved in arguments that are able to address concrete human persons with their histories of joys and sorrows in a truly persuasive manner. Only this kind of argument is capable of mobilizing the capacity of the human heart to engage imaginatively with others, recognizing what is objectively good as my own good and what objectively deserves to be loved as beloved to me.[26]

The Baroque was the style of the *Siglo de Oro* in Spain and of the Catholic Reformation, but perhaps it found its greatest expression not in Spain, not in a Catholic country, but in the great enemy of Spain, Elizabethan England, in the works of William Shakespeare. In the struggles of the seventeenth and eighteenth centuries, the Baroque was defeated, and the Catholic Church became estranged from modernity. Another modernity triumphed, the church was proclaimed anti-modern by its adversaries, and the church itself seemed to accept this judgment.

With Vatican II the church opened the search for a Christian modernity. It is not a reconciliation with, and a subordination to, the predominant form of modernity (as progressives imagine). It is not a struggle against modernity (as so-called "traditionalists" desire). It is the effort to renew the thread of another modernity, a Catholic modernity. Along the road toward a full realization of the goals of the council we must once again rediscover the greatness of Baroque culture and Latin America.[27] It is the path of a church that can give globalization the soul that it presently lacks.

The "Theology of the People"[28]

Let us return, once again, to the question we started with: What does God want us to learn from the Latin American church today? Pope Francis would say that we must learn again, in today's world,

---

[26] Antonio Martí, *La preceptiva retórica española en el Siglo de Oro* (Madrid: Gredos, 1972).

[27] Methol Ferré, "El resurgimiento católico latinoamericano."

[28] On the relationship of Pope Francis and the *teología del pueblo* tradition, see Scannone, "Pope Francis and the Theology of the People"; Luciani, *Pope Francis and the Theology of the People.*

to be missionary disciples who see the world from the point of view of the marginalized, the peripheries, the excluded, the poor, and the sinner, in order to be able to integrate them within the communion of the people of God. We must learn to say the same truth in many different languages in order to allow every people to meet this truth, and, in the process, we will become aware of new sides and dimensions and depths of this truth—who is Jesus Christ—that we now can scarcely discern. Missionary disciples create a new people. People who were foreign to one another, who hated one another, who committed injustices against one another, become friends; more than friends, they become brothers.

The "people" is simultaneously a mythical and a mystical concept. Myth is not fantasy: it is a particular story in which a universal truth becomes visible.[29] At the beginning of every people there is a singular experience of liberation. For the people of Israel, it was the exodus from the land of Egypt. For the Romans, it was the foundation of the city. The experience of liberation founds the unity of a people. In the struggle for liberation the people experience a belonging to one another. Rabindranath Tagore fittingly writes: "Thou hast brought the distant near and made a brother of a stranger."[30] This is the way nations were born.

In times of peace and abundance the people forget their myth of their original liberation and they become just a mass without any inner principle of unity. The rich oppress the poor and the poor are full of hatred against their oppressors; a people divided, they are easily enslaved by their enemies. Now and then, however, a prophet comes and reawakens the memory of their original liberation. Out of that memory the original bond is revived, internal and external oppression is conquered, and a new age of freedom begins.

Methol Ferré's understanding of "people" here is indebted to the notion of *risorgimento*, taken from Italian philosophy, particularly that of Antonio Rosmini as mediated through Augusto Del Noce.[31] Draw-

---

[29] Rodolfo Kusch, *Geocultura del hombre americano* (Buenos Aires: Fernando García Cambeiro, 1976).

[30] Rabindranath Tagore, "Poem 63," in *Gitanjali* (London: Macmillan, 1918).

[31] Augusto Del Noce's unpublished lecture on Rosmini's concept of *risorgimento*, *Rosmini e la categoria filosofico-politica di risorgimento*, can be found online at http://www.cattedrarosmini.org and http://www.fondazioneaugustodelnoce.net.

ing on Del Noce, Methol Ferré developed a transpolitical interpretation of Latin American history in which the struggle of the *libertadores*
for freedom is followed by the betrayal of the great port cities, cities
that served as inroads for the semi-colonial influence of Great Britain
and eventually grew into independent states. Subsequent Latin
American history is viewed as the struggle of the port cities to subjugate the interior, imposing on it a kind of apostasy or oblivion of
its own culture.[32] Argentinian Peronism acquires a particular relevance within this perspective: Perón succeeds in amalgamating the
criollos (natives of Spanish descent) of the interior with the new waves
of immigrants (mainly of Italian descent like the Bergoglios) and lays
a new foundation for the Argentinian nation. Perón envisaged the
continent as a *"patria grande,"* a (re)united Latin America.[33]

But the concept of "people" carries not only a mythical function
but also a mystical, or eucharistic, meaning. The missionary disciples
founded a Christian community and a new people, the people of
God. The dynamic is both similar to and different from that of the
constitution of a people as a nation. The church is a smaller community within the broader community of the nation. It radiates its
influence within the nation and contributes profoundly to bringing
its people together, molding their self-understanding as a nation
(LG 9).[34] The church also interprets the national myth that stands at
the root of the life of the nation, seeing in it a sign of the intervention
of divine providence into human history. In times of decay—of the
selfish closing in of different social sectors upon their particular
interests—the church reminds the nation of the reasons that once
inspired its unity and its appreciation of the common good. The
church, of course, is not the only agency that shapes the national
identity, and as such it must respect the role of other religious and

---

[32] Alberto Methol Ferré, *El Uruguay como problema: En la Cuenca del Plata entre
Argentina y Brasil* (Montevideo: Diálogo, 1967).

[33] Alberto Methol Ferrè, "La Integración de América en el pensamiento de Perón,"
unpublished paper, private papers of Alberto Methol Ferré, http://www.metholferre
.com/obras/conferencias/capitulos/detalle.php?id=7. To recognize the merits of
Perón does not entail a wholesale approbation of his limits and errors, especially with
regard to his economic policies.

[34] Second Vatican Council, *Lumen Gentium*, November 21, 1964, par. 9, http://www
.vatican.va/archive/hist_councils/ii_vatican_council/documents/vat-ii_const
_19641121_lumen-gentium_en.html.

cultural agents, entering with them into varying relations of alliance or of opposition. The church must also respect the role of the state that has the task of producing a synthesis of the common good, not of an abstract and timeless common good, but the common good that is concretely possible in this time and place. In other words, the church must deeply feel itself to be a national church—the Body of Christ incarnated within *this history* and in *this place*. At the same time, the church must never forget that the mission of Jesus traverses all geographical, political, and national boundaries. The church must be local and, as such, has a responsibility toward the nation, and yet, at the same time, it is universal.

The nation, often, and to a large extent, constitutes itself in the struggle against a foreign enemy: the Italians against the Austrians, the Germans against the French, the Poles against both Germans and Russians, and so forth. The church cannot suppress this reality; it must, with frankness, recognize it. At the same time, the church must keep the national conscience open to the recognition that there is a higher unity of the human family and a common good of humanity as such in which these oppositions must be reconciled: unity is more important than division. The church is and must always be local and universal at the same time.

A particular responsibility of the church is the defense of the moral order of the nation, especially in those countries in which the founding of the nation was closely linked with evangelization. The energy that moved millions and millions of women and men to love each other, to give credit to this love and to establish families, to have children and to educate them, and to work their whole lives in order that these children might live and live a better life, was generated to a large extent by their faith in the Redeemer of the world, Jesus Christ.[35] They built cities, made the land fruitful, created great works of art, and made of the earth a home for human beings. The church has the responsibility to defend the moral values that constitute the most precious inheritance of these peoples. The church, however, must know that these natural values need to be reformulated through dialogue with each new generation. Their essence does not change with the passing of time because it is grounded in human nature, but

---

[35] See Giuseppe De Luca, *Introduzione alla storia della pietà* (Roma: Edizioni di Storia e Letteratura, 1962).

the modality of their presentation does change and must be shaped through patient dialogue with each new generation and in each different cultural context.[36] This is how the church earns her title as the mother of nations.

This way of framing the relationship between church and nation was prominent in the words of St. John Paul II to the Third General Assembly of the Latin American Bishops Conference in Puebla.[37] St. John Paul II, who had already developed a Polish theology of the nation in his homilies as cardinal of Kraków,[38] there affirmed the idea of a Latin American theology. The Latin American churches had to reflect upon the event of Jesus Christ from within their own history.

If the political myth of Latin America began with the *libertadores* Simón Bolívar, José de San Martín, Bernardo O'Higgins, and others, the mystical reality of the Latin American people began with the event of Guadalupe, where the Virgin appeared to the *indio* Juan Diego. Thence began the conversion of the *indios*, the *mestizaje* (mixing) of two people that become one.[39] This is the deepest cultural layer of Latin American identity and it contains a potentiality for liberation that has yet to be fully actualized today.[40]

It is time for the Latin American churches to cease reflexively repeating and adapting European theology. It is time for the churches to become "matrices"[41] that rethink and formulate a theology as a

---

[36] For the sociology of culture that accompanies the theology of the people, see Pedro Morandé, *Pedro Morandé: Textos sociológicos escogidos*, ed. Andrés Biehl and Patricio Velasco (Santiago: Ediciones Universidad Católica de Chile, 2017).

[37] Pope John Paul II, "Opening Address to the Puebla Conference," Puebla, Mexico, January 28, 1979, http://w2.vatican.va/content/john-paul-ii/en/speeches/1979/january/documents/hf_jp-ii_spe_19790128_messico-puebla-episc-latam.html. It is important to note that the leading member of the theological consultants that prepared Puebla was Alberto Methol Ferré. When St. John Paul II arrived at Puebla he had already become familiarized with some of the concepts of the "theology of the people" through reading the preparatory documents of Puebla. The contacts between the two continued through some common friends. This is one of the many reasons why it is apparent that those who try to oppose Pope Francis and St. John Paul II do not really understand either of the men.

[38] This theology of the nation was condensed, a few months after Puebla, in Pope John Paul II, "Homily in Victory Square."

[39] See Timothy Matovina, "Theologies of Guadalupe: From the Spanish Colonial Era to John Paul II," *Theological Studies* 70 (March 2009): 61–91.

[40] See Hernan Alessandri, *Il futuro di Puebla* (Milan: Jaca Book, 1981).

[41] The expression is from Henrique C. de Lima Vaz, SJ.

critical and systematic expression of the living faith of their people.[42] The adoption of Marxism as the privileged analytical instrument for understanding history is a mistake; this proposition encountered the enthusiastic support of Bergoglio and of his Argentinian friends. They thought that Marx, Engels, and Hegel had no role to play in the vision for the peripheries of the world, especially those of Latin America. The catalyst of a true Latin American liberation could not be conceptualized in Marxist terms. Bergoglio led the Latin American church along the path established by John Paul II at Puebla up to the Fifth General Conference of the Latin American Episcopate in Aparecida.

According to Amelia Podetti,[43] the peculiar role of Latin America in world history hinges upon the fact that it is here, with an unparalleled intensity, that European Christianity becomes aware of the "other" and the periphery and is forced to confront this challenge. If this challenge is overcome in Latin America, it can also be overcome in every other part of the world. Latin America, however, is not only a challenge; it is also a bridge. It indicates a direction in which the whole church is called to move: along this path the church will become more authentically "catholic" and, at the same time, it will give a soul to globalization—accompanying and guiding the globalization of the economy with a globalization of the Spirit. To accomplish this task we must learn to think diversity within unity.

While this thinking was forged in the history of Latin America, I would go so far as to say that we must all make ourselves disciples of the great experience of faith of the Latin American church. It would be wrong, however, to imagine that we must now all become Latin Americans, as it would have been wrong to imagine in 1978 that we had all to become Polish. I am European, an Italian—I belong to a church that has long identified, in a passionate way, as the center rather than the periphery, even if it is truer to say that we are all peripheral and the center can only be Jesus. I am currently writing in English; surely the anglophone countries cannot be considered the periphery of world power today. The United States remains central, par excellence, to this system of power—politically, economically, militarily, culturally, and in many other senses. The United States

---

[42] See Pope John Paul II, "Opening Address to the Puebla Conference," sec. 1.5.

[43] See Peter Casarella's chapter in this volume, particularly pp. 198–200, which discusses Bergoglio's deep admiration for Podetti.

(and to a lesser extent today the United Kingdom) have often been seen as the custodians of an unjust world order and adversaries of attempts to build a better one. Moreover, they are the triumphant expression of Protestant and Enlightenment modernities that have defeated the Baroque. So what does it mean for us, in the United States, to become missionary disciples in the sense outlined by *Evangelii Gaudium*?

Unity Prevails over Conflict

I think that Bergoglio would ask American Catholics to be good citizens of the United States: to become aware of the role and the task of the Catholic Church in forming the self-understanding of this nation. What are the challenges to the unity of this nation today? What has been forgotten of its original mission? How should we reinterpret its foundational myth?[44] The national motto of the United States, "*e pluribus unum*," closely resembles Bergoglio's principle: "unity is more important than division." Unity is not undifferentiated; it is composed of a plurality of parts. Differences must be recognized and respected; a fair political struggle has an important role in the construction of the unity of a nation. It must, however, be oriented to the construction of a common good and not to the destruction of one's political opponents. Within the United States, the Catholic Church has integrated the Irish, the Italians, the Poles, and others. One key issue for the future of the United States today is the integration of Latinos. If the church does not do it, who will?

The original spirit of the Baroque was that of a "Catholic Reformation" rather than that of a "Counter-Reformation." The course of history, particularly the wars of religion, have created a tremendous split among Christian denominations. How might we rethink the Baroque in the light of the ecumenical spirit of the Council? A concrete response to this question cannot be severed from the need for dialogue between Latin America and Anglo-America, two parts of one continent. Diversity must be recognized but in a manner that promotes unity over conflict.

---

[44] See Richard John Neuhaus, *American Babylon: Notes of a Christian Exile* (New York: Basic Books, 2009).

Time Is More Important than Space

In the cultural wars of the recent past the church has defended the fundamental values of our civilization. We must be proud of the intellectuals and pastors who led those struggles. We must, however, ask ourselves: Is it possible to defend Christian (and natural) values in the public arena if their root—faith in the living presence of Jesus Christ—has dried up? If the root is rotten the tree will fall; we must first of all strengthen the root. We must become missionary disciples: before preaching the law we must enter into the hearts of the people. Only then will we be able to speak with authority, and only then will our people feel that the law is not an external imposition but the answer to the most profound desire of their hearts.

Realities Are More Important than Ideas

The missionary disciple takes care of people and communities of people. Human beings grow and we must follow their growth. They grow according to an inner principle that is constitutive of their personality and in constant dialogue with the Spirit of God. We can, indeed we must, have ideas and plans about the people entrusted to our care: both those who belong to our national church and those who belong to our nation. We must, however, first of all try to divine God's plan for his people and to cooperate with providence. Seldom does God's project coincide with our own, and God often chooses to let good and evil grow side by side, where we instead would eradicate the evil even at the cost of letting the good perish. Our projects and categories should always be flexible enough to adapt to God's project, and we must be ready to give them up rather than become an obstacle to the authentic development of the realities entrusted to our care. We should always keep before us the words of Isaiah 55:8-9: "For my thoughts are not your thoughts, / nor are your ways my ways, says the LORD. / For as the heavens are higher than the earth, / so are my ways higher than your ways / and my thoughts than your thoughts."

The Whole Is Greater than the Parts

You belong to a particular community; you have a particular life experience; you have "experimented" in your life and discovered truths. You want to hold on to them and you are fully justified in doing that. You must, however, never forget that we can lead our communities only if we listen to a Word that comes from above and never ceases to surprise us. People who have different and sometimes opposite temperaments, histories, and cultural heritages have an equal right as we do to participate in the one church of God, to belong to the redeemed people. More than this, each one of them adds something to my faith and is important for my personal spiritual growth in the Spirit of the Lord. The church, as well as the Truth, is not an aggregation of solo recitals but a symphony played by an orchestra, an orchestra that needs a director. If we want our contribution to be fruitful we must act according to the instructions of the director. In the Catholic Church the director is the bishop and in the last instance the pope. The force and the inspiration of each one of us comes from the unity of the church. It is good that some are conservative and others progressive, some more inclined to action and some to contemplation. There is an infinite plurality of charisms and of vocations and they are all precious, under one condition: that they be exercised within the bond of unity that in the last instance is guaranteed by the Bishop of Rome.

PART TWO

European Theology

Chapter 5

The Polarity Model: The Influences of Gaston Fessard and Romano Guardini on Jorge Mario Bergoglio[1]

Massimo Borghesi
Università di Perugia

Non coerceri a máximo, contineri tamen a minimo, divinum est[2]
(Not to be limited by the greatest,
and yet to be contained in the tiniest: this is divine)

Gaston Fessard and the Ignatian Component of the Theology of Tenderness

When I began to write *The Mind of Pope Francis: Jorge Mario Bergoglio's Intellectual Journey,*[3] one thing was clear to me: The pope had a deep and original thought that was expressed in his speeches and documents without being clearly visible. There was an underlying swell,

---

[1] This chapter was translated by Pietro Bartoli.

[2] On the so-called epitaph of St. Ignatius of Loyola, see Hugo Rahner, "Die Grabschrift des Loyola," *Stimmen der Zeit* (1947): 321–39.

[3] Massimo Borghesi, *The Mind of Pope Francis: Jorge Mario Bergoglio's Intellectual Journey*, trans. Barry Hudock (Collegeville, MN: Liturgical Press, 2018).

93

of sorts, that only occasionally came to the surface. This inkling was encouraged by two sources. The first of these was the best biography of the pontiff presently in circulation: *The Great Reformer: Francis and the Making of a Radical Pope* by Austen Ivereigh.[4] Ivereigh had the insight of analyzing the authors and ideas that accompanied Bergoglio's life and formation. He was the only one who dwelt on these issues. The other biographies, however accurate they may be, presumed that the future pope, the pastor of simple language, was in some way averse to intellectual reflection. Without realizing, they legitimated the image popular among Pope Francis's critics of a pope deprived of the cultural, theological, and philosophical formation necessary for the Petrine office. Ivereigh's research, documenting a complex picture of influences and ideas, dismantled this image. The second set of sources were his own writings from the '70s, even prior to becoming the youngest provincial of the Jesuits in Argentina. The speeches and reports of that time document the young Jesuit's efforts to guide the Society past the violent and ruthless conflict that divided Argentina between the military junta and the revolutionary guerillas. The Jesuits could not divide themselves among the opposing factions but needed to fight for the unity of a wounded people. The church, in Bergoglio's eyes, was the *complexio oppositorum* of these clashes, which, on the natural plane, could not be reconciled, but could only degenerate into irreconcilable contradictions. Catholicism, as a body of peace, was opposed to Manichean divisions and worked until the opposing poles, such as the progressives vs. the reactionaries, found a superior reconciliation that did not annul either.

This was an original perspective that reminded me, as a student of Romano Guardini's polar anthropology, of the Guardinian perspective. Of course, I knew that Bergoglio had gone to Frankfurt, Germany in 1986 for a doctoral thesis on Guardini. Guardini's name, however, was not present in his writings from the 1970s, nor in those of the first half of the 1980s. Where, then, had Bergoglio found the idea of "polar" thinking, in which the synthesis of opposing poles was entrusted to Mystery, operative in history?

Although I began to write the volume in early October 2016, I was unable to answer the question. There was no option but to ask the question of the pope himself by way of a mutual friend, Guzmán

---

[4] Austen Ivereigh, *The Great Reformer: Francis and the Making of a Radical Pope* (New York: Henry Holt, 2014).

Carriquiry. Through him, I sent Francis a collection of open-ended questions along with an explanation of the book. Surprisingly, given Bergoglio's distrust of abstract intellectual reflections, the pope responded amply and warmly. On four occasions between January and March 2018 he responded through recorded audio files to the questions I had posed. Thanks to these, a world was opened—Bergoglio's laboratory of ideas—which was otherwise inaccessible. The missing link, the connection between his polar thinking in the 1970s and his work on that of Romano Guardini in 1986, had a name: Gaston Fessard. It was the great French Jesuit, friend of Henri de Lubac (another figure important to Bergoglio[5]), who developed, influenced by the thought of Maurice Blondel and in clear opposition to Hegel, a Catholic conception of dialectics, through which Christ is the unity of slaves and free-people, men and women, Jews and pagans, and so on.[6] Fessard is *the* author at the beginning of Bergoglio's thought.[7] As Francis affirms in one of the interviews: "The writer . . . who had a big influence on me was Gaston Fessard. I've read *La Dialectique des Exercises Spirituels de Saint Ignace de Loyola,* and other things by him, several times. That work gave me many elements that later got mixed [into my thinking]."[8]

This is an important confession. The pope here offers the key to understanding the genesis of his thought as well as the common thread that holds it together. In *Dialectique,*[9] Fessard analyzes the spirituality of St. Ignatius starting from the tension between grace

---

[5] See Susan Wood's essay on the role of paradox and polarity in the ecclesiologies of de Lubac and Bergoglio in this volume, pp. 130–49.

[6] See Bishop Robert Barron's essay on the role of dialectic in Fessard's work in this volume, pp. 114–29.

[7] For more on the thought of Gaston Fessard (1897–1978) see Giao Nguyen-Hong, *Le Verbe dans l'histoire. La philosophie de l'historicité du Père Gaston Fessard,* preface by J. Ladrière (Paris: Beauchesne, 1974); Michel Sales, *Gaston Fessard, 1897–1978: genèse d'une pensée; suivi d'un résumé du «Mystère de la société» par Gaston Fessard* (Brussels: Culture et vérité, 1997); Michèle Aumont, *Philosophie sociopolitique de Gaston Fessard, S.J., «Pax nostra»* (Paris: Cerf, 2004), and *Ignace de Loyola et Gaston Fessard : l'un par l'autre* (Paris: L'Harmattan, 2006); Frédéric Louzeau, *L'anthropologie sociale du Père Gaston Fessard* (Paris: Presses Universitaires de France, 2009); Dominique Serra-Coetanea, *Le défi actuel du Bien commun dans la doctrine sociale de l'Église. Études à partir de l'approche de Gaston Fessard S.J.* (Zurich: LIT, 2016); A. Petrache, *Gaston Fessard, un chrétien de rite dialectique?*, preface by D. Pelletier (Paris: Cerf, 2017).

[8] Borghesi, *Mind of Pope Francis,* 6.

[9] Gaston Fessard, SJ, *La Dialectique des Exercises Spirituels de Saint Ignace de Loyola,* 3 vols. (Paris: Aubier, 1956–84).

and freedom, between the infinitely large and the infinitely small, between contemplation and action. The young Bergoglio would be struck by this dynamic interpretation of the *Exercises*. In it, he finds not only the formula for a dynamic open thought in tension, but also, as much as the interpretation may be unique to him, the model for a theology of tenderness. At its roots, Bergoglio's theology of tenderness depends on a profoundly Ignatian concept of the relationship between humanity and God. This is a little studied feature of the pontiff's spirituality.

It comes to light particularly clearly in his morning homily on December 14, 2017 at Santa Marta.[10] On that occasion, the pope, keeping the upcoming Christmas in mind, affirms being in front of "one of the greatest mysteries and one of the most beautiful things," that "our God has this tenderness that brings us closer and saves us with this tenderness." Francis explains, "He is the great God who makes himself small and in his smallness does not stop being great. And in this great dialectic he is small: there is the tenderness of God. The great that makes himself small and the small that is great." The unique characteristic of the pope's interpretation of the Fessardian insight here is the connection established between the category of "tenderness" and the dialectic between the great and the small. "Christmas helps us understand this fact: the little God in the manger," reaffirms Francis. "A phrase from St. Thomas comes to mind in the first part of the *Summa* [*Theologica*]. Wanting to explain 'What is divine? What is the most divine thing?,' he says: '*non coerci a maximo contineri tamen a minimo divinum est*' [not to be limited by the greatest and yet to be contained in the tiniest—this is divine]." In other words, what is divine is having ideals that are not limited, even by that which one considers greatest, but that are simultaneously contained and lived in the tiniest things of life. In essence, the pontiff explained, it is an invitation to "not be afraid of great things, but to take note of small things: this is divine, both together." The Jesuits know this line well, Francis notes, because "it was taken as one of St. Ignatius's cornerstones, as if to describe St. Ignatius's simultaneous strength and tenderness."

---

[10] Pope Francis, morning homily in the "Domus Sanctae Marthae" chapel, December 14, 2017. Italian language video from TV2000 accessible at http://youtu.be /HgtlqQyP1t0.

What Francis says here is of particular value due to the decisive influence the Ignatian motto would have on the formation of the future pontiff. The young Bergoglio had found a long commentary on the Ignatian saying in the final part of Fessard's *Dialectique* that particularly interested him.[11] The reason for this interest was, most likely, his professor of philosophy at the Colegio Máximo San José in the city of San Miguel in the province of Buenos Aires: Miguel Ángel Fiorito. Fiorito, an expert on the *Spiritual Exercises*, was the person who introduced Fessard to Bergoglio. Bergoglio, in 1981, would remember two articles by Fiorito: one from 1956, *La Opción Personal de S. Ignacio*, and one from 1957, *Teoría y Práctica de G. Fessard*.[12] The second article was primarily a commentary on the so-called Ignatian epitaph, "Not to be confined to what is great, but to be concerned with what is smaller: this is divine!"[13] Explaining the sense of it, Bergoglio writes, "we could translate it this way: 'without turning away from that which is high, we must bend down to pick up what is apparently small in the service of God,' or, 'while remaining attentive to what is further away, we must worry about what is closer.' It is applied to religious discipline . . . *and is useful for characterizing Ignatian spirituality dialectically (in the sense adopted by Fessard)*."[14] The Ignatian motto, analyzed by Fessard in *Dialectique*, became, for Bergoglio, the expression of the polar tension that animates the spirituality of St. Ignatius.[15] His reading of Fessard is guided by Fiorito, whose 1957 essay *Teoría y Práctica de G. Fessard* Francis picks up in the light of Fessard's dialectic model: "The (so-called) epitaph of St. Ignatius has two complementary phrases . . . the first phrase, *non coerceri a maximo, contineri tamen a minimo, divinum est*, highlights a fundamental characteristic of Ignatian spirituality . . . because it dialectically expresses—that is, by the opposition of contraries—the

---

[11] Fessard, *Dialectique des Exercises Spirituels*, 1:307–41.

[12] Miguel Ángel Fiorito, "La Opción Personal de S. Ignacio," *Ciencia y Fe* 12 (1956): 23–56; "Teoría y Práctica de G. Fessard," *Ciencia y Fe* 13 (1957). The two articles are cited in Jorge Mario Bergoglio, "Farsi custodi dell'eredità" (June 1981) in Pope Francis, *Nel Cuore di Ogni Padre: Alle Radici Della mia Spiritualità* (Milan: Rizzoli, 2016), 282, n. 4.

[13] Fiorito, "La Opción Personal de S. Ignacio," 43–44.

[14] Pope Francis, *Nel Cuore di Ogni Padre*, 282, n. 4. Emphasis mine.

[15] See Fessard, *Dialectique des Exercises Spirituels*, 1:210ff.

fundamental dynamism of the holy soul of Ignatius, who points always to the highest ideal, God, but is at the same time attentive to the smallest details of the divine plan."[16]

Bergoglio constantly recalled the Ignatian maxim, which he read in both Fessard and Fiorito. As pope, he would say, "I was always struck by a saying that describes the vision of Ignatius: *non coerceri a maximo, contineri tamen a minimo, divinum est*. I thought a lot about this phrase in connection with the issue of different roles in the government of the church, about becoming the superior of somebody else: it is important not to be restricted by a larger space, and it is important to be able to stay in restricted spaces. This virtue of the large and small is magnanimity. Thanks to magnanimity, we can always look at the horizons from the position where we are. That means being able to do the little things of every day with a big heart open to God and to others. That means being able to appreciate the small things inside the large horizons, those of the Kingdom of God."[17]

The dialectic of great and small, the tension that characterizes the faith and spirituality of St. Ignatius, becomes a focal point of Bergoglio's thought. In fact, through Fiorito, Fessard's concept of "dialectic" in the *Spiritual Exercises* became a point of reference for the young student. It was this perspective that opened him to further studies important for his formation. Fiorito and Fessard had helped

---

[16] Fiorito, "Teoría y Práctica de G. Fessard," 350–51, cited in Borghesi, *Mind of Pope Francis*, 11.

[17] Pope Francis with Antonio Spadaro, *My Door Is Always Open: A Conversation on Faith, Hope and the Church in a Time of Change*, trans. Shaun Whiteside (London: Bloomsbury, 2014), 21. On the Ignatian "epitaph," see Jorge Mario Bergoglio, "Condurre nelle grandi e nelle piccole circostanze," *Boletín de Espiritualidad* 73 (October 1981). In his "Letter on Inculturation, to the Whole Society" of May 14, 1978, Father General Pedro Arrupe recalls the Ignatian maxim, "The Ignatian spirit was once summed up in this sentence: 'Non cohiberi a maximo, contineri tamen a minimo, divinum est.' In our context, this maxim challenges us to hold on to the concrete and the particular, even to the last cultural detail, but without renouncing the breadth and universality of those human values which no culture, nor the totality of them all, can assimilate and incarnate in [a] perfect and exhaustive way" (Pedro Arrupe, "Letter on Inculturation, to the Whole Society," in Pedro Arrupe, *Other Apostolates Today*, vol. 3, Selected Letters and Addresses, ed. Jerome Aizala, SJ [St. Louis: Institute of Jesuit Sources, 1981], 171–81 at 176). The maxim was also studied by Hugo Rahner, "Die Grabschrift des Loyola," *Stimmen der Zeit* (February 1947): 321–39.

him intuit the "polarity," the contrast of opposites, that guides the Ignatian spirit. Everything follows from this intuition. It is important to detect that Francis's theology of tenderness also stems from this intuition. It is a theology that unites the Ignatian idea of "an ever-greater God," with Philippians 2:6-11, with the idea of the Lord who assumes the conditions of a slave. The theology of tenderness is a theology of the lowering of the Lord to become a servant, who *becomes small in order to communicate with the small.* Salvation comes thusly, not through force and power, which are also attributes of God, but through the weakness of the Son. *God chooses tenderness as the method of salvation.* Tenderness is found in the dialectic of great and small, in the great that becomes small, and the small that becomes great. Only in the logic of the Incarnation, in the lowering of God to the condition of a servant as a supreme sign of love for humanity, is the logic of tenderness comprehensible. Bergoglio's theology, then, springs from the reimagining of the Ignatian epitaph. In it, he finds his explanation for the paradoxical relationship between God and humanity, steered by mercy, that develops in Christian logic.

The Society of Jesus as a Synthesis of Opposites

About twenty years pass between 1962–1964, the period of first contact with Fessard, and 1986, the year of his arrival in Germany for a thesis on Romano Guardini's polar anthropology. It is a tragic period in Argentinian history, divided between revolution and military oppression. In that dramatic context, Bergoglio develops the intuition about a "polar" Christian life, lifted from Fessard's "dialectic" of the *Spiritual Exercises*, into a guiding interpretive criterion. Polarity is at the center of Ignatian spirituality. So writes the young Jesuit provincial in 1976: "The Ignatian vision is the possibility of harmonizing opposites, of inviting to a common table those concepts that seem irreconcilable, because it brings them to a higher place where they can find their synthesis."[18]

---

[18] Jorge Mario Bergoglio, "*Fede e giustizia nell'apostolato dei gesuiti*," in Pope Francis, *Pastorale Sociale*, ed. Marco Gallo, Italian trans. A. Taroni (Milan: Jaca Book, 2015), 246.

Such a synthesis was the fruit of the Ignatian concept of historical memory. "In the end, when St. Ignatius mentions memory, *a conception of unity* is in play. It is therefore possible to synthesize in unity the diversity of the times. This is what happened in our land: The Jesuits came to you with a great history, sixteen centuries of church, and with a very clear position regarding the religious problematic that was debated at the time in Europe, and they made a synthesis with the era of our natives. That synthesis was history."[19] This synthesis was the encounter between the Spaniard and the indigenous Americans, an encounter whose history includes light and darkness, but one that Bergoglio affirmed despite the strong indigenist ideology of the 1970s.

> The subsequent history of the Jesuits will then be marked by a unity capable of shaping the synthesis of opposites. Unity through reduction is relatively easy but not lasting. It is more difficult to forge a unity that does not annul differences or reduce conflict. It is the search for this latter unity that marks the Society's work of evangelization. It chose the *indio*, a viable project of justice, without forgetting the instruction of the Spaniards and the creoles of the cities. It brought to these lands the Spanish predilection for baroque art, but with the [indigenous] Americans—who according to Carpentier were already baroque, even in their geography—produced an art that, while clearly bearing Spanish origins, displayed at the same time an American originality. Responding to the Enlightenment, which gave birth to the pseudo-unity of Europe based on a kind of reason that was blind to transcendence, the Society transmitted the Gospel without rationalism or ingenuity, but with a solid intellectual foundation harmonized with fidelity to revelation and the magisterium of the church. If, on the one hand, it avoided subjectivist mysticism, on the other it knew how to nourish the people with a simple devotion, not at all lacking in affective elements. Nor did it fear, in guiding consciences, to be judged lax or casuist, succeeding in synthesizing the traditional morality of the body of the church with concrete existence. It is this fidelity to a charism of discernment that the Jansenist rigidity had never been able to understand.[20]

---

[19] Bergoglio, "*Fede e giustizia nell'apostolato dei gesuiti*," 246.
[20] Bergoglio, 246–47.

This passage illustrates Bergoglio's thought. It demonstrates his vision of the Society of Jesus as a place of encounter, dialogue, and synthesis among peoples. It highlights the difference between the abstract universalism of Enlightenment reason and the concrete universalism of Catholicism; the latter takes real people, including the dimension of the heart, into account. He demonstrates the relevance of the seventeenth-century controversies between the moral reflection of the Jesuits, which was concerned with the concrete, and the rigid and inhuman reflection of Jansen's disciples. At the center lies the idea of *"a unity that does not annul differences or reduce conflict."*[21] It is a unity in tension that recognizes the value of polarity, resisting the temptation to bring resolution through conflation or contradiction. Although Bergoglio's doctrine of polarity was not fully theoretically formulated, it is already essentially present. *Unity that does not annul differences* is already a dialectical concept that, unlike the Hegelian model, ends with a synthesis that is not reached simply through reason but through a higher principle provided by God, who is "ever greater." Such a synthesis always represents an encounter between grace and nature, God and humanity, otherness and freedom. The discovery of the 1960s, that of dialectical tension as the soul of Ignatius's *Exercises*, now takes its place within a larger Christian commitment in the world. Christians are called to be a source of unity within the divisions of history, to bear the tragedies of their time by opening them to the "ever greater" God. Catholic universality is polyphonic, capable of integrating differences without erasing them. Hegel's immanent universality, on the other hand, is fated, despite its attempts to distance itself from the abstraction of the Enlightenment, to resolve—or better *dissolve*—the "particular."[22] The Society of Jesus, in its intellectual confrontation with modern Idealism, is called to enact a synthesis between past and future, between immanence and transcendence. "Remembrance of the past and having the courage to open new spaces to God are united solidly in the Society, knowing that domes can never be raised if solid foundations are not built first. In other words, the goal of drawing all things in Christ—that is to say, to the universality of the church—cannot be accomplished in the

[21] Bergoglio, 246–47, emphasis mine.
[22] See Massimo Borghesi, *L'era dello Spirito: Secolarizzazione ed escatologia moderna* (Rome: Studium, 2008), 73–113.

absence of a transcendence that paradoxically recognizes the topography of the various immanences called to be drawn together and transcended."[23]

The "concrete," the universal-particular, arises from a transcendence that integrates and unifies the immanent pluriformity of multiplicity. It represents an antinomy that the Jesuits live: *the tension between Catholic universality and its particular inculturation.* As Bergoglio said in 1980, "both of these realities guarantee that we stand firmly on the frontier, which is typical of us Jesuits. Universality gives us horizons beyond the limits of localism; inculturation forces us to take seriously the 'space' that has been entrusted to us. These realities constitute an antinomy. A 'localist' province has already begun to die, as it lives far from the border. A province that lives universality without inculturation confuses Jesuit universalism with an abstract spirituality."[24] *Bergoglio here offers us the key to understanding the genesis of one of his polar couples: globalization and localization.* It is an antinomy that the Jesuit conscience knows well.

Bergoglio's antinomic and dialectical vision of the Christian's presence in the world is reaffirmed in his opening address to the provincial congregation in 1978. Here, the order's Argentine leader affirms that "*an indication* that we are well grounded in the Lord is that we are able to *maintain the antinomies* that constitute *being Jesuit,* and that classically are summarized in the formula 'contemplation in action.' "[25] To clarify the formula, he describes four antinomies characteristically maintained by "men of synthesis."[26] The first is based in "an attitude of *availability* and, at the same time, of *apostolic constancy. . . .* The inculturation that the Society of Jesus requires of us calls for an interior agility capable of recognizing the constants and the variables, together with a great austerity of contemplation that keeps us from confusing what is solid with what is yielding. In simpler terms, living this antinomy in a salvific manner is a discipline;

[23] Bergoglio, "Fede e giustizia nell'apostolato dei gesuiti," in Bergoglio, *Pastorale Sociale,* 247.

[24] Bergoglio, "Criteri di azione apostolica," *Boletín de Espiritualidad de la Compañia de Jesús,* January 1980, in Bergoglio, *Pastorale Sociale,* 61, n. 15.

[25] Bergoglio, "Discorso di aperture alla Congregazione pronvicial," in Bergoglio, *Pastorale Sociale,* 252.

[26] Bergoglio, 252.

it is Ignatian indifference; it is allowing ourselves to be guided by the Lord."[27]

The second mode of being of the man of synthesis is based in the tension between the union of minds and apostolic dispersion: "Space is another reality in which the Jesuit's ability to support antinomies is demonstrated. On the one hand he is a member of the body, of a *communitas*; but this is a community *ad dispersionem*. This antinomy is maintained by attaining not just any unity but the unity 'of hearts,' like that of soldiers who fight in the trenches of the kingdom."[28]

The third mode spans the memory of the past and the courage to face the future. Here, our relationship with time comes into play, which challenges both those who want to reduce history to a "restoration shop" and those who desire a "laboratory of utopias": "neither one thing, nor the other: neither traditionalists, nor utopians."[29] In order to transcend this (false) opposition, Bergoglio says, the Jesuit must

> resort to the "classic," which is very different from the easy recourse to what is "traditional," to the empty traditionalism that is concerned only with maintaining peace . . . but which is actually like the peace one finds at a tomb. By "classics," we refer to those powerful moments of experience and religious and cultural reflection that make up history because, in some way, they touch the irreversible events of the journey of a people, of the church, of the Christian. It is a matter of always having before our eyes the fundamental nucleus around which our identity is constituted (see Hebrews 10:32ff; 13:7ff), in order to be able to fulfill, without deviating from our identity, the steps that concrete and current historical situations demand from us. We are inspired by the "classics" to bring forward these two apparently antinomian attitudes that reflect our way of being: *remembering the past and having the courage to open new spaces to God*. The "classics" have provided the strength to find synthesis in moments of conflict. These are not easy "compromises" or cheap "irenicism." These are the syntheses that, without denying the contrary elements that cannot be simply combined in such crises, find resolution

[27] Bergoglio, 252–53.
[28] Bergoglio, 253.
[29] Bergoglio, 253.

at a higher level, through a mysterious journey of understanding and of fidelity to what is perennial in history. For this reason, the "classic" possesses this double virtue of being faithful to this history and of inspiring new paths to be undertaken.[30]

The last antinomy to be held in tension is that between piety and apostolic zeal. The young provincial's guiding idea is that of the Society of Jesus as a *coincidentia oppositorum*. With a dramatic awareness that sociopolitical conflict and ideologies tend to build insurmountable walls, profound hatreds, and victims, Bergoglio fought for the unity of the church and of the people. He did so by beginning with a *Catholic*, rather than Hegelian, conviction that sees the synthesis of opposites as the ideal goal. For Hegel, the particular is only apparently "conserved" in the universal. In a Catholic dialectic, the concrete universal indicates the *care for the particular*, the awareness that the smallest is the greatest in the kingdom of God. *Non coerceri a maximo, contineri tamen a minimo, divinum est.* This kind of synthetic capacity is missing in Idealism and in the subsequent ideologies founded on the sacrifice of the finite, the limited, and the contingent. Authentic totality, which opposes totalitarianism, does not break anyone or anything.

The Polar Philosophy of Romano Guardini

In 1986, Bergoglio traveled to Germany, to the Sankt Georgen Graduate School of Philosophy and Theology in Frankfurt, for a doctoral thesis on Romano Guardini.[31] As he will later confess, it was the first time he confronted the author's writing directly.[32] The theme,

---

[30] Bergoglio, 255. The reference to the "classics" as a bridge between memory and future explains the reform of the juniorate undertaken by Bergoglio at the Colegio Máximo, according to which the students would study, in addition to the European classics, those of Argentine literature also, from *El gaucho Martín Fierro* to Borges. On Bergoglio's favorite authors, see Pope Francis, *My Door Is Always Open*, 111–15. As a young man, Bergoglio was professor of literature and psychology at the Institute of the Immaculate Conception in Santa Fe, Argentina, in 1964 and 1965. On his teaching at that time, see the recollections of his former students in Jorge Milia, *Maestro Francesco: Gli allievi del Papa ricordano il loro professore* (Milan: Mondadori, 2014).

[31] On Guardini's philosophy, see Massimo Borghesi, *Romano Guardini: Dialettica e antropologia* (Rome: Studium, 1990), and *Romano Guardini: Antinomia della vita conoscenza affettiva* (Milan: Jaca Book, 2018).

[32] See Borghesi, *Mind of Pope Francis*, 101.

remembers Pope Francis, "was Guardini's first book of philosophy, *Der Gegensatz*, 'polar opposition,' the study that Guardini did on 'concrete-living.' I worked on that book with the help of Guido Sommavilla's study, which became for me the translator of Guardini and, at the same time, an authentic Guardinian thinker. The title of my thesis was *Polar Opposition as Structure of Daily Thought and of Christian Proclamation*. But it was not yet completely worked out."[33]

The thesis, for reasons also tied to Bergoglio's personal situation at the time, would not be completed. Nevertheless, he would continue to work on it between 1990 and 1992 in Cordoba, even considering, in 2011, bringing it to completion when he resigned as bishop of Buenos Aires. He would not reach his goal. This did not prevent, however, his theoretical reflection on the Guardinian model of polarity from continuing and developing richly.[34]

Guardini confirmed an already established idea. Nevertheless, he contributed to the deepening and broadening of the Bergoglian conceptual framework. Through Bergoglio's doctoral thesis, even though it was never completed, Guardini became his second teacher, who equipped him with the categories with which to face ecclesiology, society, and politics. Moving between Fessard and Guardini, Bergoglio found himself in a current of nineteenth-century Catholic thought beginning with the Tübingen School and Adam Möhler and continuing with Guardini, Erich Przywara, de Lubac, and Fessard. This school of thought understands the church as *coincidentia oppositorum*, as the tension between united opposites. This same conception is found in a man who might be called the third teacher of Bergoglio, Alberto Methol Ferré (1929–2009), who was also deeply influenced by Fessard's concept of dialectics.[35]

The pope's explanations of his thesis do not explain whether his original project included the other major Guardinian themes that, as seen in *Laudato Si'*, influenced Bergoglio: criticism of the technocratic paradigm, and the indiscriminate accumulation of uncontrolled power, developed by Guardini in *Das Ende der Neuzeit* (The End of the Modern World) (1950) and *Die Macht* (Power and Responsibility)

---

[33] Borghesi, 104.

[34] See Chapter 3, "The Theory of Polar Opposition," in Borghesi, 101–41.

[35] On Methol Ferré's thought, see Borghesi, *Mind of Pope Francis*, 85–99, 143–96.

(1951).[36] In fact, the most cited author in *Laudato Si'* is none other than Guardini. The thought of the Italo-German thinker, with his system of "concrete-living," is clearly an essential point of reference for Francis. Bergoglio found, in Guardini, the confirmation of a "synthesizing" and "complete" model, a "catholic" paradigm analogous to his own, capable of both explaining and embracing the contrasting personal, social, and political principles that tend to crystalize into contradictory dialectics, harbingers of dangerous conflict. As he confessed to Antonio Spadaro:

> Opposition opens a path, a way forward. Speaking generally, I have to say that I love oppositions. Romano Guardini helped me with an important book of his, *Der Gegensatz*. . . . He spoke of a polar opposition in which the two opposites are not annulled. One pole does not destroy the other. There is no contradiction and no identity. For him, oppositions are resolved at a higher level. In that resolution, however, the polar tension remains. The tension remains, it is not cancelled out. Limits must be overcome, not negated. Oppositions are helpful. Human life is structured in oppositional form. And we see this happening now in the church as well. The tensions are not necessarily resolved and ironed out, they are not like contradictions.[37]

Bergoglio's clarification as pope is important. It explains *what* the former Jesuit provincial might have found in the Italo-German thinker: the idea of life, both personal and communal, as a necessary

---

[36] Romano Guardini, *The End of the Modern World: A Search for Orientation* (Wilmington, DE: ISI Books, 1998; first Eng. ed., New York: Sheed and Ward, 1957), orig. *Das Ende der Neuzeit* (Basel: Hess, 1950); *Power and Responsibility: A Course of Action for the New Age*, trans. Elinor C. Briefs (Chicago: Henry Regenery, 1961), orig. *Die Macht* (Würzberg: Werkbund, 1951).

[37] Antonio Spadaro, "Le orme di un pastore: una conversazione con Papa Francesco," Introduction to Jorge Mario Bergoglio, *Nei tuoi occhi è la mia parola: Omelie e discorsi di Buenos Aires 1999–2013* (Milan: Rizzoli, 2016), xix. Bergoglio directed his friend and disciple Diego Fares, currently professor of metaphysics at the Universidad del Salvador and the Pontificia Universidad Católica of Buenos Aires, to Guardini's book: "Bergoglio opened the intellectual path to the study of Romano Guardini and Hans Urs von Balthasar, on whose phenomenology of truth Fares wrote his doctoral thesis" (Antonio Spadaro, "L'amicizia è questione di un momento," foreword to Diego Fares, *Papa Francesco è come un bambù: alle radici della cultura dell'incontro* [Milan: Àncora–La Civiltà Cattolica, 2014], 8). Spadaro's statement is indirectly confirmed by Fares: "I am well aware of the admiration that Pope Francis has for Romano Guardini" (Spadaro, "L'amicizia è questione di un momento," 17).

polar tension of opposites, as an oppositional rather than contradictory tension. Opposites constitute the lifeblood of "concrete-living," they render unity mobile and dynamic. Contradiction, on the other hand, like that between good and evil, requires decision and choice: evil is not the counter-pole of good, as gnosis would have it; it is its negation. The distinction between *opposition (Gegensatz)* and *contradiction (Widerspruch)* is crucial because it allows us to think of the Catholic *communio* not as flat, uniform unity but a dynamic, polyform reality that need not fear the loss of its unity. Ecclesial unity is not a monolithic block in which unity comes from on high in a fixed and direct manner. It does not fear accommodating different poles and reconciling them in the strength of the Spirit, who unites everything as in a musical symphony. *Communio* is realized in a *dialogical* form, in the patient weaving that does not pretend to deny but maintains peculiarities and varied sensibilities. It is the idea of church that Bergoglio has and had in 1986, grounded in Guardini's philosophical anthropology.

In his polar "system" Guardini proposed a set of opposites that he identified as the *categorical* (subdivided into *intra-empirical* and *trans-empirical*) and the *transcendental*. As Bergoglio remembers,

> Guardini presents the *polar oppositions* as real and living. One can experience this structurally as fullness-form, act-structure, and individuality-totality tensions. Guardini characterizes these oppositions as *intra-empirical* categories. A deeper (I would say reflexive) level of tensions comes in the relationship between a person's experience and interiority. This *trans-empirical* reality is expressed in the opposites of production-disposition, originality-rule, and interiority-transcendence. Finally, Guardini synthesizes the tensions found in all the others, the *trans-empirical* polar tensions: unity-multiplicity and similarity-difference. That is to say: one must see these tensions between opposites as *indivise et inconfuse* [not divided yet not conflated]. It is necessary to maintain their differences and their resemblance, their unity and multiplicity, and this is possible through *measure* and *rhythm*. On a gnoseological level, the fundamental tension is between intuition and concept, a tension that allows us to see all these tensions as *indivise et inconfuse*.[38]

---

[38] Jorge Mario Bergoglio, "Necessità di un'antropologia politica: Un problema pastorale," *Stromata*, January–June 1989, in Pope Francis, *Pastorale Sociale*, 292, n. 5.

In comparison to Guardini's framework, Bergoglio's model is simple. It gathers all the Guardinian polar principles into three fundamental pairs:

A. Polarity: Fullness (time)-Limit (moment)
   1. Time is superior to space.
   2. Unity is superior to conflict.

B. Polarity: Idea-Reality
   3. Reality is superior to ideas.

C. Polarity: Globalization-Localization
   4. The sum is superior to the part.[39]

The first polar pair, fullness-limit, corresponds to Guardini's second pair of intra-empirical opposites, *fülle-form* (fullness-form), while the third, globalization-localization, corresponds to the third of the intra-empirical ones, *einzelheit-ganzheit* (individuality-totality). Only the second polar pair, idea-reality, does not have a parallel in the Guardinian set of categories:

> *Reality* is. *Idea* is elaborated, induced. [Idea] is instrumental in the understanding, perceiving, and engaging with reality. Between the two there must be dialogue—a dialogue between reality and the explanation of it that I produce. This represents another *bipolar* tension, which rejects an autonomy of idea and word with respect to reality in which the idea is dominant (from which are derived idealisms and nominalisms). Nominalisms never synthesize. At most they classify, cite, or define, but they do not unite. What unites is reality illuminated by reason, idea, and the intuitive perception [underlying them].[40]

This is an important development on Guardini. Bergoglio's *realism*, his meeting point with Thomism and the distinctively Christian

---

[39] The three polar pairs, coupled with the four principles, are found in Bergoglio, *Nosotros como ciudadanos, nosotros como pueblo. Hacia un bicentenario en justiciar y solidaridad 2010–2016* (Buenos Aires: Claretiana, 2011), Italian trans., *Noi come cittadini noi come popolo. Verso un bicentenario in giustizia e solidarietà 2010–2016* (Milan: Jaca Book, 2013), 59–69. See also *Evangelii Gaudium* 221–37.

[40] Bergoglio, *Noi come cittadini, noi come popolo*, Italian trans. *Nosotros como ciudadanos, nosotros como pueblo*, 65.

grounding of his critique of Gnosticism, is articulated in the principle "Reality is superior to ideas." The broadening of the Guardinian framework does not put the original model in question. On the contrary, in the interview *My Door Is Always Open* with Fr. Spadaro, the bipolar tensions mentioned by Francis are apparently not limited to three. He seems to be open to other oppositions present in the Guardinian framework. Among these is that between immanence and transcendence (*immanenz–transzendenz*), the third *trans-empirical* pair important for family, society, the state, and the church. Every "structure," including all social bodies (and the church), must have a *trans-empirical* point, a point of rupture, that breaks its tendency for immanence and closure. This is also important for the Jesuits, the religious order of the pontiff.

> The Society is an institution in tension, always fundamentally in tension. A Jesuit is a person who is not centered in himself. The Society also looks to a center outside itself; its center is Christ and his church. So, if the Society centers itself in Christ and the church, it has two fundamental points of reference for its balance and for being able to live on the margins, on the frontier. If it looks too much in upon itself, it puts itself at the center as a very solid, very well "armed" structure, but then it runs the risk of feeling safe and self-sufficient. The Society must always keep before itself the *Deus semper maior*, the always greater God. . . . This tension constantly takes us out of ourselves.[41]

Being brought "out" of oneself is the precondition of any successful effort at avoiding *clericalism*, the celebration of oneself. The Christian is, by definition, decentered. Their place is at the margins. Only Christ can live at the "center." Christ represents Guardini's *trans-empirical* point, the vanishing point that prevents withdrawal, closure, and bureaucratic crystallization. These correspond to and are reinforced by a "systematic," completed, repetitive way of thinking. As we have already seen in Guardini, the knowledge of the living-concrete can be modulated only in a polar tension between concept and intuition, between the rational and the superrational. This is what Guardini called "perception" or "vision" (*Anschauung*). For Bergoglio,

---

[41] Pope Francis, *My Door Is Always Open*, 23.

> When you express too much, you run the risk of being mis-
> understood. The Society of Jesus can be described only in nar-
> rative form. Only in narrative form do you discern, not in a
> philosophical or theological explanation, which allows you
> rather to discuss. The style of the Society is not shaped by discus-
> sion, but by discernment, which of course presupposes discus-
> sion as part of the process. The mystical dimension of discernment
> never defines its edges and does not complete the thought. The
> Jesuit must be a person whose thought is incomplete, in the sense
> of open-ended thinking.[42]

Living thought, both rational and intuitive, is "open." Thus, it is
clear, the concept of polarity guides the entirety of Bergoglian thought.
It is not limited to the social context. There are many references to
bipolar structures in the Spadaro interview: contemplation-action,
people-hierarchy, gentleness-strength, primacy-collegiality, male-
female, and past-present.[43] To these Francis adds the fundamental
bipolarity between theology and pastoral care in his video message
for the Pontifical Catholic University of Argentina:

> Not infrequently a kind of opposition is constructed between
> theology and pastoral care, as if they were two opposite, separate
> realities that have nothing to do with one another. Not infre-
> quently, we identify doctrine with the conservative, the retro-
> grade; and, on the other side, we think that pastoral care is an
> adaptation, a reduction, and an accommodation, as if they had
> nothing to do with each other. Thus, we create a false opposition
> between the so-called "pastorally-minded" and the "academics,"
> those who are on the side of the people and those on the side of
> doctrine. We create a false opposition between theology and
> pastoral care; between the believer's reflection and the believer's
> life; life, then, has no space for reflection and reflection finds no
> space in life. The great fathers of the church, Irenaeus, Augustine,
> Basil, and Ambrose, to name a few, were great theologians be-
> cause they were great pastors. One of the contributions of the
> Second Vatican Council was seeking a way to overcome this
> divorce of theology and pastoral care, between faith and life. I

---

[42] Pope Francis, 24.
[43] Pope Francis, 25.

dare to say that it revolutionized, to some extent, the status of theology—the believer's way of doing and thinking.[44]

In this way, we can understand the meaning of *agonic/organic reflection* that puts bipolar tensions, unresolvable poles that occasionally require synthesizing processes, at the center. Bergoglio's "dialogical thinking" does not represent, from this point of view, an irenic solution defined by easy optimism but the result of ontological reflection. *The ontology of polarity requires dialogical thinking, directed toward a synthetic horizon, that resists a "contradictory" interpretation of its poles.* The framework is that of a "catholic" thought that understands the church and life as a *complexio oppositorum*, an agonizing struggle to overcome conflicts, to prevent the resolution of polarities into Manichean contradictions. This thought has its roots in the mystery of the church. As Henri de Lubac, an author dear to Bergoglio, writes:

> Multiple or multiform, she is nonetheless *one*, of a most active and demanding unity. She is a people, the great anonymous crowd, and still—there is no other word—the most personal of beings. Catholic, that is, universal, she wishes of her members to be open to everything and yet she herself is never fully open but when she is withdrawn into the intimacy of her interior life bent in the silence of adoration. She is humble and she is majestic. She professes a capacity to absorb every culture, to raise up to their highest values; at the same time, we see her claim for her own, the homes and hearts of the poor, the undistinguished, the simple and destitute masses. Not for an instant does she cease— and her immortality assures continuity—to contemplate him who is at once crucified and resurrected, the man of sorrows and lord of glory, vanquished by, and savior of, the world. He is her bloodied spouse and her triumphant master.[45]

[44] Pope Francis, "Video Message to Participants in an International Theological Congress Held at the Pontifical Catholic University of Argentina," Buenos Aires, September 1–2, 2015, http://w2.vatican.va/content/francesco/en/messages/pont -messages/2015/documents/papa-francesco_20150903_videomessaggio-teologia -buenos-aires.html.

[45] Henri de Lubac, *The Church: Paradox and Mystery*, trans. James R. Dunne (Staten Island: Alba House, 1969), 2; orig. *Paradoxe et Mystère de L'Eglise* (Paris: Aubier- Montaigne, 1967).

For de Lubac, as for Bergoglio, "the Church is *complexio opposito-rum*," a mystical unity in which "the impact of the *opposite* hides the unity of the *complexio*."[46] The church is a universal paradox of that which, on the immanent plane, is inexorably divided. Both de Lubac and Bergoglio come, indirectly, from the school of Adam Möhler, first through Fr. Pierre Chaillet, then through Guardini. From Möhler, the author of *Die Einheit in der Kirche* (1825) and *Symbolik* (1832), comes the possibility of a Catholic thought that matches up with the church's difficulties in the era of globalization. Catholicism is the beating heart of thought in tension, not static, between unity and distinction. In the words of the pope:

> In other words, the same Spirit creates *diversity and unity*, and in this way forms a new, diverse and unified people: the *universal* Church. First, in a way both creative and unexpected, he generates diversity, for in every age he causes new and varied charisms to blossom. Then he brings about unity: he joins together, gathers and restores harmony: "By his presence and his activity, the Spirit draws into unity spirits that are distinct and separate among themselves" (Cyril of Alexandria, *Commentary on the Gospel of John*, 11, 11). He does so in a way that effects true union, according to God's will, a union that is not uniformity, but *unity in difference*.
>
> For this to happen, we need to avoid *two* recurrent *temptations*. The first temptation seeks *diversity without unity*. This happens when we want to separate, when we take sides and form parties, when we adopt rigid and airtight positions, when we become locked into our own ideas and ways of doing things, perhaps even thinking that we are better than others, or always in the right, when we become so-called "guardians of the truth." When this happens, we choose the part over the whole, belonging to this or that group before belonging to the Church. We become avid supporters for one side, rather than brothers and sisters in the one Spirit. We become Christians of the "right" or the "left," before being on the side of Jesus, unbending guardians of the past or the avant-garde of the future before being humble and grateful children of the Church. The result is diversity without unity. The opposite temptation is that of seeking *unity without*

---

[46] De Lubac, *The Church*, Italian trans., *Paradosso e mistero della chiesa* (Brescia: Queriniana, 1968), 12.

diversity. Here, unity becomes uniformity, where everyone has to do everything together and in the same way, always thinking alike. Unity ends up being homogeneity and no longer freedom. But, as Saint Paul says, "where the Spirit of the Lord is, there is freedom" (2 Cor 3:17).[47]

---

[47] Pope Francis, homily, "Holy Mass for the Solemnity of Pentecost," June 4, 2017, http://press.vatican.va/content/salastampa/en/bollettino/pubblico/2017/06/04 /170604a.html.

Chapter 6

Gaston Fessard and Pope Francis

Bishop Robert Barron

Archdiocese of Los Angeles

Introduction

Those searching out the principal intellectual sources for Pope Francis's thinking and pastoral activity would probably look first to Romano Guardini, the theologian and philosopher around whom Jorge Mario Bergoglio's doctoral research centered. However, when Massimo Borghesi posed the question to Pope Francis himself, the answer came back unambiguously: "The writer . . . who had a major influence on me was Gaston Fessard. I read many times his *Dialectic of the Spiritual Exercises of St. Ignatius of Loyola* along with other things of his. He gave me so many of the elements that later got mixed [into my own thinking]."[1]

Though crucial in the intellectual formation of Pope Francis, Gaston Fessard is not well known in this country, even, I daresay, in academic circles. Many of his colleagues and intellectual peers are widely read still: Henri de Lubac, Jean Danielou, Teilhard de Chardin, Hans Urs von Balthasar, Romano Guardini. But Fessard has been largely forgotten. We might proffer a number of explanations for this:

[1] Pope Francis, quote in Massimo Borghesi, "How Francis Thinks," Il blog di Massimo Borghesi, February 9, 2018, https://www.massimoborghesi.com/how-francis-thinks-il-the-tablet-dedica-la-copertina-al-volume-sul-pensiero-del-papa/.

the density of his style, his preoccupation with ideologies, namely, Nazism and communism, that are no longer at the forefront of our concern, his somewhat dated Hegelianism, but Pope Francis's emergence provides a rich opportunity to rediscover and reappropriate this exceptionally interesting and important figure.

A Biographical Sketch

Because Gaston Fessard is not a household name, I thought it would be useful, as we get underway, to provide at least a sketch of his biography and principal themes. Fessard was born in 1897 and joined the Society of Jesus at the tender age of sixteen in 1913. Like so many of his generation, he was profoundly marked by the cataclysm of the First World War, in which he actively participated as a soldier between 1917 and 1918. He received a classical formation in philosophy, especially in the Thomist mode, but as a young Jesuit, he became interested in German idealism, especially Fichte and Schelling. While he was in Germany in 1926, he bought, from a sidewalk bouquiniste, a copy of Hegel's *Phaenomenologie des Geistes*, and it is fair to say that the encounter with the great German philosopher would decisively influence his life.

During the 1930s, very much under the influence of Hegel's dialectical method, he commenced his massive commentary on the *Spiritual Exercises* of St. Ignatius. This, his *chef d'oeuvre*, would appear eventually in three volumes, the last of which was published posthumously in 1984. Between 1934 and 1938, Fessard participated in the famous seminars on Hegel offered by the Russian-born French philosopher Alexandre Kojève. These lectures were followed by most of the leading French intellectuals of the mid-twentieth-century: Jacques Lacan, Georges Bataille, Jean-Paul Sartre, Maurice Merleau-Ponty, and Raymond Aron, among many others. At the end of the lecture series, Fessard, who had become a friend of Kojève, intervened to contest the master's atheistic interpretation of Hegel. So impressed was he by the younger man's intellectual acumen, Kojève commented that, if he so desired, Fessard would become the greatest Marx specialist writing in French.[2] Like Lacan, Fessard benefitted especially

---

[2] Hugh Gillis, "Gaston Fessard and the Nature of Authority," *Interpretation* 16, no. 3 (Spring 1989): 447.

from Kojève's recuperation of Hegel's treatment of the master/slave dynamic. The amplification of this idea, following a prompt from St. Paul, would become eventually the central thematic template of Fessard's thought.

In 1937, Fessard published a text entitled *La main tendue: Le dialogue catholique-communiste est-il possible?*, which proposed a strenuous argument against those Catholics who were encouraging a rapprochement with communism. I will return to this theme in some detail later in this essay, but suffice it to say for the moment that Fessard felt that communism amounted, not simply to a social theory, but to a rival and entirely secular religion. To balance his opposition to communism, Fessard turned in the late 1930s and early '40s to an equally vigorous attack on Nazism (*France, prends garde de perdre ton âme*), and in 1945, he summed up his opposition to both forms of totalitarianism in *France, prends garde de perdre ta liberté*. Throughout the 1950s and turbulent '60s, Fessard continued to comment on Hegel, Marx, and Kierkegaard and to engage the question of Catholic "progressivism," which he took to be an updated but still dysfunctional attempt to reconcile Catholicism and Marxist social theory.

He undertook a major study of his friend and colleague Raymond Aron in the 1970s, but this book was published only after Fessard's death. The last text that he prepared was *Église de France, prends garde de perdre ta foi*, in which he once again took up the issue of communism, proving that the engagement with this enormously influential philosophy was, along with the study of Hegel, the golden thread of his intellectual life. Gaston Fessard died on Sunday morning, June 18, 1978, while working at his desk at Ponte Vecchio in Corsica.

Philosophy of History

In order to grasp the thought of Fessard, we must explore the conceptual apparatus that he conceived early in his career and that he used, fairly consistently, throughout his writings on a variety of subjects. From Hegel's meditations on the relationship between pure spirit and absolute spirit, Fessard derived a fundamentally dialectical understanding of the movement of history. He furthermore took in Hegel's notion of the master/slave relationship as key to the process by which spirit comes to self-possession, but, as I suggested above, he amplified this through the influence of St. Paul's great text from his letter to the Galatians: "There is no longer Jew or Greek, there is no longer slave or free, there is no longer male and female; for all of you are one in Christ Jesus" (Gal 3:28). Jesus breaks down the walls that separate these three elemental pairs, and hence he is the resolution of the principal dialectical tensions that govern history.

Therefore, along with the master/slave dialectic, there is the male/female tension and, most important, the play between Jew and Greek. And these three correspond to the basic dimensions of history, namely, the natural (male and female), the human (master and slave), and the supernatural (Jew and pagan). The last of the three controls and orders the first two, so that everything depends upon the navigation of one's relationship to the supernatural. At the physical, instinctive, and biological level, the dialectic between men and women holds sway. Following Hegelian prompts, Fessard appreciates that a man comes to self-possession precisely in relationship to a woman, and the inverse is true as well. And the mutual surrender and self-discovery of each finds concrete expression in the child that results from their union. This dialectical play becomes dysfunctional when it devolves, as it frequently does, into forms of domination, violence, and subjugation. It ought to tend in the direction of love and mutual self-gift, but this will happen only when it is placed consciously in relation to the call of God.

The second tension—the one massively studied by Hegel and so many of his disciples, especially Marx—is the master/slave rapport. Fessard learned the basic dynamics of this relationship from Kojève's lectures. The master emerges through a willingness to risk his life and safety in the context of a dangerous world, and this act of courage enables him to subjugate others for his own purposes. Hence the slave emerges, accepting domination as a means of avoiding violent death. However, the slave comes to self-possession through labor on behalf of the master, which gives him (the slave) a mastery over nature. And this in turn provides a sort of leverage vis-à-vis the one who dominates and brings about a reversal, the master coming to depend upon the achievement of the slave. According to Hegel, much of human society and civilization is conditioned by this dialectical dynamic, and it is not difficult to see the ample use that Marx would make of it in his analysis of the play between the proletariat and the bourgeoisie in a capitalist political economy. Fessard borrowed from Hegel the idea that, ultimately, the master/slave relationship should evolve, by slow steps, to become the friendship of citizens within the state, but once more, he appreciated that this evolution would be complete only when something like supernaturally inspired love comes to obtain in place of domination and subjugation.

The play between Jew and Greek is the dialectic that most fascinated Fessard and that he appreciated as most important in the work of discerning the movement of history. In using this pair of terms, Fessard is speaking of the supernatural order, which is to say, the relationship to God, whether we understand that as pertaining to the individual or to the society. Fessard held that this dialectic plays itself out in a fourfold way, corresponding to the attitudes of Jews and Greeks prior to Christ and after Christ. Before Jesus, the two options are the *Juif élu* (the elected Jew) and the *païen idolatre* (the idolatrous pagan); and after Jesus, the two options are the *Juif incrédule* (the unbelieving Jew) and the *païen converti* (the converted pagan).[3] To examine all of the permutations and combinations of these relationships would take us too far afield. So I will focus, as Fessard usually does, on the first pair.

The elected Jew is in right relation to the true God but in a restricted and tribal manner, whereas the idolatrous pagan is in a positive relation to philosophy and beauty but out of step with the true God. Christ, who is a Jew and a son of the Mosaic Law as well as the incarnation of the Logos, represents, accordingly, the overcoming of the split between Jew and Greek. In him, as Paul points out in Romans 9–11, Israel finds the deepest meaning of its election, and Greeks find themselves properly and fully ordered to the Logos which they had always been seeking through their philosophy and mythology. Again, love is the resolution, for Christ, as Paul teaches, breaks down the wall of hatred that separates Jew from gentile (Eph 2:14).

What remains key for Fessard—and here he differs from Hegel, who consistently operates within a somewhat determinist framework—is that the resolution of the various dialectical tensions always happens through freedom. A person faces the option between truth and falsity, between being and nonbeing, ultimately between accepting or rejecting God's will, and upon the choice of the individual

---

[3] Ana Petrache, *Gaston Fessard, un chrétien de rite dialectique?* (Paris: Les Éditions du Cerf, 2017), 86.

agents, everything depends. Here the influence of the Ignatian exercises, which we will examine in greater detail anon, is, once again, obvious.

Critique of Totalitarianisms

As we saw, Fessard remained, throughout his writing career, preoccupied with the rival totalitarianisms that bedeviled the twentieth century, namely, National Socialism and communism. He lived through a time when a considerable number of European Christians seemed to be making peace with Nazism, especially in the context of Vichy France. And from the 1930s through the '70s, he wrestled with Catholics who felt that it was possible, even desirable, to make common cause with communism. Fessard saw both totalizing systems as pseudoreligions, borrowing many elements from Christianity but distorting them. His great no to both the extreme right and the extreme left made him suspect to many in the French intellectual and religious establishment, and, I would venture to say, helps to explain why he is not widely read today.

It is first important to point out that Fessard saw both totalitarianisms as a reaction to the excessive individualism promoted by Enlightenment rationalism. The political movements that grew up out of the Enlightenment—in both Europe and America—were conditioned by an almost exclusive interest in the rights and privileges of the individual. Thomas Jefferson's rather vague appeal to the "pursuit of happiness" on the part of each individual witnesses to the breakdown of any thick sense of the common good. The extremism of liberal democracy gave rise to an excessive reaction in the twentieth century in favor of the collective and the general—one putting a stress on race and the other on class.

One is reminded of the speculation of Fessard's contemporary, Paul Tillich, who spoke of the oscillation between individualization and participation that tends to mark every society. The Nazism against which Tillich fought so strenuously represented excessive "participation" (*ein Volk, ein Reich, ein Führer*), whereas the liberal democracies represented excessive "individualization." Very much in the manner of Fessard, Tillich held that such tension is resolvable, not through cultural or political evolution, but only through the grace of God, who stands beyond the one and the many. One is put in mind as well of Hannah Arendt, who said that the "atomization" of society through modern liberalism excited a counterreaction in the direction of a mobilization of the masses through a common cause.[4] It seemed impossible to build a real society on the basis of such abstract ideas as liberty and equality and the universality of rights. Some sort of grounded solidarity was required, and the totalitarianisms provided it, however dysfunctionally. The problem was that they did so through a form of idolatry, that is to say, a substitute religion or a "political religion," in Raymond Aron's language. And this is precisely why both Nazism and communism stood so resolutely against Christianity, unlike the liberal democracies, which at least tolerated it.

The basic form of their idolatry, Fessard argued, was the placing of humanity and the temporal good as the supreme value, the triumph of the proletariat in the case of communism, and the dominance of the master race in the case of Nazism. In his more specific criticisms, Fessard took advantage of his tripartite hermeneutic. Most famously, he analyzed both Nazism and communism in terms of the master/slave dynamic. Within capitalism, the proletariat plays the role of the slave, but in the great reversal of the revolution, the proletariat overthrows the capitalist and establishes, not a new master/slave relationship, but rather the end of private property and the oppressive system that protects it. The "classless" society proposed by Marx is hence, Fessard concluded, the universalization of the attitude of the slave. By the same token, Nazism employs the master race of Aryans to eliminate the subordinate slave races and hence to establish a raceless society, or, if you will, a society made up entirely of masters. In point of fact, these immanentist and idolatrous systems can never resolve the tension between master and slave, except through the greatest and most brutal violence—as became startlingly clear in the twentieth century. It is, as St. Paul saw so clearly, only in Christ that the tension between master and slave is resolved, only through a breaking down of the wall of hatred.

We find a similar one-sidedness in regard to the male/female dichotomy. Fessard's analysis depends upon an analogy he makes between masculinity and the state and femininity and the society. In

---

[4] Hannah Arendt, *The Origins of Totalitarianism* (San Diego: Harcourt, 1968), 316–17.

Nazism, the state is absolutized to such a degree that the mediating institutions of the society are effectively abolished, whereas in communism, which involves the complete withering away of the state, the society—the arena of family, work, and community—is hyperemphasized. Hence the former is all male and the latter all female. Here is Fessard's summary: "On one side, the Master Race reveals itself through its interdiction of all sexual commerce with the slave nations, as a man without a woman; on the other side, the classless society is as a woman without a man, due to its exclusion of the power of the State."[5] Once more, it is only in the mutual surrender to the will and purposes of God that men and women—as well as the masculine and feminine dimensions of public life—find their equilibrium.

Finally, Fessard analyzes the two totalitarianisms under the rubric of Jew and Greek. Both Nazism and communism represent a secularized and hence idolatrous messianism. Nazism corresponds to paganism in its desire to conquer the world through reliance upon its own powers, much in the manner of the Roman Empire. It is a messianism of the master race. Communism, on the other hand, corresponds to Judaism in its stress upon the categories of fall, redemption, and messianic intervention, but the messianism in this case is one of class, the proletariat taking the role of the Suffering Servant. In point of fact, communism and Nazism combine the negative poles of the Jew/pagan split, namely, the unbelieving Jew and the unconverted pagan; whereas the church, according to the Pauline dictum, combines the positive poles of elected Jew and converted pagan.

Now since Nazism faded from the scene in 1945, but communism continued to assert itself in Europe to the end of Fessard's days, the Jesuit spent a considerable amount of time and effort unpacking the dynamics of communism as a false religion. The most fundamental difference between right- and left-wing interpretations of Hegel is that the former appreciates the chief protagonist of history as the divine spirit, which comes to itself through the vagaries and conflicts of history, while the latter sees the principal subject as the proletariat, which gradually comes to consciousness through the struggle against various forms of oppression. On the left-wing or Marxist reading, the proletariat functions as the messianic culmination of the process

---

[5] Petrache, *Gaston Fessard*, 224.

of history and hence as the means by which the definitive revolution is fostered and the era of pure communism ushered in. In one sense, the proletariat is the Son or the Suffering Servant, who bears the sins of the people; and in another sense, it is the Spirit whose mission is to transform the world.

This inversion or transposition of Christian themes can be seen throughout the Marxist enterprise. Hence, salvation comes, not through the right rapport between human beings and God, but rather through the right rapport between humanity and nature. Fessard insists: "For the disciples of Marx, the essential unity of man and nature . . . plays exactly the same role that the unity of God and man does for Christians."[6] (Fessard, incidentally, was one of the first European scholars to do extensive research into Marx's early texts, especially the *Economic and Philosophical Manuscripts of 1844*, in which the young revolutionary explores the deep alienation from nature that occurs through capitalism). Further, the original sin is no longer disobedience to God, but rather the establishment of private property, which leads to a variety of alienations; salvation happens through the fomenting of class war, and so forth. Fessard argued throughout his career that Marxism is predicated upon a fundamental contradiction, namely, that the clash of master and slave will end with the supremacy of the proletariat, when history gives absolutely no warrant for this confidence. But his more basic difficulty is that the entire project involves the rejection of God and hence the establishment of what amounts to a false religion.

Some of Fessard's interlocutors, following a more or less Leninist line, argued that atheism is the core supposition of the Marxist program. Others, more influenced by the writings of the early Marx, held that it functions as a corollary to the economic critique. In a word, they opined, people engage in the neurotic self-alienation described by Feuerbach, precisely because they are suffering from a more basic alienation from nature and from their own best selves, this latter estrangement produced by private property. But in any case, Fessard maintained, atheism is at the very least close to the center of Marxism. When he turned his attention to the so-called "progressive" Catholics of the 1960s and '70s, Fessard complained bitterly that they supposed

[6] Petrache, 157.

that one could do Marxist economics without adopting atheism.[7] Such an interpretive move, on his reading, was just naïve. And he particularly scored the progressives for abandoning the social teaching of the Catholic Church, which teaches the complementarity of social classes and which proposes, in fact, a far more convincing account of history than Marxism.

The Link to Ignatius

The turn to the church's social doctrine and to its spiritual reading of history allows us to explore Fessard's intense relationship with the *Exercises* of St. Ignatius. As a Jesuit, he had followed the exercises on retreat and had used them to guide others, and as an academic, he had made the formal study of the *Exercises* one of his principal preoccupations. At the heart of Ignatius's classic text, on Fessard's reading, is the play between two freedoms, divine and human. It is most important, he argues, that in the famous *Suscipe* prayer, Ignatius invites God to take not only his "memory, understanding, and will," the well-known Augustinian triplet, but also his "liberty." This addition makes the text peculiarly modern. And it provides the hermeneutical key to reading the entire project.

Unlike Hegel and Marx, who saw history as the unfolding of largely abstract forces, Ignatius saw it as a function of the playing out of two liberties, God's free offer of grace and our equally free acceptance or rejection of that offer. The novelty of Fessard was to take the Ignatian analysis of the individual's relation to grace and apply it to the social and political arena. The same sort of discernment of spirits that takes place in the former setting ought to obtain in the latter as well. We remark the similarity to von Balthasar here. The great Swiss theologian, like Fessard, thoroughly trained in the Ignatian tradition, opposed what he called "epic" theology to "lyrical" theology, the former marked by abstraction and the latter by concrete engagement of freedoms. The *Theodramatik*, the second panel of von Balthasar's great theological triptych, is entirely predicated upon the play between infinite and finite freedom, precisely in the manner of our theologian.

---

[7] Petrache, 171.

Key to the discernment of the divine will, at either the personal or social level, is the so-called "Principle and Foundation," in which St. Ignatius lays out the entire *raison d'etre* of the human being: "Man is created to praise, reverence, and serve God our Lord, and by this means to save his soul."[8] Therefore, the drawing of all people together in the common praise of God, forming thereby one mystical body, is the goal that ought to lure any and all decisions in the social order: "This unity of all men destined to form one body, that of the New Man, at the end of history: that is what grounds the jurisdiction of the Church of all the temporal order and obliges us to have a social doctrine."[9] In a word, the fundamental decisions that we make in regard to God will govern the decisions that we make at the political, familial, and social levels. Discerning the difference between a choice born of our attachments and one born of our acquiescence to the divine will is the heart of the matter. Another condition for the possibility of correct discernment is the right ordering of temporal and spiritual goods, the former always subordinate to the latter. For Fessard, as for Ignatius, everything in the created or social order exists, finally, for the sake of salvation. Accordingly, if a society consistently ignores the demands of God and prioritizes wealth, power, and privilege, it will, in short compass, devolve into chaos and corruption.

Here an important distinction between Hegel and Ignatius is clear. Like the Jesuit founder, Hegel was interested in discerning the "will" of God in history, but for the philosopher this was a matter of looking backward to see how Spirit actually had evolved through the conflicts of time, whereas Ignatius always looks forward, to determine how God is calling the individual and the society toward the *magis* (the ever greater) praise of God.

As in the personal order, so in the social, a kind of spiritual direction is required. Certainly, "clerics" of liberalism and of the great totalitarianisms were (and are) thick on the ground; their ideological texts are widely available and carefully studied; and their perspectives are on general offer in the popular culture. The church's task, for Fessard, is to provide authentic spiritual direction to those engaged in the political and economic life of a given society and to help

---

[8] Ignatius of Loyola, *The Spiritual Exercises of St. Ignatius*, trans. Louis J. Puhl, SJ (New York: Random House, 2000), 12.

[9] Petrache, *Gaston Fessard*, 244.

them discern the relevant spirits. To be sure, this intervention on the part of the church will not always be welcome, but it provides the leavening that a society needs in order to realize its potential, even at the natural level.

Fessard and Francis

Though Pope Francis has never laid out in a systematic way precisely how Gaston Fessard has influenced his own thinking and practice, I believe that, once we have grasped some of the French Jesuit's basic positions, it is easy enough to see multiple connections. I might draw attention first to Jorge Mario Bergoglio's consistent anticommunism. Though he is customarily seen, at least in the West, as a man of the political left, it is clear that Bergoglio/Pope Francis has steadily resisted the temptation to embrace a straightforwardly Marxist position or approach to economics. To Andrea Tornielli he said, unambiguously enough, and deftly summing up hundreds of pages of Fessardian analysis, "The Marxist ideology is wrong."[10]

Indeed, when the Marxist option of Latin American liberation theology was clearly on the table, Bergoglio consciously moved in another direction, embracing what he termed *la teología del pueblo*. Uneasy with a Marxist reading of the people in purely economic terms, Bergoglio read *el pueblo* culturally and religiously, taking their concrete practices and aspirations as starting points. He was also unhappy with the elitism and condescension of European-trained academics instructing the people of Latin America, and furthermore he saw the danger in embracing a point of view that construed class warfare as inevitable. This *teología del pueblo* approach came to rich expression in the documents of the Puebla Conference of 1979 in which the evangelization of the culture and the valorization of popular religiosity were emphasized, over and against standard-issue themes of liberation theology. Bergoglio has remained, over the past four decades, a fervent advocate of the teaching of Puebla. Very much in the spirit of Fessard, he has fretted that liberation theology tends

---

[10] Pope Francis, "Never Be Afraid of Tenderness," interview by Andrea Tornielli, *Vatican Insider—La Stampa* (Turin), December 14, 2013, http://www.lastampa.it/2013/12/14/esteri/never-be-afraid-of-tenderness-5BqUfVs9r7W1CJIMuHqNeI/pagina.html.

to reduce the question of salvation to a this-worldly matter. And this unease can be seen clearly in his resistance to the dominant understanding of the mission of the Jesuits in the period after the council when the Order came perhaps too strongly under the influence of the 32nd General Congregation, which effectively shifted the purpose of the Jesuits from "the defense and propagation of the faith" to "the promotion of justice."

That said, there is no question that Bergoglio/Francis is also a sharp critic of an unfettered capitalism that would make an idol of wealth and would foster, very much along master/slave lines, an "economy of exclusion" (EG 53). This citation from *Evangelii Gaudium* is representative of many similar comments that Pope Francis has made around the world: "The worship of the ancient golden calf has returned in a new and ruthless guise in the idolatry of money and the dictatorship of an impersonal economy" (EG 55). The Fessardian element is clearly visible in the use of the term "idolatry." Pope Francis is not launching here so much an economic or sociological critique as a spiritual one, using the Principle and Foundation of Ignatius's *Exercises* in order to expose a phony religiosity. That same criterion of the right relationship between spiritual and material goods is neatly employed in another passage from *Evangelii Gaudium*, critical of a capitalism free of moral constraint: "Behind this attitude lurks a rejection of ethics and a rejection of God. Ethics has come to be viewed with a certain scornful derision. It is seen as counterproductive, too human, because it makes money and power relative" (EG 57). What the good Jesuit director knows, of course, is that money and power are among the worldly values that must indeed be relativized in relation to the goods of the soul.

It would be useful at this point to cast a glance toward a philosophical friend of Jorge Mario Bergoglio who played a role in drawing the future pope's attention toward Gaston Fessard, namely, the Uruguayan *tomista silvestre*, Alberto Methol Ferré. A consistent theme in Methol Ferré's writing is that the "messianic atheism" (*ateismo messianico*) of Marxism, prompted in large part by the individualism of the liberal democracies, has been succeeded by a "libertine atheism" (*ateismo libertino*). Very much in line with Fessard, Methol Ferré saw Marxism as involving the transposition of Christian messianism into a purely economic key, whereby the proletariat plays the role of Christ and God has been shunted from the stage entirely. A devotee of G.K. Chesterton and the social teaching of the church, Methol Ferré would obviously find these moves unacceptable, but he was equally unhappy with the pleasure-driven individualism that seemed the triumphant successor of Marxism. Though belief in God was not formally proscribed in the West, the dominant attitude in that cultural framework is often, if I might borrow the terminology of Pope St. John Paul II, a "practical atheism,"[11] the living of one's life as though God does not exist. This sort of reading, born of an Ignatian discernment of spirits at the cultural and economic levels, undergirds many of Pope Francis's statements regarding excessive individualism, materialism, an economy that "kills" (EG 53), and so forth. It is not the market itself that Francis excoriates, but a godless market, one turned in on itself, no longer governed by moral and spiritual laws. And this brings him close indeed to John Paul's criticism of a capitalism that is "not circumscribed within a strong juridical framework which places it at the service of human freedom in its totality, and which sees it as a particular aspect of that freedom, the core of which is ethical and religious."[12]

Another Fessardian theme, mediated to Francis through Methol Ferré, is that of the danger of a detached and ahistorical religiosity. Animated by the Ignatian command to "find God in all things" and by his generally incarnational approach to spirituality, Fessard saw the movement of grace within the political and economic realms. And this attitude inspired Methol Ferré to be suspicious of certain evangelical churches that had become influential in Latin America. Here is the Uruguayan's rather frank assessment: "The world of the protestant sects within an evangelical matrix is an ahistorical place, in which grace is punctual, personal, interrupting mechanically and with an absolute verticality. This is why the adherents of the sects don't normally have an historical consciousness and don't feel the necessity to have one; they don't require an historical reading of the signs of the times and thus don't cultivate one. The sects are a

[11] Pope John Paul II, general audience, April 14, 1999, par. 1, https://w2.vatican.va/content/john-paul-ii/en/audiences/1999/documents/hf_jp-ii_aud_14041999.html.

[12] Pope John Paul II, *Centesimus Annus*, encyclical letter, May 1, 1991, par. 42, https://w2.vatican.va/content/john-paul-ii/en/encyclicals/documents/hf_jp-ii_enc_01051991_centesimus-annus.html.

world without history."[13] And here, from *Gaudete et Exsultate*, is Pope Francis's variation on the same theme: "The other harmful ideological error is found in those who find suspect the social engagement of others, seeing it as superficial, worldly, secular, materialist, communist or populist. . . . We cannot uphold an ideal of holiness that would ignore injustice in a world where some revel, spend with abandon and live only for the latest consumer goods" (GE 101). Both are riffing on motifs central to Gaston Fessard.

A final Franciscan theme that I would identify as Fessardian is the deep respect for freedom even as the church goes about its work of evangelization. Pope Francis would heartily agree with St. John Paul II that, at its best, the church never imposes, only proposes.[14] Again and again, Papa Bergoglio rails (and that *is* the appropriate word) against "proselytism," by which he seems to mean an aggressive, overbearing, hyper-rationalistic manner of spreading the faith. The fundamental problem with this approach is that it does not honor the freedom of the one to be addressed. The true evangelist, Pope Francis implies, imitates the divine master, who, in freedom, awakens an answering freedom, who proposes a path but never compels obedience. If divine providence were an imposition, then nothing like human discernment of spirits would be required, at either the personal or political level. As with the woman at the well, or with the man born blind, or with Zacchaeus, the Lord invites and engages errant freedom—and delights in the free response he elicits.

Conclusion

There is much more that can and should be said, but allow me to draw this already too lengthy essay to a conclusion. What became especially clear to me in researching this chapter is that Papa Bergoglio found in Gaston Fessard a kindred spirit precisely in the measure that he found him to be a true son of St. Ignatius. Having learned the discernment of spirits as a young man and having made the study

[13] Alberto Methol Ferré and Alver Metalli, *El Papa y el Filósofo* (Buenos Aires: Editorial Biblos, 2013), 132.

[14] Pope John Paul II, *Redemptoris Missio*, encyclical letter, December 7, 1990, par. 39, http://w2.vatican.va/content/john-paul-ii/en/encyclicals/documents/hf_jp-ii_enc_07121990_redemptoris-missio.html.

of the *Exercises* his principal pursuit, Fessard read the signs of his own times with extraordinary perceptiveness, always alert to the ways God was engaging human freedom as well as the manner in which sinners tend to abuse that freedom. This double focus seems equally at play in the mind of Jorge Mario Bergoglio, making him one of the most insightful readers of the present moment.

Chapter 7

Pope Francis and the Ecclesiology of Henri de Lubac

Susan K. Wood, SCL

Marquette University

Pope Francis and Henri de Lubac, both Jesuits, are kindred spirits despite differences in age, culture, and work in the church—one a pastor and the other a scholar and academic. Three ecclesial themes prominent in the thought of Pope Francis exhibit a certain parallelism with and, at times, find a source in the thought of Henri de Lubac: (1) the use of paradox or dialectic to describe the church, such as unity that does not annihilate particularity, a concept that echoes de Lubac's concept of catholicity; (2) Pope Francis's condemnation of spiritual worldliness, which evokes de Lubac's ideal of a man of the church; and (3) the pope's devotion to Mary as Mother of the Church, which, while less evident in his theological writing, emerges through his pastoral action of establishing a memorial to her with this title in the liturgical calendar.

Even though Henri de Lubac is one of the Jesuit influences on the thought of Francis, it is important to note that the literary genres of the two men differ significantly: Pope Francis, as priest, bishop, cardinal, and pope, issues pastoral statements, whether they be apostolic exhortations such as *Evangelii Gaudium* (2013) and *Gaudete et Exultate*

(2018), or encyclicals such as *Lumen Fidei* (2013)[1] and *Laudato Si'* (2015). Henri de Lubac's work is within the genre of academic theology. This is to say that de Lubac's theology involves more theory, and Francis's work is more geared toward application to the life of the church, although the essays within this collection demonstrate that they are grounded in a sophisticated philosophical and theological framework. Henri de Lubac provides part of this framework, so it is not surprising that some of the principles of de Lubac's ecclesiology can be seen in Pope Francis's writing, pastoral decisions, and actions.

Understanding Paradox and Dialectic in the Thought of de Lubac and Pope Francis

Pope Francis employs a dialectical method of thinking evocative of de Lubac's notion of paradox. Massimo Borghesi has shown how Pope Francis's dialectical thought, evident from the 1970s, has its roots in Ignatian spirituality and the thought of men such as Erich Przywara, Henri de Lubac and Gaston Fessard, the last through the Uruguayan Thomist Alberto Methol Ferré, who applied dialectical thought to the church.[2] Bergoglio found within Ignatian spirituality

---

[1] The encyclical *Lumen Fidei* (2013) was begun under his predecessor, Pope Benedict XVI, and redacted and completed by Pope Francis.

[2] Alberto Methol Ferré, "La Chiesa, popolo fra i popoli," in Methol Ferré, "Il risorgimento cattolico latinoamericano," 148–49: "It would be fully superhuman to fully understand the *coincidentia oppositorum* that the church is. Some real dimensions always remain in the shadows or are forgotten. The church has essentially two poles, born of the Spirit of God and of Jesus Christ in the Apostles. It is visible and invisible, in a single, indissoluble breath. Ecclesiologies tend to emphasize one or the other of the poles: at certain times they lean toward 'spiritualization,' at other times toward 'incarnation.' Placing emphasis on a single pole leads to deviation and heresy; if a rectifying, corrective movement is not permitted, it becomes contradictory opposition. One's hold on neither of the two poles can be released, yet it is humanly impossible not to give a certain supremacy to one of them. The balance is always unstable, moving, being restored. If allowed to break, the church cannot 'breathe' and then either dissolves into abstract mysticism or gets bogged down in institutional forms. Spirit without institution or institution without Spirit—both are false oppositions that destroy the church. An ever-present risk. Perennial temptations. The ecclesiological movement of this century becomes clear; it is a movement from full visibility to pure anonymity. The visible extremities, without Spirit, harden and freeze history. The invisible extremities move the church away from historical reality, becoming ahistorical idealisms, subjectivisms of 'beautiful soul,' narcissism in imaginary

a synthesis of contrasts and oppositions: a spiritualism outside of history and an activism in the world, mysticism and asceticism, contemplation and action, and doctrine and practice. For Francis, mysticism is the point of synthesis within these polarities, the point of unity that prevents the polarities from becoming dualisms. Francis told Fr. Spadaro, "Ignatius is a mystic, not an ascetic."[3] After 1986, his thought was increasingly influenced by the polar oppositions developed by Romano Guardini. The subject of his doctoral thesis was entitled "Polar Opposition as Structure of Daily Thought and of Christian Proclamation," although he never completed it.[4]

Henri de Lubac's notion of paradox differs from a dialectic that tends toward a synthesis of two opposites. De Lubac comments, "Paradox is the reverse of what, properly perceived, would be synthesis."[5] Paradox does not seek to resolve the tension between opposites, but is the intermediate state that awaits not synthesis, but fullness. De Lubac distinguishes between paradox and dialectic, saying that paradox is more realist, more modest, less tense, and less hurried. In de Lubac's thought, paradox does not lead to synthesis but to an ever renewed paradox. Paradox concerns the real, what is objective, rather than the ideal. For him, paradox is embedded in creation, for de Lubac says, "The universe itself, our universe in growth, is paradoxical." Examples of paradox include the incarnation, Christ the God-man, the joy in suffering of those in purgatory, and God who is both immanent and transcendent. From these examples, one can see that one pole of the paradox does not cancel out the other

---

'authenticities' masquerading as prophetisms beyond the visible, historical church." Cited and translated in Massimo Borghesi, *The Mind of Pope Francis: Jorge Mario Bergoglio's Intellectual Journey*, trans. Barry Hudock (Collegeville, MN: Liturgical Press, 2018), 88. The original Spanish-language version of the article is published as Alberto Methol Ferré, "El resurgimiento católico latinoamericano," in CELAM, *Religión y cultura: Perspectivas de la evangelización de la cultura desde Puebla* (Bogotá: CELAM, 1981), 63–124. See also Alberto Methol Ferré, *La dialectica hombre-naturaleza* (Montevideo: IEPAL, 1966).

[3] Pope Francis with Antonio Spadaro, *My Door Is Always Open: A Conversation on Faith, Hope and the Church in a Time of Change*, trans. Shaun Whiteside (London: Bloomsbury, 2013), 27.

[4] Bergoglio's doctoral thesis focused largely on Romano Guardini's 1925 book *Der Gegensatz: Versuche zu einer Philosophie des Lebendig-Konkreten*, 4th ed. (Mainz: Matthias-Grünewald, 1998). First published 1925 by Matthias-Grünewald (Mainz).

[5] Henri de Lubac, *Paradoxes of Faith* (San Francisco: Ignatius Press, 1987), 9.

pole; nor does one seek a resolution in a synthesis that somehow combines both poles in a new reality. The distinction and opposition remain in tension. De Lubac comments that in a sense no progress is made, and "we are ever going from 'beginnings to beginnings.'"[6]

A similarity between de Lubac's notion of paradox and Francis's use of dialectic is that the two poles are not contraries or contradictions. That is, they do not function against one another. This is where the thought of both de Lubac and Francis differs from Hegelian dialectic based on contradiction and contrasts. In de Lubac's words, "They do not sin against logic, whose laws remain inviolable: but they escape its domain. They are the *for* fed by the *against*, the *against* going so far as to identify itself with the *for*; each of them moving into the other, without letting itself be abolished by it and continuing to oppose the other, but so as to give it vigor."[7]

Massimo Borghesi describes Bergoglio's thought as a "symphony of opposites," a "*coincidentia oppositorum*" such as is expressed in the work of Johann Adam Möhler, Erich Przywara, Romano Guardini, and Henri de Lubac. Bergoglio's thought seeks a unity within the paradox. Borghesi describes Bergoglio's thought, as influenced by Gaston Fessard, in these words: "Bergoglio fought for a synthesis of the oppositions that lacerated the historical reality—not 'meet in the middle' synthesis, nor a mere 'centrist' solution, but a theoretical/practical/religious attempt to propose an antinomian unity, an agonic solution achieved by way of the contrast. It is, therefore, a dialectical view in which reconciliation is not interested, as in Hegel, to philosophical speculation, but to the Mystery that acts in history."[8] Bergoglio seeks a resolution of opposites in a transcendent or "mystical" point that operates through the church, much along the line of Adam Möhler and the nineteenth-century ecclesiologies of the Tübingen school.[9] Möhler famously distinguished between "contrariety" (*Gegensatz*) and "contradiction" (*Widerspruch*). The notion of "contrariety" would characterize the dialectical paradigm of de Lubac and Bergoglio within the context of the church.

---

[6] De Lubac, 10.
[7] De Lubac, 12.
[8] Borghesi, *Mind of Pope Francis*, xxiv.
[9] Borghesi, 68.

Another similarity in Bergoglio and de Lubac is that their use of paradox ties together unity and distinction. In *Catholicism* de Lubac writes:

> Unity is in no way confusion, any more than distinction is separation. For does not distinction imply a certain connection, and by one of the most living bonds, that of mutual attraction? True union does not tend to dissolve into one another the beings that it brings together, but to bring them into completion by means of one another. The Whole, therefore, is "not the antipodes, but the very pole of Personality." "Distinguish in order to unite," it has been said, and the advice is excellent, but on the ontological plane the complementary formula, unite in order to distinguish, is just as inevitable.[10]

De Lubac applies this paradox of unity and distinction to the church in *The Church: Paradox and Mystery*: "Multiple or multiform, she is nonetheless *one*, of a most active and demanding unity."[11] For de Lubac, the mystery of the church "can only be expressed in a series of antithetical, or if you prefer, dialectical sentences" such as: "The Church is of God (*de Trinitate*) and she is of men (*ex hominibus*); she is visible and invisible; she is of this earth and this time, and she is eschatological and eternal."[12]

Bergoglio's dialectical thinking originates in the 1960s with the dialectical tension that characterizes the faith and spirituality of Ignatius of Loyola as analyzed by Gaston Fessard's work, *La Dialectique des "Exercises Spirituels" de Saint Ignace de Loyola* and by an article by the Jesuit Karl-Heinz Crumbach, "Ein ignatianisches Wort als Frage an unseren Glauben" ("A Word of Ignatius as a Question to Our Faith").[13] Through these authors Bergoglio became aware of the polar tension that undergirds all Ignatian theology. The paradox

---

[10] Henri de Lubac, *Catholicism: Christ and the Common Destiny of Man*, trans. Lancelot C. Sheppard and Elizabeth Englund, OCD (San Francisco: Ignatius Press, 1988), 303, referring to Jacques Maritain, *Distinguer pour unir, ou, Les degrés du savoir* (Paris: Desclés, 1932).

[11] Henri de Lubac, *The Church: Paradox and Mystery*, trans. James R. Dunne (Staten Island: Alba House, 1969), 2; orig. *Paradoxe et Mystère de l'Eglise* (Paris: Aubier-Montaigne, 1967).

[12] De Lubac, *The Church*, 23.

[13] Borghesi, *Mind of Pope Francis*, 12–13.

within the vision of Ignatius that captures Bergoglio's imagination is: *non coerceri a maximo, sed contineri a minimo divinum est* ("not to be limited by the greatest and yet to be contained in the tiniest—this is the divine").[14] The work of Fessard was also well known by de Lubac since they had been fellow students during the years of their Jesuit formation, and de Lubac had published some of Fessard's work.[15]

Within this theology based on the Ignatian dialectic, the tension between polar opposites is maintained rather than dissolving into a dualism of two separate levels, two parallel lines that never meet.[16] As Borghesi observes, "The Ignatian dialectic keeps firmly in place the two ends of the chain: the action of the person and the grace of God. It unites them in a way that Henri de Lubac identified as *paradox*: 'Trust in God as though the success of things depends on you and not on God; work, however, as though you did nothing, but God alone did everything.' "[17] Theological examples of this paradox reminiscent of the theology of de Lubac would be the relationships between nature and grace, between grace and freedom, and between divine and human action. However, Bergoglio values these tensions as questions that must be lived rather than as abstract dogmas. This is where reality becomes greater than an idea, one of the principles that as Pope Francis he will develop in *Evangelii Gaudium.*

Paradox in de Lubac's Ecclesiology

In *Paradoxe et Mystère de L'Eglise*, de Lubac asserts that the church itself is both paradox and mystery.[18] Echoing the thought of Möhler and Guardini, de Lubac describes the church as a complex of opposites. The clash between these opposites hides the unity within them.[19] The opposites within the church are communities of Christians who differ in their mentality, in their ways of living and thinking about

---

[14] Interview with Antonio Spadaro, SJ, in *America Magazine*, "A Big Heart Open to God," September 30, 2013, https://www.americamagazine.org/faith/2013/09/30/big-heart-open-god-interview-pope-francis.

[15] Henri de Lubac, *At the Service of the Church: Henri de Lubac Reflects on the Circumstances That Occasioned His Writings* (San Francisco: Ignatius Press, 1993), 166–67.

[16] Borghesi, *Mind of Pope Francis*, 15.

[17] Borghesi, 18–19.

[18] De Lubac, *Paradoxe et Mystère de L'Eglise*.

[19] De Lubac, 11.

their faith, each professing an equal fidelity to the church while opposing each other in almost everything. De Lubac observes that "it is at such a point that a good observer was able to argue recently that the profession of the Catholic faith, far from being a principle of unity, seemed to be more a principle of division."[20] This description, written shortly after the Second Vatican Council, is an apt description of the ecclesial landscape today. Beyond these differences among various Christians, de Lubac notes that people tell him that the church is holy, but he sees it full of sinners. People say that the church's mission is to save a people from earthly cares by reminding them of their eternal vocation, while all the while it ceaselessly busies itself with earthly things as if we were permanently ensconced in this world. One speaks of the open universality of the church while often its members timidly gather themselves into closed groups just as all human beings have a tendency to do. Those church members who found comfort in the unchanging nature of the church despite the vicissitudes of history found themselves disconcerted with the suddenness of the change and renewal immediately after the Council. Such is the paradox of the church.

Underneath this diversity, however, lies a paradoxical unity. According to de Lubac a consideration of the relations between distinction and unity leads to a better understanding of the agreement between the personal and the universal.[21] He says, "The paradox is this: the distinction between the different parts of a being stands out the more clearly as the union of these parts is closer."[22] The church, despite its diversity, is one. Its unity consists in its identity as the sacrament of Christ. Christ, fully human fully divine, is himself the primordial paradox. Thus the fundamental unity underlying all earthly paradox is itself paradox. De Lubac said that Augustine indefatigably preached unity, a unity that won over every force of division, a unity that is love and by which love is the last word.[23]

Within this unity, the church is paradoxically at once visible and invisible, organized society and mystical participation, institution and communion, human and yet of God. De Lubac's concept of the

---

[20] De Lubac, 11.
[21] De Lubac, *Catholicism*, 327–28.
[22] De Lubac, 328.
[23] De Lubac, 26.

church reflects this paradox. The point of departure for considering the structure of the church is neither the papacy, the episcopacy, the presbyterate, nor the laity, but the Eucharist. If one were to give priority to one of the marks of the church in de Lubac's thought, that mark would be unity, a unity inseparably linked with the concept of the church as the Body of Christ. The Body of Christ is one; the body which is the church is one, and the source of that unity is the Eucharist, which is one although celebrated on many altars.[24] Thus the structure of the church derives from its worship.

As with so much of de Lubac's thought, there is the dialectical tension between two poles. With reference to church structure, the problem of relating the universal church and the particular church is not to resolve the tension between one and the other, but to articulate the reciprocal relationship between the two.

When de Lubac speaks of the universal church, he uses "universal" to suggest his idea of the meaning of "Catholic": "The idea of an organic whole, of a cohesion, of the firm synthesis, of a reality which is not scattered, but, on the contrary, turned out towards the center which assumes its unity."[25] The center toward which the "Catholic" is turned is the particular church. It is the center precisely because it is the place of the Eucharist. Thus the universal church is not a diffuse, generalized entity, an idealized concept or simply the sum total of particular churches. It is defined in terms of a center that transcends the local particularity of that center. This center will provide the basis for de Lubac's distinction between the local and the particular church: the particular church being defined by its eucharistic center and the local church being a collectivity of particular churches, but a collectivity that itself does not possess a eucharistic center. An example of a particular church would be a diocese and an example of a local church would be the American church as represented by the United States Conference of Catholic Bishops.

The particular church is identified or circumscribed as a community gathered around a bishop, but here again the authority of the bishop derives from his sacramental function and consecration rather

---

[24] See Walter Kasper, "The Unicity and Multiplicity of Aspects in the Eucharist," *Communio* 12 (1985): 115–38.

[25] Henri de Lubac, *The Motherhood of the Church* (San Francisco: Ignatius Press, 1982), 174.

than from an administrative delegation of authority. Thus de Lubac describes a particular church as "the coming together of baptized people around the bishop who teaches the faith and celebrates the Eucharist. It is, as *Lumen Gentium* says in brief in no. 26, 1, the 'altar community under the sacred ministry of the bishop.' "[26] One consequence of this characterization of the particular church in terms of eucharistic worship is that its boundaries are not determined geographically, but by "the mystery of faith."[27] This means that in de Lubac's view, church structures must be interpreted within a sacramental rather than a pragmatic or functional framework.

Given this eucharistic identification of the particular church, the universal church is related to the particular church as the Eucharist is related to its manifold celebrations. That is, the particular church is the universal church: "In each particular church is present essentially, 'mystically,' the entire universal church since Christ is there through the Eucharist celebrated by the bishop; but equally, each particular church exists fully only in the 'one, single, and Catholic' church."[28] This identification is possible because of the identification between Christ in the Eucharist. Implicit within the identification is the designation of the church as the Body of Christ. Thus where Christ is, there is the church, and not otherwise.

Precisely because of the eucharistic center of the church, the universal church does not result from an addition or federation of particular churches. Nor does a particular church result from a division of the universal church.[29] The relationship is rather organic and mystical.[30] Therefore, the particular church is the universal church in the sense that it is the particular, concrete place in which the universal church is found. Thus the unity between the particular church and the universal church is not the unity of a plurality of churches, but the unity of the one church that finds concrete, historical objectification in a plurality of particular churches and only there.

---

[26] Henri de Lubac, "Particular Churches in the Universal Church," in *Motherhood of the Church*, 192.

[27] De Lubac, "Particular Churches in the Universal Church," 193.

[28] Henri de Lubac, *De Lubac: A Theologian Speaks* (Los Angeles: Twin Circle Publishing Co., 1985), 20.

[29] De Lubac, *Motherhood of the Church*, 203, 207.

[30] De Lubac, 203.

In addition to the analysis based on the Eucharist just described, another conceptual tool for considering this relationship is his concept of the "concrete universal." According to this concept, the universal only has existence through the particular. The particular is not an instance of the universal, but that which is universal only has existence in the particular. Thus, the universal church has concrete existence, properly speaking, only in the particular churches, with the result that "every local church is nothing but the manifestation of that Body of Christ which is equally present, the same in every place, in all the others."[31]

We have seen that paradox provides the structure of much of de Lubac's ecclesiology, especially in terms of the theme of unity and diversity and that of universality and particularity. What holds the center within this paradox is Christ, who himself is the ultimate paradox of the God-man and his presence in the Eucharist.

Paradox within the Thought of Pope Francis

Pope Francis articulates four principles in *Evangelii Gaudium* that guide his whole approach to life. These four principles can be translated into an ecclesiology within Francis's thought: (1) Time is greater than space; (2) unity prevails over conflict; (3) realities are more important than ideas; (4) the whole is greater than the part. While Pope Francis clearly weighs one element of each doublet as being more important than the other, they nevertheless represent polarities in his thought.

Time Is Greater than Space

Beginning with the first principle, *time is greater than space*, "'time' has to do with fullness as an expression of the horizon which constantly opens before us, while each individual moment has to do with limitation as an expression of enclosure" (EG 222). Here we have the polarity, dialectic, or paradox of the present moment set against a future horizon: the first is an experience of limitation while the second is an experience or expectation of fullness. Here one thinks of the relationship between the "already" and the "not yet" of a pilgrim

---

[31] De Lubac, 181, 202.

church which reaches its fullness and completion only eschatologically (LG 48). Furthermore, "giving priority to time means initiating processes rather than possessing spaces" (EG 223). It means "to give priority to actions which generate new processes in society and engage other persons and groups who can develop them to the point where they bear fruit in significant historical events" (EG 223). Pope Francis has done this with the revisions he initiated of the procedures of the synods of bishops, his creation and use of the eight cardinals who serve as his councilors, and his reform of curial offices and procedures.

Unity Prevails over Conflict

Pope Francis's second principle, *unity prevails over conflict*, originated in his experience of the conflict dividing church and society in Argentina in the 1970s. Unity prevails over conflict insofar as it is possible to build communion amid disagreement. Pope Francis comments, "solidarity, in its deepest and most challenging sense, thus becomes a way of making history in a life setting where conflicts, tensions and oppositions can achieve a diversified and life-giving unity" (EG 228). Here it is important to note that unity encompasses diversity and that solidarity does not necessarily embrace conflict, tension, and opposition. Pope Francis continues, "this is not to opt for a kind of syncretism, or for the absorption of one into the other, but rather for resolution which takes place on a higher plane and preserves what is valid and useful on both sides" (EG 228). Once again, polarity and paradox do not erase the polarities, but encompass diversity and difference within a higher plane. The very fact that Francis speaks of a kind of resolution distinguishes his thought from de Lubac, for whom there is no resolution or synthesis.

Realities Are More Important than Ideas

Third, *realities are more important than ideas* because realities are what things simply are. Ideas and ideals must be put into practice. Here there is correspondence between de Lubac and Francis, for de Lubac states that "paradox exists everywhere in reality, before existing in thought."[32] For him, the word "paradox" specifies "things

---

[32] De Lubac, *Paradoxes of Faith*, 12.

themselves, not the way of saying them."[33] Words must become fruitful in justice and charity.

Francis's statement that realities are more important than ideas echoes de Lubac's citation of Pope St. Paul VI's encyclical *Ecclesiam Suam* (1964), which says, "The mystery of the Church is not a truth to be confined to the realms of speculative theology. It must be lived, so that the faithful may have a kind of intuitive experience of it, even before they come to understand it clearly."[34] Mystery is something lived before it is thought. The experience of mystery is more important than the idea of mystery.

The Whole Is Greater than the Part

Fourth, *the whole is greater than the part* within the tension between globalization and localization, but neither pole must be eliminated. Pope Francis's vision of the whole begins with the universal communion of all of creation. In *Laudato Si'* he comments, "As part of the universe, called into being by one Father, all of us are linked by unseen bonds and together form a sublime communion which fills us with a sacred, affectionate and humble respect" (LS 89). This communion requires care for the least and the weakest creature.

Francis's fourth principle, "the whole is greater than the part," is developed in terms of the paradox of universality and catholicity in tension with locality and particularity with respect to the particular churches in the universal church. The "whole is not only greater than the part," but the whole exists in the part within a paradoxical relationship. One item on Francis's agenda is to return more decision-making to the local church.

Pope Francis is exercising the principle of subsidiarity through his use of synods and by directing decision-making to episcopal conferences and local churches rather than perpetuating the tendency in the twentieth century for these decisions to be made in Rome for the church universal. In *Evangelii Gaudium* he explicitly writes, "I am conscious of the need to promote a sound 'decentralization'" (EG 16). For example, his apostolic letter issued *motu proprio* entitled *Magnum Principium* (2017) modifying Canon 838, which deals with

---

[33] De Lubac, 12.

[34] De Lubac, *Paradox et Mystère de l'Eglise*, 30, citing Pope Paul VI, encyclical *Ecclesiam Suam*, August 6, 1964, par. 37.

the translation of liturgical texts, was one of the first examples of this. The translation of liturgical texts must deal with the paradox that while these texts must accurately reflect the doctrine common to the church universal and must reflect the entire Catholic faith, nevertheless, because these ritual texts are also oral communication, they must reflect the language usage of a particular time and place. While affirming the competency of the Apostolic See with regard to liturgical texts, Pope Francis issued the regulation that "it pertains to the Episcopal Conference to faithfully prepare versions of the liturgical books in vernacular languages suitably accommodated within defined limits, and to approve and publish the liturgical books for the regions for which they are responsible after the confirmation of the Apostolic See."[35]

Another instance of referring decisions to a local church is found in his comments about being open to the possibility of ordaining married men to the presbyterate. He has said that this should come in response to calls from the local churches rather than from the initiative of the Vatican.

Spiritual Worldliness

Another influence of de Lubac on Pope Francis consists in their common opposition to "spiritual worldliness." According to de Lubac, spiritual worldliness is that condition wherein "moral and even spiritual standards should be based, not on the glory of the Lord, but on what is the profit of man; an entirely anthropocentric outlook would be exactly what we mean by worldliness."[36] The category of spiritual worldliness directly applies to careerism within the hierarchy and Pope Francis's admonitions to his brother priests and bishops.

When asked in an interview what the worst thing that could happen in the church might be, Pope Francis responded, explicitly citing

---

[35] Pope Francis, apostolic letter *motu proprio, Magnum Principium*, September 3, 2017, can. 838, par. 3, https://press.vatican.va/content/salastampa/en/bollettino/pubblico/2017/09/09/170909a.html.

[36] Henri de Lubac, *The Splendor of the Church* (San Francisco: Ignatius Press, 1999), 377 (French original: *Méditation sur l'Église* [Paris: Montaigne, 1953]).

de Lubac: "spiritual worldliness."[37] Henri de Lubac's description of the opposite of spiritual worldliness is found in his description of a "man of the church."[38] He is far from being caught up in "all coteries and all intrigue, maintaining a firm resistance against those passionate reactions from which theological circles are not always free."[39] His spirit is " 'charitable rather than quarrelsome,' in distinction from every kind of 'spirit of fraction' or mere sectarianism, whether the aim of it be to evade the authority of the church or, on the contrary to make a corner in it."[40] The quality of character that counters the spiritual worldliness described by Pope Francis is illustrated by the humility of the ecclesiastical man described by de Lubac, a man whose greatest fear is "of imposture and this more in the sphere of the sacred than in any other."[41]

Pope Francis and Henri de Lubac share a formation in Ignatian spirituality. The humility of the ecclesiastical man described by de Lubac is expressed in these words of Pope Francis: "If, as we said, the core of Jesuit identity is found—as St. Ignatius says—in adhering to the cross (through poverty and humiliation), the cross as true *triumph*, then the fundamental sin of the Jesuit will be precisely the caricature of the triumph of the cross: a *triumphalism* that sits at the heart of all his actions; the 'myth of success,' the search for himself, for his own things, for his own opinion, for the admiration of people, for power."[42] For Pope Francis, the resolution of the tension between earth and heaven, between humanity and God lies in the mystery of the cross, which is the culmination of the whole set of polar tensions.[43] As Borghesi puts it, Bergoglio tells us that "loyalty to the cross is freedom from power."[44]

---

[37] Cited in *The Catholic World Report*, September 21, 2018, https://www.catholic worldreport.com/2013/03/28/pope-francis-and-henri-de-lubac-sj/.

[38] De Lubac, *Splendor of the Church*, 241–57.

[39] De Lubac, 250.

[40] De Lubac, 251.

[41] De Lubac, 256.

[42] Pope Francis, "Che cosa sono i gesuiti?," in Jorge Mario Bergoglio, *Chi sono i gesuiti: Storia della Compagnia di Gesù* (Bologna: EMI, 2014), 38, cited by Borghesi, *Mind of Pope Francis*, 235.

[43] Jorge Mario Bergoglio, "Servizio della fede e promozione della giustizia," *Stromata*, January–June 1988, in Bergoglio, *Pastorale sociale*, 89, cited by Borghesi, *Mind of Pope Francis*, 235.

[44] Bergoglio, "Servizio della fede e promozione della giustizia."

Spiritual worldliness is not just a personal character flaw; it militates against evangelization because instead of going out of itself to proclaim the gospel, the church turns in on itself and becomes self-referential. Pope Francis stated, "The evils that, in the passing of time, afflict the ecclesiastical institutions have a root in self-referentiality, in a sort of theological narcissism."[45] Pope Francis addressed spiritual worldliness in *Evangelii Gaudium* 93–97, where he defined it as "seeking not the Lord's glory but human glory and personal well-being" (EG 93). He described two forms of this ecclesial affliction. The first consists in a "subjective faith whose only interest is a certain experience . . . which keeps the person imprisoned in his or her own thoughts and feelings." The second is "the self-absorbed promethean neopelagianism of those who ultimately trust only in their own powers and feel superior to others because they observe certain rules or remained intransigently faithful to a particular Catholic style from the past" (EG 94). The first form is reminiscent of certain contemporary spiritualities that seem to be self-referential rather than focused on a relationship with the divine. This first form of spiritual worldliness is characterized by an obsession with programs of self-help and is perhaps best characterized as a spiritual navel-gazing. It focuses on consolations and self-knowledge, an examination of the self, rather than an encounter with Jesus Christ and a discernment of mission. The object of spirituality should never be one's spirituality, but a personal encounter with Christ. As Pope Francis says in *Evangelii Gaudium*, "I invite all Christians, everywhere, at this very moment, to a renewed personal encounter with Jesus Christ, or at least an openness to letting him encounter them; I ask all of you to do this unfailingly each day" (EG 3).

The second form of spiritual worldliness, as Pope Francis says, leads "to a narcissistic and authoritarian elitism, whereby instead of evangelizing, one analyzes and classifies others, and instead of opening the door to grace, one exhausts his or her energies in inspecting and verifying" (EG 94). Here one thinks of the ecclesial polarities wherein each camp engages in self-justification and criticism of the other from a position of self-righteousness. He notes that in both

---

[45] Cardinal Bergoglio's speech to the 2013 conclave to elect the new pope, published by Sandro Magister, "Le ultime parole di Bergoglio prima del conclave," March 27, 2013, http://magister.blogautore.espresso.repubblica.it.

cases one is not really concerned about Jesus Christ or others and says that these are both examples of an "anthropocentric immanentism." This second form of spiritual worldliness is characterized by concern with social and political gain, by a concern to be seen in a social life full of appearances, meetings, dinners, and receptions, and driven by a business mentality.

Spiritual worldliness "can only be healed by breathing in the pure air of the Holy Spirit who frees us from self-centeredness cloaked in an outward religiosity bereft of God" (EG 97). The antidote to spiritual worldliness is companionship with the poor. Pope Francis illustrated this quality when, as Cardinal in Buenos Aires, he was seldom present at gatherings or functions in the Barrio Norte, a region of wealthy Argentinians living in sumptuous mansions and high-rises, but he regularly walked the streets in the southern zone in Villa 21 where "forty-five thousand people were jammed into 175 acres, in brick and corrugated iron houses squeezed up against each other on narrow dusty streets zigzagged by feral kids and stray dogs."[46] Pope Francis's program of evangelization begins with the poor at the margins of both the church and society.

Pope Francis is a living example of this ecclesiastical man who remains silent in the face of his critics, who preaches evangelization to the poor, who does not implicate his predecessor popes in the scandals that swirl around him. One of Francis's agendas is reform not only of the curia, but of the episcopacy. In *Evangelii Gaudium*, he famously stated that "evangelizers should take on 'the smell of the sheep'" (EG 24). In his 2014 Christmas address to the cardinals he identified fifteen "curial diseases."[47] Two of these relate directly to spiritual worldliness: first, the disease of rivalry and vainglory wherein appearances, the color of clothes (one thinks here of the color scarlet), and titles of honor become the primary object of life; and second, the disease of worldly profit, of forms of self-exhibition whereby an apostle turns his service into power and his power into a commodity in order to gain worldly profit or even greater power.

[46] Austen Ivereigh, *The Great Reformer: Francis and the Making of a Radical Pope* (New York: Henry Holt and Company, 2014), 304.

[47] Pope Francis, "Presentation of Christmas Greetings to the Roman Curia," December 22, 2014, http://w2.vatican.va/content/francesco/en/speeches/2014/december/documents/papa-francesco_20141222_curia-romana.html.

Pope Francis develops this last point further, saying, "This is the disease of persons who insatiably try to accumulate power and to this end are ready to slander, defame and discredit others, even in newspapers and magazines. Naturally so as to put themselves on display and to show that they are more capable than others. This disease does great harm to the Body because it leads persons to justify the use of any means whatsoever to attain their goal, often in the name of justice and transparency!"[48] These words were uttered in December 2014, but they ring prophetic today in the light of the controversy regarding (former) Cardinal Theodore McCarrick and the accusations of Archbishop Carlo Maria Viganò and the ecclesiastical polarization that it occasions.

Finally, an ecclesiastical man, particularly an Ignatian one, "thinks and feels with the church" (*sentire cum ecclesia*). When asked in an interview by Antonio Spadaro what this means to him, Pope Francis answered with the image of the church from *Lumen Gentium* 12, the holy, faithful people of God: "The people themselves are the subject. And the church is the people of God on the journey through history with joys and sorrows. *Sentire cum ecclesia*, therefore, is my way of being a part of this people."[49] He then developed the notion of an infallibility "in believing" (*in credendo*)[50] through a supernatural sense of the faith of all the people walking together. His "thinking with the church" involves a dialogue among the people and the bishops and the pope. For him, "this church with which we should be thinking and feeling is the home of all, not a small chapel that can only hold a small group of select people."[51] It is a field hospital where ministers accompany sinners and heal wounds. Structural and organizational reforms are secondary to this primary work of mercy. The ecclesiastical man is not a bureaucrat, but a pastor; pastors must be "able to support the movement of God among their people with patience, so that no one is left behind."[52] Perhaps returning to a dialectical framing of the tension between a multitude of doctrines on the one hand

---

[48] Francis, "Presentation of Christmas Greetings."

[49] Francis, *My Door Is Always Open*, 49.

[50] Developing LG 12, "The entire body of the faithful, anointed as they are by the Holy One, cannot err in matters of belief."

[51] Francis, *My Door Is Always Open*, 51.

[52] Francis, 55.

and a pastoral presence to sinners on the other hand, Francis finds a resolution in a "proclamation in a missionary style" that "focuses on the essentials, on the necessary things: this is also what fascinates, and is a more attractive proposition, what makes the heart burn, as it did for the disciples at Emmaus." The solution he seeks is for the Gospel's proposal to be "simpler, profound or, more radiant," for "it is from this proposition that moral consequences then flow."[53] Holding the dialectic in tension means not choosing one pole over the other; thus, critics that suggest that his pastoral approach is a denial of doctrine miss the entire structure of his thought.

Mary, Mother of the Church

Finally, both Pope Francis and Henri de Lubac share a devotion to Mary as Mother of the Church. Pope Francis inserted the Memorial of the Blessed Virgin Mary, Mother of the Church, into the Roman Calendar on the Monday following Pentecost Sunday. Veneration of Mary as Mother of the Church is not original to either Pope Francis or Henri de Lubac; its ancient roots reach back to St. Augustine and St. Leo the Great. *Lumen Gentium*, while devoting a section to the Blessed Virgin and the Church (LG 60–65), never explicitly refers to her under the title "Mother of the Church," although it identifies her motherhood as being in the order of grace, citing St. Ambrose, who taught that "the Mother of God is a type of the church in the order of faith, charity, and perfect union with Christ" (LG 63).[54] The council develops an analogy between Mary and the church, stating, "For in the mystery of the Church, which is itself rightly called mother and virgin, the Blessed Virgin stands out in eminent and singular fashion as exemplar both of virgin and mother" (LG 63). Furthermore, it affirms that in her "the Church has already reached that perfection" whereby she was "a model of that motherly love with which all who join in the Church's apostolic mission for the regeneration of humanity should be animated" (LG 65). In 1964, at the conclusion of the third session of Vatican II, St. Paul VI formally declared Mary "Mother of the Church."

---

[53] Francis, 58.
[54] Citing St. Ambrose, *Expos. Lc.* II, 7: PL 15, 1555.

During the jubilee year of 1975 the church inserted into the Roman Missal a votive Mass for Mary under the title *Beata Maria Ecclesiae Mater*, Blessed Mary Mother of the Church. On February 11, 2018, the Congregation for Divine Worship and the Discipline of the Sacraments issued the decree on the celebration of the Blessed Virgin Mary Mother of the Church in the General Roman Calendar. The decree comments that Pope Francis took this action to "encourage the growth of the maternal sense of the Church in the pastors, religious and faithful as well as a growth of genuine Marian piety."[55]

References to Mary as Mother of the Church occur in the writings of Pope Francis. He concludes his encyclical *Lumen Fidei* (2013) with a prayer to Mary, Mother of the Church.[56] In his apostolic exhortation *Evangelii Gaudium* (2013), he attributes to Mary, Mother of the Church the very possibility of a new evangelization since she joined the disciples in praying for the Holy Spirit at Pentecost (Acts 1:14): "Without her we could never truly understand the spirit of the new evangelization" (EG 284). He ends the apostolic exhortation with another prayer to Mary in which he refers to her as a pure icon of the church, asking her to pray that the church "may never be closed in on herself or lose her passion for establishing God's kingdom" (EG 288).

While the prevalence of references to Mary as Mother of the Church in Catholic tradition precludes a relationship of cause to effect with respect to the influence of Henri de Lubac on Pope Francis's use of the title "Mary, Mother of the Church," a strong correlation exists between the two Jesuits in this regard. The second part of de Lubac's book, which in French is entitled *Les églises particulières dans l'Église universelle,* is entitled *La maternité de l'Église.*[57] The English edition inverts the two parts and entitles the volume *The Motherhood of the*

---

[55] Congregation for Divine Worship and the Discipline of the Sacraments, "Decree on the Celebration of the Blessed Virgin Mary Mother of the Church in the General Roman Calendar," February 11, 2018, http://www.vatican.va/roman_curia/congregations/ccdds/documents/rc_con_ccdds_doc_20180211_decreto-mater-ecclesiae_en.html.

[56] Pope Francis, encyclical, *Lumen Fidei*, June 29, 2013, par. 60, http://w2.vatican.va/content/francesco/en/encyclicals/documents/papa-francesco_20130629_enciclica-lumen-fidei.html.

[57] Henri de Lubac, *Les églises particulières dans l'Église universelle* (Paris: Aubier, 1971).

Church.[58] De Lubac's *The Splendor of the Church* contains a chapter entitled *"Ecclesia Mater"* and another one on "The Church and Our Lady."[59] The motherhood of the church is thus a prominent theme in his ecclesiology, and he reflects on Mary as the image of the maternity of the church.[60] For him, "Mary is the 'ideal figure of the Church,' the 'sacrament' of her, and the mirror in which the whole Church is reflected."[61] The maternity of Mary "carries the Church within her, so to speak."[62] Her maternity is the type of the maternity of the church itself. She does not just give birth to the church by engendering disciples, which would be a relation of cause to effect. Her maternity is not just the instrumental cause of the church, but is an icon, type, or symbol of the nature of the church as itself maternal. De Lubac consequently develops a parallelism between Mary and the church such that Mary is mother of the church, but also the church itself, the whole Christian community, is mother.[63]

Conclusion

Pope Francis has frequently commented on how much he admires Henri de Lubac. Both Jesuits share an intuition of the profoundly paradoxical and dialectical nature of the church and of the spiritual life. Behind this commonality lies their commonality of being steeped in the spirituality of St. Ignatius and the dialectical character of his thought, who was likewise the source of their abhorrence of spiritual worldliness. Both shared a devotion to Mary under the title "Mother of the Church." For both, one an academic, the other a pastor, the church is the subject of their theological reflection and pastoral service.

[58] De Lubac, *Motherhood of the Church.*
[59] De Lubac, *Splendor of the Church.*
[60] De Lubac, 321.
[61] De Lubac, 320.
[62] De Lubac, 320.
[63] De Lubac, *Motherhood of the Church*, 77.

Chapter 8

An Encounter That Becomes Method: The Influence of Hans Urs von Balthasar and Luigi Giussani in the Theology of the Post–Vatican II Popes

Rodrigo Guerra López

Centro de Investigación Social Avanzada (CISAV)

Introduction

The absence of study in Europe, in the United States, and in some other parts of the world of Latin American philosophers and theologians is widespread. I sometimes get the impression that some scholars consider Latin American thought to represent an inferior or derivative reflection, as opposed to the "real" work being carried out in such countries as Germany, France, and even Italy. This would be nothing more than an anecdotal observation were it not, in my opinion, such an important factor in understanding what is happening in regard to Pope Francis.

When St. John Paul II was elected pope, a special effort needed to be made in order to understand his teaching in the context of his intellectual and pastoral background. For many, it was necessary to study the history of Christians in Poland and the various philosophical traditions at the roots of Karol Wojtyła's thinking, as well as to master his own arduous philosophy in order to understand in depth the true meaning and scope of, for example, his *Redemptor Hominis, Laborem Exercens*, or what would eventually be known as the "theology of the body." Scholars such as Rocco Buttiglione, Massimo Serreti, Tadeusz Styczen, Angelo Scola, and others undertook remarkable work to explore and explain, work that continues to bear fruit today. In my opinion, a similar effort must be made in the case of Jorge Mario Bergoglio, SJ. How many misunderstandings could be avoided if we better understood our pope's intellectual and pastoral biography! In the major academic institutions dedicated to the dissemination and deeper understanding of the pontifical magisterium, professors and students have scarcely begun to undertake serious and systematic study of the writings of Bergoglio and his most beloved authors, such as Lucio Gera, Rafael Tello, Juan Carlos Scannone, or Alberto Methol Ferré, not to mention the "theology of people" or the magisterium of the Latin American episcopate.

Massimo Borghesi has written a book in which he deals with this concern to a large extent: *The Mind of Pope Francis: Jorge Mario Bergoglio's Intellectual Journey*.[1] With a huge amount of data and information coming from interviews with Francis himself, Borghesi shows not only the pope's intellectual roots but also the gradual maturing of his thought over time. This book is an important resource for understanding the intellectual and pastoral foundations of the current pontificate, and for avoiding misunderstandings and misjudgments.

Just as in order to understand the theoretical background of John Paul II's magisterium it is necessary to study rigorously the *sui generis* way in which he reformulated realistic phenomenology and critically interpreted authors such as St. Thomas Aquinas, Kant, and Max Scheler, so, too, is careful study needed of the philosophical and theological premises of Pope Francis and his interpretation of Romano Guardini, Henri de Lubac, Michel de Certeau, or Gaston Fessard.

Current Controversies about Francis

One point where lack of sympathy and understanding for Francis's thought is evident is in debates over continuity in the magisterium

---

[1] Collegeville, MN: Liturgical Press, 2018.

of John Paul II, Benedict XVI, and Francis. For example, in the controversy over Francis's apostolic exhortation *Amoris Laetitia*, one of the most recurrent objections was that it betrays the doctrine of the apostolic exhortation *Familiaris Consortio* or the encyclical *Veritatis Splendor*. This is surely not the first time that some have tried to oppose the current magisterium to that of the past, and it surely is not the last time.

In the summer of 2016, Rocco Buttiglione and I were teaching in a summer program in a small town near Vienna. After talking about the debate surrounding *Amoris Laetitia*, we deemed it appropriate to converse with Cardinal Schönborn in his house. Later, we would also speak with others by telephone. A few days later, we decided to write. While we differed in language and approach, we nonetheless agreed in our conviction that by taking a thoughtful, and not merely repetitive, understanding of the magisterium of John Paul II, one must affirm the rationality, thoroughness, and truth of Pope Francis's position regarding persons who live in an irregular situation in their marriage, and their eventual access to the sacraments of reconciliation and the Eucharist. There is a true "creative fidelity" to the deposit of the faith shared by Francis and the preceding popes: the indissolubility of marriage or the doctrine about the essential elements that constitute a sin as "mortal" are not in debate. The true question is to discover how the deposit of faith should best be understood, and how one should respond, in the light of the Gospel, to the numerous historical and cultural needs, proper to each person in each period, at the pastoral level and eventually at the normative level.[2]

Days after publishing our respective texts in *L'Osservatore Romano*, a former student of Buttiglione's and my classmate during my doctoral studies, Jaroslaw Merecki (currently a professor at the Pontifical John Paul II Institute in Rome), wrote a critical response to my text

---

[2] See Rocco Buttiglione, "The Joy of Love and the Consternation of Theologians," in *L'Osservatore Romano*, July 19, 2016, http://www.osservatoreromano.va/en/news /joy-love-and-consternation-theologians; Rodrigo Guerra, "The Relevance of Some Reflections by Karol Wojtyła for Understanding 'Amoris Laetitia': creative fidelity," in *L'Osservatore Romano*, July 22, 2016, http://www.osservatoreromano.va/en/news /relevance-some-reflections-karol-wojtyla-understan.

published in Sandro Magister's news service.[3] My response to him[4] dared to reflect upon the need for a "hermeneutics of continuity": the present magisterium must be interpreted in the light of the preceding magisterium, but the preceding magisterium can also be illuminated by the present one. These two methodological moments are not symmetric. Each one has its peculiarities, which—unfortunately, for reasons of time—we cannot explain here. I simply point out that an exclusive insistence on the former is equivalent to imprisoning and freezing the new contributions of Pope Francis within previous categories and arguments, negating the innovative aspects of his teaching. Likewise, an exclusive emphasis on the latter leaves the magisterium of Francis without its organic foundations, thus conveying rupture hermeneutics.

As the months went by, we wrote other texts explaining various questions concerning the moral theology and philosophical ethics present in *Amoris Laetitia*, including responses from Buttiglione and myself to the doubts (*dubia*) of four cardinals.[5] As the debate intensified, however, the idea grew stronger in me that behind all these "doubts" there dwelled problems concerning some of the central elements of faith itself.

The doctrinal debate over *Amoris Laetitia* has not yet been extinguished, but it has diminished significantly. Following the publication of Rocco Buttiglione's *Risposte amichevoli ai critici di* Amoris Laetitia (Friendly Responses to the Critics of *Amoris Laetitia*), it is hard to accuse Pope Francis of being guilty of adhering to "situational ethics" or any kind of relativism.[6] We can now affirm with peace of mind that the discernment of each irregular case that presents itself in pastoral praxis is a practice that is faithful to the constant doctrine of the church, since not every single "objective situation of grave sin"

---

[3] Jaroslaw Merecki, "Fidelity That Is Too Creative Becomes Infidelity," in Sandro Magister, "Second Challenge to L'Osservatore Romano. Merecki vs. Guerra López," August 4, 2016, http://chiesa.espresso.repubblica.it/articolo/1351351bdc4.html?eng=y.

[4] Rodrigo Guerra, "Aprender los unos de los otros," in *Chiesa Espresso On Line*, August 18, 2016, http://chiesa.espresso.repubblica.it/articolo/1351355.html.

[5] See Rocco Buttiglione, *"Amoris Laetitia.* Risposte ai critici," in *Lateranum* 83 (2017): 191–239; Rodrigo Guerra, "Para comprender *Amoris Laetitia*," in *Medellín* 43, no. 168 (May–August 2017): 409–47.

[6] Rocco Buttiglione, *Risposte amichevoli ai critici di* Amoris Laetitia (Milan: Ares, 2017).

always and by definition involves "mortal sin." However, new subjects and issues absorb the energies of Francis's detractors: sexual abuse by the clergy, the agreements of the Holy See with China, the concept of "synodality," the Synod on Young People, and so on. In all these controversies, it is growing increasingly clear that the critics harbor within themselves a certain dissatisfaction toward the Second Vatican Council and with some of the theological emphases of the last few pontiffs.

The Theological Landscape of the Post–Vatican II Pontiffs

For the aforementioned reasons, the subject on which I have been asked to write for this book could not be more providential: the influence of Hans Urs von Balthasar and of Luigi Giussani on the post–Vatican II popes. It appears to me that underlying the discontent of recent critics toward Francis's papacy is a certain problem with subjects on which these two authors have meditated with singular dedication, and which have profoundly impacted the theological landscape of the Catholic Church over the last sixty years.

The widely varied intellectual influences on each pope[7] are part of their personal stories and surely also a part of the providential path that God chooses when he gives us a new pontiff. Nevertheless, these influences do not explain everything. Each pope seeks to exercise his own *munus docendi* with faithfulness to the deposit of faith and with an organic and creative continuity with the teaching of his predecessors. Thus when analyzing the magisterium of a pope, it is necessary to use a method that exceeds a mere reconstruction of a "theologian's" intellectual biography and takes into account the global evolution of the church at that moment in history.

To trace the influence of von Balthasar and Giussani among the recent popes one must recognize, in some schematic fashion, that the discussions raised within Vatican II echoed a varied theological landscape: on one side neo-Thomists, on the other, transcendental

---

[7] Studies of the thought of the last three popes include Rocco Buttiglione, *Il pensiero dell uomo che divenne Giovanni Paolo II* (Milan: Mondadori, 1998); Aidan Nichols, *The Thought of Benedict XVI: An Introduction to the Theology of Joseph Ratzinger* (New York: Burnes & Oates, 2005); Borghesi, *Mind of Pope Francis*.

Thomists, and, in a third group, those who sought to promote the *ressourcement* of the fathers of the church and the integration of the spiritual life as a constitutive dimension of theological method.[8]

Tracey Rowland has commented that in strategic terms, the "great losers" in the council were the neo-Thomists.[9] But the "alliance" of the two other groups was rather ephemeral. By 1972 the differences between the group surrounding the journal *Communio* and that surrounding the journal *Concilium* were already quite apparent.

Communio had been founded by Hans Urs von Balthasar, Joseph Ratzinger, Henri de Lubac, Marie-Joseph Le Guillou, Louis Bouyer, and Jorge Medina, among others. It is feasible that the name of the journal emerged through the meeting of von Balthasar and Luigi Giussani, founder of the movement *Communion and Liberation*, who had invited von Balthasar to preach spiritual exercises in Einsiedeln in 1971.[10] Karol Wojtyła participated to some extent in this group through his interest in French Catholicism and his closeness to Henri de Lubac, who had written the prologue to the French edition of one of the most important works of the Polish philosopher and future pope.[11] With time Wojtyła would also foster a great appreciation toward von Balthasar, naming him cardinal in 1988, as well as toward Giussani, to whom the then Archbishop of Kraków was introduced in 1965 through Francesco Ricci.

The lives of von Balthasar, Giussani, Ratzinger, and Wojtyła were interwoven. Four extraordinary men, of diverse ages and nationalities, each one with a distinct philosophical-theological approach but united by a similar sensitivity on key subjects: a renewed metaphysical thought; a critical and differentiated reading of modernity; an ecclesiology of the church as the people of God; a pedagogy centered on the encounter with the living person of Jesus Christ; a renewed

---

[8] The term *ressourcement* comes from the publication of the church fathers in the collection *Sources Chrétiennes*.

[9] Tracey Rowland, *Ratzinger's Faith: The Theology of Pope Benedict XVI* (Oxford: Oxford University Press, 2008), 23.

[10] See Joseph Ratzinger, "Communio: un programa," lecture given in the Pontifical Gregorian University, May 28, 1992; see also Alberto Savorana, *The Life of Luigi Giussani*, trans. Mariangela Sullivan and Christopher Bacich (Montreal: McGill-Queen's University Press, 2018), 433, and references cited there.

[11] Karol Wojtyła, *Amour et responsabilité. Étude de morale sexuelle*, preface by Henri de Lubac (Paris: Societé d'Editions Internationales, 1965).

appreciation of the importance of the spiritual life for its own sake and as a source for theology; and a Marian emphasis, not only in their personal lives, but in their theology itself.

The case of Jorge Mario Bergoglio, SJ is a bit different. He enters this universe through the reading of St. Augustine, Romano Guardini, Henri de Lubac, and von Balthasar himself, as Massimo Borghesi has documented. Likewise, his sympathy for Giussani is perceptible: he presented four of his books in Buenos Aires: *The Religious Sense* in 1999, *The Attraction of Jesus Christ* in 2001, *Why the Church?* in 2005, and *Is It Possible to Live This Way?* in 2008.

We cannot pretend to provide an exhaustive examination of the direct influence of von Balthasar and Giussani on the postconciliar popes. For this, several doctoral dissertations would surely be needed. What we can do is to indicate how some themes very typical of von Balthasar and Giussani are perceptible in the papal magisterium of the last forty years.

Theological Aesthetics

A first topic, typically associated with von Balthasar but present also in Giussani as part of his pedagogy of faith, is theological aesthetics. If theology is true to its point of departure, the incarnation, it discovers that it has always been a reflection on the presence of Jesus Christ—on his radical appearance in history—and for that reason, it discovers that it is a theological aesthetics.

Von Balthasar refers to the notion of "form" (*Gestalt*) that is revealed in the mystery of faith. The incarnation allows God to develop a phenomenological capacity unprecedented in history. Jesus Christ has been made manifest: he came and made possible an encounter. He came but now he is gone. Is faith, then, a mere recollection of his passage through the world? The answer to this question is negative: Jesus Christ remains and is contemporary.

> Christ is not a "being," but the manifestation of Being, of the Father . . . Christ is the visibility of God, and the brother is the visibility of Christ. That is why Christian love for the brother is the concrete proof that we love God. . . . [Here] faith is not primarily understood in a negative way as a "not yet," but in a positive way, such as opening up and abandoning oneself to the

absolute truth of the present, and in which it is described without hesitation as a knowledge: "We know that we have passed from death unto life" (1 John 3:14).[12]

This knowledge is about a present reality! My concrete flesh that should be dead lives today. And this life that I can experience, is not my creation but something given, something that comes from outside. Thus, I verify that Jesus Christ is the resplendent form of God (*splendor formae*). This form is only seen when I open myself with stupor to the immensity of its content: "The form that manifests itself is only beautiful because the satisfaction it provokes is based on the fact that the truth and the profound goodness of reality are shown and given to us, and this showing and giving of reality reveals itself to us as something infinitely and inexhaustibly valuable and fascinating. As a revelation of depth, its manifestation is, at the same time and in an inseparable way, two things; real presence of depth, of everything, and real reference, beyond itself, to this depth."[13]

Giussani shares this perspective. Beauty is the presentation of the innate attraction of the truth. If the truth does not summon, does not provoke, or does not attract, the true human condition cannot respond: "Beauty is the ultimate correspondence with the expectation that we have and which constitutes us, with the expectation of the heart. It is the splendor of truth."[14] Giussani continues, "It is beauty that leads us to the truth, to desiring and searching for the true. The truth . . . is the last thing . . . destiny. . . . Beauty allows our eyes, on the one hand, to identify a sign that claims us; on the other, it makes it possible for us to experience dissatisfaction, to experience that it is not complete . . . that it is unfinished. And, in fact, it refers you to the true, to the last."

One might hear in von Balthasar and Giussani the echoes of a theory of the transcendental properties of being. These, however, are not given academic treatment as a formal topic in metaphysics, but

---

[12] Hans Urs von Balthasar, *Gloria I* (Madrid: Encuentro, 1985), 218–19 (Spanish translation of original German *Herrlichkeit eine theologische Ästhetik*, vol. 1, *Schau der Gestalt* [Einsiedeln: Johannes, 1961]). Translated into English by Erasmo Leiva-Merikakis as *The Glory of the Lord: A Theological Aesthetics*, vol. 1: *Seeing the Form*, 2nd ed. (San Francisco: Ignatius, 2009).

[13] Von Balthasar, *Gloria I*, 111.

[14] Luigi Giussani, *Afecto y morada* (Madrid: Encuentro, 2004), 64.

they belong to an existential method that allows us to discover the persistence of Jesus Christ in history. God *is* revealed in Jesus Christ. This is how the ultimate foundation of everything exhibits its consistency and its permanent commitment to our lives: by immersing itself in temporality and fragment, and, from that limitation, announcing a horizon that exceeds everything.

For Karol Wojtyła, too, this approach is not foreign to his personal and intellectual education. In such works as *The Acting Person* he develops a phenomenological approach that allows him to understand that the way to the truth runs through a careful exploration of experience through reason.[15] Through experience, the reality of the world and the reality of the person unfold in their multiple dimensions, inviting reason to accept its truth and eventually to interpret—without violating—the constitutive structures of being. For Wojtyła, when taking the road that goes from the phenomenon to the foundation, it is very important to learn to "stop before the irreducible," that is, to respect with amazement and astonishment realities that are explained only by contemplating them in themselves. As pope, he used this philosophical method to read the revealed data and affirm:

> In perceiving that all he had created was good, God saw that it was beautiful as well. The link between good and beautiful stirs fruitful reflection. In a certain sense, beauty is the visible form of the good, just as the good is the metaphysical condition of beauty. This was well understood by the Greeks who, by fusing the two concepts, coined a term which embraces both: *kalokagathia*, or beauty-goodness. On this point Plato writes: "The power of the Good has taken refuge in the nature of the Beautiful."[16]

---

[15] We prefer the Polish-Italian edition of *The Acting Person* instead of Ana-Teresa Tyemeniecka's translation: Karol Wojtyła, *Persona e Atto. Testo polacco a fronte*, ed. Giovanni Reale and Tadeusz Styczen (Milan: Bompiani, 2001). English translation by Adrezej Potocki, Karol Wojtyła, *The Acting Person* (Dordrecht: D. Reidel, 1979). See also: Rocco Buttiglione, *Il pensiero dell'uomo che divenne Giovanni Paolo II* (Milan: Mondadori, 1998); Rodrigo Guerra, *Volver a la persona. El método filosófico de Karol Wojtyła* (Madrid: Caparrós, 2002).

[16] Pope John Paul II, "Letter of His Holiness Pope John Paul II to Artists," April 4, 1999, sec. 3, http://w2.vatican.va/content/john-paul-ii/en/letters/1999/documents/hf_jp-ii_let_23041999_artists.html.

John Paul II continues:

> God became man in Jesus Christ, who thus becomes "the central point of reference for an understanding of the enigma of human existence, the created world and God himself." This prime epiphany of "God who is Mystery" is both an encouragement and a challenge to Christians, also at the level of artistic creativity. From it has come a flowering of beauty which has drawn its sap precisely from the mystery of the Incarnation. In becoming man, the Son of God has introduced into human history all the evangelical wealth of the true and the good, and with this he has also unveiled a new dimension of beauty, of which the Gospel message is filled to the brim.[17]

Joseph Ratzinger likewise has a deep appreciation for von Balthasar, calling him "a teacher of faith."[18] As pontiff he declared:

> In the death and resurrection of Jesus, the mystery of God's Trinitarian love is revealed in its fullness. The reality of the faith finds here its unsurpassable *beauty*. In the *drama* of the Paschal Mystery, God fully lives out his act of becoming man, but at the same time he makes man's action meaningful and gives concrete form to the engagement of the Christian in the world. Von Balthasar saw in this the *logic* of revelation. God becomes man so that man might experience communion of life with God. In Christ is offered the ultimate truth, the definitive answer to the question that everyone asks himself about the meaning of life. Theological aesthetics, dramatics and logic make up the trilogy in which these concepts find ample room [for development] and principled application. I can testify that his life was a genuine search for truth, which he understood as a search for the true Life. He looked everywhere for signs of the presence of God and of his truth: in philosophy, in literature, in religions, always managing to break through the circuitous reasoning that often holds the mind a prisoner of itself, and opening it up to the horizons of the infinite.[19]

---

[17] John Paul II, sec. 5.

[18] Joseph Ratzinger, "Funeral Homily for Msgr. Luigi Giussani," Milan Cathedral, February 24, 2005, published in *Communio* 31, no. 4 (Winter 2004): 685–87.

[19] Pope Benedict XVI, "Message to the Participants of the International Convention on the Occasion of the Centenary of the Birth of the Swiss Theologian Hans Urs von

And some years later, Benedict XVI will insist:

> The beauty of Christian life is even more effective than art and imagery in the communication of the Gospel message. In the end, love alone is worthy of faith, and proves credible. The lives of the saints and martyrs demonstrate a singular beauty which fascinates and attracts, because a Christian life lived in fullness speaks without words. We need men and women whose lives are eloquent, and who know how to proclaim the Gospel with clarity and courage, with transparency of action, and with the joyful passion of charity.[20]

In his homily for Luigi Giussani's funeral Ratzinger comments: "Fr. Giussani grew up in a home poor—so to speak—as far as bread was concerned, but rich with music, and thus from the start he was touched, or better, wounded, by the desire for beauty. He was not satisfied with just any beauty, a banal beauty, rather he looked for Beauty itself, infinite Beauty, and thus he found Christ: in Christ true beauty, the path of life, the true joy."[21]

Pope Francis, on the other hand, tries to overcome formalism in his ontology, the abstract thought that tends to split the rational and the sensible; the particular and the universal; truth, the good, and beauty. Bergoglio has a Thomistic mind strongly marked by a rigorous epistemological realism: reality always has primacy over the idea. Real, concrete being is the root and source of the transcendental properties. He often roots his reflections on various topics, including those of a social and political order, in these ontological foundations, but he always seeks to give them an existential character that makes them meaningful for real people:

> Abstract reflection runs the risk of ruminating on abstract or abstracting objects, dazzled by a sterile search for truth and forgetting that the aim of all human reflection is real being as such

---

Balthasar," October 6, 2005, https://w2.vatican.va/content/benedict-xvi/en/messages/pont-messages/2005/documents/hf_ben-xvi_mes_20051006_von-balthasar.html.

[20] Pope Benedict XVI, Address after screening the film "Art and Faith—*Via Pulchritudinis*," October 25, 2012, http://w2.vatican.va/content/benedict-xvi/en/speeches/2012/october/documents/hf_ben-xvi_spe_20121025_arte-fede.html.

[21] Ratzinger, "Funeral Homily for Msgr. Luigi Giussani."

and therefore only one, from which one cannot separate the three fundamental elements of being which the philosophers define as the transcendentals: truth, goodness, and beauty. They must be together. Within the citizen there must develop a dynamic of truth, goodness, and beauty. If one element is missing, being breaks down, becomes idealized, becomes an idea; it is not real. They have to go together. They must not be broken up.[22]

On several occasions Bergoglio reminded educators that Jesus Christ, "the way, truth and life," is the true master and teacher one must follow. Jesus Christ is the real synthesis of what is sometimes learned in a purely conceptual way. In the splendor of the truth that I discover in a person, in the beauty of an encounter, human beings can find the truth, not only in a theoretical way, but truth that responds to life—that sets us free:

By shining in beauty, the truth gives us in this light its logical clarity. The good that appears as beautiful brings with it the evidence of its duty to be fulfilled. How many abstract rationalisms, and extrinsicist moralisms, would see here the possibility of their cure if they opened themselves to think reality first as beautiful, and only later as good and true! . . . The glow of the encounter produces that metaphysical "stupor" of human and divine revelation. . . . Only those who are dazzled by beauty can initiate their students in contemplation. Only those who believe in the truth they teach can ask for truthful interpretations. Only those who live in goodness—which is justice, patience, respect for diversity in the task of teaching—can aspire to form the hearts of the people entrusted to them. The encounter with beauty, goodness, truth, fills us with a sense of abundance and produces a certain ecstasy in itself. What fascinates us takes us out of ourselves and seizes us. The truth thus found, or rather, that encounters us, makes us free.[23]

Bergoglio, it seems, reaches these intuitions from within his pastoral praxis, which guides his reflection upon Giussani and von Balthasar.

---

[22] Jorge Mario Bergoglio, *Nosotros como ciudadanos, nosotros como pueblo: hacia un bicentenario en justicia y solidaridad: 2010–2016* (Buenos Aires: Claretiana, 2013), 41–42.

[23] Jorge Mario Bergoglio, "Mensaje a las comunidades educativas," April 23, 2008, http://www.arzbaires.org.ar/inicio/homilias/homilias2008.htm#educacion.

At times Bergoglio's thoughts on the subject seem to reflect a creative appropriation of von Balthasar's work in *Wahrheit*.[24]

Francis did not forget these convictions upon assuming the Chair of Peter. The pope has often repeated an expression of Benedict XVI: "It is not by proselytizing that the Church grows, but 'by attraction.'"[25]

The Gospel cannot be imposed; it must be offered to the heart by the force of its beauty. Only by revealing its beauty is freedom respected and the person invited to respond along a path of one's own discernment. In the end, the *via pulchritudinis* is the one that arouses sincere affection and adhesion.

> Every form of catechesis would do well to attend to the "way of beauty" (*via pulchritudinis*). Proclaiming Christ means showing that to believe in and follow him is not only something right and true, but also something beautiful, capable of filling life with new splendor and profound joy even in the midst of difficulties. Every expression of true beauty can thus be acknowledged as a path leading to an encounter with the Lord Jesus. This has nothing to do with fostering an aesthetic relativism which would downplay the inseparable bond between truth, goodness and beauty, but rather a renewed esteem for beauty as a means of touching the human heart and enabling the truth and goodness of the Risen Christ to radiate within it. If, as Saint Augustine says, we love only that which is beautiful, the incarnate Son, as the revelation of infinite beauty, is supremely lovable and draws us to himself with bonds of love. So a formation in the *via pulchritudinis* ought to be part of our effort to pass on the faith. (EG 167)

[24] Particularly, I think, in the section devoted to "the truth, the good and the beautiful": Hans Urs von Balthasar, *La esencia de la verdad* (Buenos Aires: Sudamericana, 1955), 242–52 (German original: *Wahrheit*, vol. 1: *Wahrheit der Welt* [Einsiedeln: Benziger, 1947], which is incorporated into his *Theologik* series as *Theologik*, vol. 1: *Wahrheit der Welt* [Einsiedeln: Johannes, 1985]). English translation available as *Theo-Logic*, vol. 1: *The Truth of the World* (San Francisco: Ignatius, 2001).

[25] For example, Pope Francis paraphrases Benedict XVI's expression in "Homily at Mass for the Opening of the Fifth General Conference of the Latin American and Caribbean Bishops," Aparecida, May 13, 2007, http://w2.vatican.va/content/benedict -xvi/en/homilies/2007/documents/hf_ben-xvi_hom_20070513_conference-brazil .html; in *Evangelii Gaudium* 15.

Christianity as Event

A second theme relates to the essence of Christianity. The concrete experience of the encounter with Jesus Christ was slowly transformed by a process of conceptualization and formalization, eventually leading to the immanentizing reduction of the Christian faith to a purely subjective human experience. Hegel took a first step in this direction by locating the Christian fact in its entirety within the confines of the flow of history. In this way, the transcendent and gratuitous dimension of Jesus Christ is canceled and only a moral example remains (that in some way was already contained in what previously existed). Within this perspective, God dies so that the purely human survives—an ironic interpretation of Jesus's death on the cross, we might say.

Feuerbach, a disciple of Hegel, will suggest not only that the Christian fact is purely intra-historical but that God himself is the result of the deepest subjective yearnings of the human condition.[26] His thinking will influence various authors, such as David Friedrich Strauss, and some trends within contemporary philosophical anthropology and Christology. The Christ of faith is a myth; its real referent is the good example of a dead person. The Christianity that Hegel had argued was the pinnacle of the historical evolution of human consciousness further devolved into a purely formal construction that expresses in the best of cases that the essence of Christianity is ethical.

Much more is needed to do justice to this complex intellectual process, which has had many philosophical, theological, and cultural derivations, but one important point can be seen.[27] While many (including myself, at one point) would have pointed to Marx and his children as the victors of the great modern battle between materialism and idealism, a more attentive analysis of modernity (following Augusto del Noce and Massimo Borghesi) suggests that Hegel's spiritual posterity is in some sense more powerful than that of Marx. A Christianity without Christ, in which there is no gratuitous irruption of gift and the empirical, the corporeal, and the concrete are not decisive, dissolves within the *pleroma* of ideas and values *ad usum*:

---

[26] See Ludwig Feuerbach, *The Essence of Christianity* (Mineola, NY: Dover, 2008).

[27] See, among others: Massimo Borghesi, *Hegel: La cristologia idealista* (Rome: Studium, 2018).

apparently correct, but profoundly dull. In a word, values and ideas, however beautiful, exalted, and promising they may be, do not save.

Here is where we can appreciate the intellectual and spiritual harmony of the popes after Vatican II, and the influence that von Balthasar and Giussani, directly or indirectly, had in some decisive aspects of their magisterium. It is telling, in this respect, to recall how many years after Feuerbach published his book on *The Essence of Christianity*, Romano Guardini dared to face the same challenge of identifying the essence of the faith, answering the question thus:

> Christianity is, ultimately, neither a doctrine of truth nor an interpretation of life. It is this, but none of this constitutes its core essence. Its essence is constituted by Jesus of Nazareth, by his existence, his work and his concrete destiny; that is, by his historical personality. Something similar . . . is experienced by everyone to whom another person acquires essential meaning. For him or her, it is not "humanity" or "the human" that is important, but this concrete person. It determines everything else, more profoundly and broadly the more intense the relationship is. It can even be that everything—the world, destiny, and the commitment itself—passes through the beloved person, that he or she is contained in everything, that he or she is seen in everything and everything receives its meaning from him or her. In the experience of a great love, everyone comes together in the I-Thou relationship, and everything that happens becomes an event within its scope. The personal element to which love ultimately refers, and which represents the highest among the realities of the world, penetrates and determines everything else: space and landscape, stone, tree and animals.[28]

Later in the same work he says: "The decisive moment in the order of salvation, however, is Christ himself. Not his doctrine, nor his example, nor the divine power operating through him, but plain and simple his person."[29]

The essence of Christianity is Christ: an irreducible, nonderivable personal reality. In more abbreviated terms: Christianity is an "Event"

---

[28] Romano Guardini, *La esencia del cristianismo: Una ética para nuestro tiempo* (Madrid: Cristiandad, 2006), 16–17 (German original: *Das Wesen des Christentums* [Würzburg: Werkbund, 1938], originally published as "Das Wesen des Christentums," *Die Schildgenossen* 9 [1929]: 129–52).

[29] Guardini, *La esencia del cristianismo*, 45.

(*Ereignis*). In the same way that one's biographical description, which presents the facts of one's life in terms common to other human beings, can never fully explain the person, the person of Christ is emptied of its real content when only his humanity, his conduct, his kindness is considered, but his specificity as a unique, unrepeatable and unsubstitutable subject that bursts into history is not recognized.

We mention these fundamental elements of Guardini's theology not only because he is an author particularly appreciated by John Paul II, Benedict XVI, and Pope Francis, but because especially in this regard his contribution to the theology of von Balthasar and Giussani was decisive.

The notion of an event has a complex philosophical and theological meaning. In common language, an "event" is something that typically happens in an unforeseen manner, a provocation that first demands to be recognized before a response can even be formulated. An event is something that is placed before me in a nondeterministic way, opening a space of novelty in the ordinary chain of causes and effects that the universe typically offers me. The event that breaks in to my experience has a certain degree of incomprehensibility. It is there but I do not fully realize why it is there. My response to this data (*datum*) that is a gift (*donum*) is amazement and stupor.

The most significant events in life, such as finding the beloved man or woman, the birth of a child, the merciful forgiveness we receive after having offended someone, are a mystery. Their occurrence is experienced as something dark and luminous at the same time. Dark, because they overtake us and we hardly understand how they have come to be. Luminous, because they reconfigure life: they allow us to perceive the meaning of reality in a new way. To repeat Guardini's words cited above: "In the experience of a great love . . . everything that happens becomes an event within its scope."

Hans Urs von Balthasar will follow this path. Throughout his theological exploration of the beauty and drama of Christian revelation, we find the fundamental category "event" used to articulate the distinctiveness of Christianity:

> The decisive difference consists in this: that the event of salvation through which man arrives to the salvific relationship with God develops in history; God does not make a sign or say a word to man, but converts man himself, with all his uncertainty,

weakness, and imperfection, in the language with which he expresses the word of full salvation. . . . If this has happened, historical existence has been given a place, without being deprived of value, or reduced to pure appearance, or without having to deny it, in the movement of the return to God. The Christological synthesis realized here differs radically from any synthesis elaborated by the mythical imagination; its strength is—beyond all expectation and all imagination—in the resurrection from death.[30]

Luigi Giussani, on the other hand, will make the "event" the pedagogical key to the renewal of the Christian experience:

We must correct the way in which faith is normally conceived. The new beginning of the Christian experience, and therefore of every relationship, is not born of a cultural point of view . . . a discourse . . . but it happens experimentally: It is an act of life that sets everything in motion! The beginning of faith is not an abstract culture, but something that comes before [that]: an event. Faith is becoming aware of something that has happened . . . a new reality from which, in reality, everything starts.[31]

Elsewhere Giussani will also say:

The positive response to this dramatic dispersion in which society makes us live is an event. Only an event—and let us stop at that for the moment without qualifying the term further—can render the "I" clear and consistent in all its constituent factors. . . . In *Notre jeunesse*, Péguy said: "An event is always whatever is most unexpected." An event, then, is "something," which suddenly introduces itself: the unpredictable, the unforeseen, the non-consequence of antecedent factors. . . . But above all (and this is what interests us now), "event" is the only category capable of defining what Christianity is (Christianity totally boils down to this category): Christianity is an event. . . . "The real

[30] Hans Urs von Balthasar, *El todo en el fragmento* (Madrid: Encuentro, 2008), 79–80 (German original: *Das Ganze im Fragment : Aspekte der Geschichtstheologie* [Einsiedeln: Benziger, 1963]. English translation, *A Theological Anthropology* [New York: Sheed and Ward, 1967]).

[31] Luigi Giussani, "Io e i ciellini, la nostra fede in faccia al mondo," interview by Gian Guido Vecchi, *Corriere della Sera*, October 15, 2004, http://www.corriere.it/Primo _Piano/Cronache/2005/02_Febbraio/22/corriere.shtml.

drama of the Church that likes to call itself modern (the real drama of Christians who want to be modern) is the attempt to modify the wonder of the event of Christ by means of rules." This was an admirable comment of John Paul I (because of this observation alone—and nothing like it can be found elsewhere— his month-long pontificate would prove providential). Christ is a happening, an event, a fact which, first of all, fills us with wonder.[32]

John Paul II did not use the category "event" in more than a generic way throughout his magisterium. The concept, however, defines the architecture of his programmatic encyclical *Redemptor Hominis*:

> Against the backdrop of the ever-increasing processes in history—in our time . . . the various systems, ideological concepts of the world, and regimes—Jesus Christ becomes, in a way, present once again, despite all his apparent absences, despite all the limitations of the presence and institutional activity of the Church. Jesus Christ becomes present with the power of that truth and that love that are expressed in him with unique and unrepeatable fullness, despite the brevity of his life on earth and his even briefer public activity.[33]

It is Benedict XVI who places the notion of "event" in the first paragraph of his encyclical *Deus Caritas Est*, and with it he not only affirms the centrality of Jesus Christ as an absolute novelty in history but also lays the foundations for an acute critique of moralism, that is to say, the ethical reduction of Christianity to the values and aristocratic circles of modern-day Pelagians: "Being Christian is not the result of an ethical choice or a lofty idea, but the encounter with an event, a person, which gives life a new horizon and a decisive direction."[34]

---

[32] Luigi Giussani, *He Is If He Changes: Notes from Conversations with Young People*, supplement no. 7/8 to *30 Days*, 7–8 (Rome: 30Giorni, 1994), 12–16.

[33] Pope John Paul II, encyclical, *Redemptor Hominis*, March 4, 1979, par. 13, http://w2.vatican.va/content/john-paul-ii/en/encyclicals/documents/hf_jp-ii_enc_04031979_redemptor-hominis.html.

[34] Pope Benedict XVI, encyclical, *Deus Caritas Est*, December 25, 2005, par. 1, http://w2.vatican.va/content/benedict-xvi/en/encyclicals/documents/hf_ben-xvi_enc_20051225_deus-caritas-est.html.

Indeed, for Joseph Ratzinger, Christianity is an event; it is the presence of a divine person within human history who refuses to be interpreted as a justification for Pharisaic behavior. The numerous evangelical passages in which the novelty of Jesus Christ transcends a legalistic misuse of the ancient law strongly support this view. In fact, for Ratzinger, the loss of awareness of this fundamental aspect of the nature of Christianity immediately translates into a moralistic claim, that is, the ethical reproach of the other who does not behave according to the norm. It is very important to look at the internal logic of this. When the truth of Christianity, for example, in the order of moral life, is proclaimed without Jesus Christ, mercy is lost and in the name of a supposed ethical correction the other is condemned and the doors are closed to a new beginning. St. Augustine had already faced this challenge in his debate with the Pelagians: "This is the horrendous and hidden poison of your error: that you claim to make the grace of Christ consist in his example and not in the gift of himself."[35]

Ratzinger, who deeply loves St. Augustine, affirms: "The temptation to turn Christianity into a kind of moralism and to concentrate everything on man's moral action has always been great . . . indeed even in our own day. . . . Augustine teaches that Christian holiness and rectitude do not consist in any superhuman greatness or in some superior talent. If that were the case, Christianity would become a religion for just a few heroes or chosen groups."[36]

We all know how this perspective enriched the entire document of the Fifth General Conference of the Latin American Episcopate held in Aparecida, Brazil. We are all becoming aware that the themes of Christianity as an event and the criticism of liberal and conservative moralisms were central at Aparecida and go a long way toward explaining the mood of the Latin American church and the profile of our current pontiff. This is evident in the concluding document of Aparecida, the essence of which, in my opinion, is found in sections 11 and 12:

---

[35] St. Augustine, *Contra Iulianum*, 2, 146 (PL 45, 1202).
[36] Joseph Ratzinger, "Presentation of the Book *The Power and the Grace*," *30Days* 5 (2005), http://www.30giorni.it/articoli_id_8926_l3.htm.

The church is called to a deep and profound rethinking of its mission and to relaunch it with fidelity and boldness in the new circumstances of Latin America and the world. It cannot retreat in response to those who see only confusion, dangers, and threats, or those who seek to cloak the variety and complexity of situations with a mantle of worn-out ideological slogans, or irresponsible attacks. What is required is confirming, renewing, and revitalizing the newness of the Gospel rooted in our history, out of a personal and communal encounter with Jesus Christ that raises up disciples and missionaries. That depends not so much on grand programs and structures, but rather on new men and women who incarnate that tradition and newness, as disciples of Jesus Christ and missionaries of his Kingdom, protagonists of new life for a Latin America that seeks to be rediscovered with the light and power of the Spirit.[37]

A Catholic faith reduced to mere baggage—to a collection of rules and prohibitions, to fragmented devotional practices, to selective and partial adherence to the truths of the faith, to occasional participation in some sacraments, to the repetition of doctrinal principles, to bland or anxious moralizing—that does not convert the life of the baptized, cannot withstand the trials of time. Our greatest danger is that of "*the gray pragmatism of the daily life of the church in which everything apparently continues normally, but in reality the faith is being consumed and falling into meanness.*"[38] We must all start again from Christ, recognizing that "*being Christian is not the result of an ethical choice or a lofty idea, but the encounter with an event, a person, which gives life a new horizon and a decisive direction.*"[39]

Pope Francis has given us *Evangelii Gaudium*. Much is collected there of what was discussed and discerned in Aparecida, where Bergoglio was elected to chair the committee that drafted the final document. In a certain sense *Evangelii Gaudium* represents the appropriation of the pontifical magisterium of the entire path of the Latin American church in its efforts to be faithful to Vatican II in a

---

[37] CELAM, Aparecida: Concluding Document, sec. 11–12.

[38] Joseph Ratzinger, "The Current Situation of Faith and Theology: Meeting with the Doctrinal Commissions of Latin America," Guadalajara, Mexico, May 7, 1996, sec. 7, http://www.vatican.va/roman_curia/congregations/cfaith/incontri/rc_con_cfaith_19960507_guadalajara-ratzinger_en.html.

[39] Pope Benedict XVI, *Deus Caritas Est* 1; cf. Pope Francis, *Evangelii Gaudium* 7.

creative, prophetic, and joyful way. And, of course, in a certain sense, *Evangelii Gaudium* also demonstrates the Argentine pope's familiarity with Guardini, von Balthasar, and Giussani:

> When preaching is faithful to the Gospel, the centrality of certain truths is evident and it becomes clear that Christian morality is not a form of stoicism, or self-denial, or merely a practical philosophy or a catalogue of sins and faults. Before all else, the Gospel invites us to respond to the God of love who saves us, to see God in others, and to go forth from ourselves to seek the good of others. Under no circumstance can this invitation be obscured! All of the virtues are at the service of this response of love. If this invitation does not radiate forcefully and attractively, the edifice of the Church's moral teaching risks becoming a house of cards, and this is our greatest risk. It would mean that it is not the Gospel which is being preached, but certain doctrinal or moral points based on specific ideological options. The message will run the risk of losing its freshness and will cease to have "the fragrance of the Gospel." (EG 39)

In his presentation of Giussani's book *The Attraction That Is Jesus*, Bergoglio says:

> Everything in our life, today just as in Jesus' time, begins with an encounter. An encounter with this man, the carpenter of Nazareth, a man like all men and yet different. The first ones, John, Andrew, and Simon, felt as if Jesus gazed into their very depths, read in their innermost being, and in them sprang forth a surprise, a wonder that instantly made them feel bound to him, made them feel different. . . . We cannot understand this dynamic of encounter which brings forth wonder and adherence if it has not been triggered . . . by mercy. Only someone who has encountered mercy, who has been caressed by the tenderness of mercy, is happy and comfortable with the Lord. I beg the theologians who are present not to turn me in to the *Sant'Uffizio* or to the Inquisition; pushing things a bit, however, I dare to say that the privileged locus of the encounter is the caress of the mercy of Jesus Christ on my sin.[40]

---

[40] Jorge Mario Bergoglio, "Presentation of Luigi Giussani, *El atractivo de Jesucristo*," Buenos Aires, April 27, 2001, http://archivio.traces-cl.com/Giu2001/argent.htm.

In front of this merciful embrace—I continue along the lines of Giussani's thought—we feel a real desire to respond, to change, to correspond, and a new morality arises, an ethics that is born of the encounter. Christian morality is not a titanic effort of the will, the effort of someone who decides to be consistent and succeeds, the solitary response in the face of the challenges of the world. No. Christian morality is simply the heartfelt response to a surprising, unforeseeable, "unjust" (I shall return to this adjective) mercy, the mercy of one who knows me, knows my betrayals and loves me just the same, appreciates me, embraces me, calls me again, hopes in me, and expects from me. This is why the Christian conception of morality is a revolution: it is not a never-falling-down but an always-getting-up-again.

As we shall see, this authentic Christian conception of morality that Giussani presents has nothing to do with the spiritualistic-type quietisms of which the shelves of today's religious supermarkets are full. Trickery. Nor with the Pelagianism so fashionable today in its different, sophisticated manifestations: "Pelagianism, underneath it all, is a remake of the Tower of Babel. The spiritualistic quietisms are efforts at prayer and immanent spirituality which never go beyond themselves. Jesus is encountered, just as 2,000 years ago, in a human presence, the Church, the company of those whom he assimilates to himself, his Body, the sign and sacrament of his presence."[41]

For Bergoglio, everything is grace. And grace precedes us. Privileging the encounter with Jesus Christ becomes the methodological expression of the recognition of the primacy of grace. Encounter, therefore, is the essential modality of the communication of faith. In a culture that, most often, is built apart from God, Christianity has to risk presenting itself in its essential form. The kerygma is not the natural law nor any ideal of decency. The kerygma is the resurrected Jesus Christ who has overcome my sin and my death. This means that when I evangelize I do not preach my own coherence but I proclaim that someone greater than my incoherence has picked up my broken pieces and has forgiven me. This announcement is not that of a chair of theology but an invitation to live a friendship: the friendship that constitutes the *ekklesia*, the church.

---

[41] Bergoglio, "Presentation of Luigi Giussani."

By Way of Conclusion: Mary, Figure of the Church

I would not like to end these brief reflections without pointing out that the influence of von Balthasar and Giussani on John Paul II, Benedict XVI, and Francis can be perceived in many other subjects. There is the influence of von Balthasar in Benedict XVI, for example, regarding the charismatic and the institutional in the church, some elements of the critique of certain theologies of liberation, and the so-called "kneeling theology" or the theology of Holy Saturday. Also, Giussani's influence on Francis is felt in his understanding of Pelagianism, Gnosticism, the religious sense, and other matters.

While we cannot discuss all of these issues, one issue worthy of a little more of our attention is how von Balthasar conceives of Mary as a figure of the church. In the third volume of his *Theo-Drama*, von Balthasar reflects on the archetypal figure of the Virgin Mary, whom he considers to be the true symbol of the church, as a constitutively feminine reality.[42] Based on the fathers and tradition, von Balthasar presents the Virgin as the woman who personifies and is the model-synthesis of the church, because of her essentially nuptial abandonment to God. Mary's whole life is encompassed in her *fiat*, her perfect consent that allows everything. By doing so, the Word of God takes full possession of her body and soul. She becomes a bride and the Mother of God incarnate.

John Paul II in *Mulieris Dignitatem* will work on these same ideas:

> The Council has confirmed that, unless one looks to the Mother of God, it is impossible to understand the mystery of the Church, her reality, her essential vitality. Indirectly we find here a reference to the biblical exemplar of the "woman" which is already clearly outlined in the description of the "beginning" (cf. Gen 3:15) and which proceeds from creation, through sin to the Redemption. In this way there is a confirmation of the profound union between what is human and what constitutes the divine economy of salvation in human history. The Bible convinces us of the fact that one can have no adequate hermeneutic of man, or of what is "human," without appropriate reference to what is "feminine."[43]

---

[42] Hans Urs von Balthasar, *Theo-Drama: Theological Dramatic Theory*, vol. 3: *Dramatis Personae: Persons in Christ* (San Francisco: Ignatius, 1993).

[43] Pope John Paul II, apostolic letter, *Mulieris Dignitatem*, August 15, 1988, par. 22, http://w2.vatican.va/content/john-paul-ii/en/apost_letters/1988/documents/hf_jp-ii_apl_19880815_mulieris-dignitatem.html.

Benedict XVI, for his part, is convinced that from the moment of her fiat, Mary began to take us all into her womb. This vocation and maternal mission of the Virgin with regard to believers is made explicit with Jesus's words from the cross: "Woman, here is your son" (John 19:26):

> The Son of God thus fulfilled his mission: born of the Virgin in order to share our human condition in everything but sin, at his return to the Father he left behind in the world the sacrament of the unity of the human race (cf. *Lumen Gentium* 1): the family "brought into unity from the unity of the Father and the Son and the Holy Spirit" (Saint Cyprian, *De Orat. Dom.*, 23: PL 4, 536), at whose heart is this new bond between the Mother and the disciple. Mary's divine motherhood and her ecclesial motherhood are thus inseparably united.[44]

Similarly, Pope Francis will insist: "The important thing is that the Church be a woman, that has this attitude of a bride and of a mother. When we forget this, it is a masculine Church. Without this dimension, it sadly becomes a church of old bachelors, who live in this isolation, incapable of love, incapable of fecundity. Without the woman, the Church does not advance—because she is a woman. And this attitude of woman comes from Mary, because Jesus willed it so."[45]

A theological aesthetics that allows us to rediscover the revelation of the attractive beauty of Jesus Christ as the core of evangelization, and a personalist understanding of Christology that helps us to encounter the startling mercy of Jesus Christ that provokes all of our affection and transforms our life, culminates with meditation on Mary and the church. Mary is the Mother of God and our Mother. With tenderness and patience, she leads us to her Son, thus helping us to live more intensely within her as brothers and sisters to one another. The church, that great friendship that Jesus builds by giving his life for us, has in Mary the paramount paradigm.

---

[44] Pope Benedict XVI, "Homily, Mass before the Shrine of Meryem Ana Evì," Ephesus, November 29, 2006, citing *Lumen Gentium*.

[45] Pope Francis, "Homily," Chapel, Casa Santa Marta, *Memorial of the Blessed Virgin Mary, Mother of the Church*, May 21, 2018, https://www.vaticannews.va/en/pope-francis/mass-casa-santa-marta/2018-05/pope-francis-mass-santa-marta-mary-church-woman-mother.html.

I cannot refrain from mentioning, as a Mexican, that the post-conciliar popes have insisted that when contemplating Our Lady of Guadalupe we each discover that we are looked at; in her eyes the mystery of our persons and our peoples can be revealed. In her eyes we can rediscover our dignity, often wounded, and we can recover our brotherhood, often fractured. In these dramatic moments of pain for the pope and for the church, it may be important to turn to Our Lady of Guadalupe as a providential way of recovering our communion. In Mary, the negative, the division, and the evil have not prevailed. On the contrary, she is precisely a victory over everything that seems to be threatening the life of society and the church. Every grace passes through her hands, every grace—including that of Peter's ministry—whom she holds in a very special way, as von Balthasar used to teach.[46]

---

[46] See Hans Urs von Balthasar, *The Office of Peter and the Structure of the Church* (San Francisco: Ignatius, 1986) (Original German edition: *Der Antirömische Affekt* [Freiburg im Breisgau: Herder, 1974]).

PART THREE

A North American Theology
of the People

Chapter 9

Pope Francis, Theology of the People, and the Church in the United States

Peter J. Casarella

University of Notre Dame

Two ironies come to mind when I think about the relationship between *la teología del pueblo* of Pope Francis and the church in the United States. First, there is the name itself. The "theology of the people" is like *la nouvelle théologie*. The term was generated by critics as a way of disparaging a new development in a certain sector of church life and theology.[1] Today the "theology of the people" is touted as a badge of honor among the proponents of Pope Francis's thought and pontificate, and I include myself among its admirers. The second irony has to do with its origins in the Southern Cone of Latin America and its transfer to the see of Rome. Obviously, the traces in the pontificate of what began in the Southern Cone and was once offered to the Latin American church more generally are just that—traces. There are indeed many traces, and the *teología del pueblo* is the most fruitful matrix for interpreting the distinct accents of the theology of Pope Francis. The exercise of the office of Peter is, however, a new home

---

[1] According to Scannone, the term "Argentine theology of the people" was coined by Juan Luis Segundo of Uruguay to criticize it and adopted by Sebastián Politi to promulgate it. Scannone, *La teología del pueblo: Raíces teológicas del papa Francisco* (Maliaño: Sal Terrae, 2017), 25–26.

for the theology of the people, and the holder of that office is under no compulsion to maintain the same line of theological reflection that he held previously. But the interesting point here is that Jorge Mario Bergoglio never visited the United States prior to his election as pope.[2] As bishop of Buenos Aires Bergoglio seems to have known about its realities mainly from the visits of US bishops and other leaders to Latin America. In this sense, the intricacies of the church life in the United States were largely foreign to Pope Francis at the outset of his pontificate. I am not at all suggesting that this is still the case. But I do think that the precise connections between the reform impulse of Archbishop Bergoglio and its impact on the US Catholic Church would have been very difficult to predict had Bergoglio not become pope and had he not actually visited the United States as pope. The visit to the US was, therefore, a watershed moment in the translation of *teología del pueblo* to our ecclesial context in this country.

A further challenge in the interpretation concerns the fact that the current pontiff does not emerge from a school of theology in any formal sense. Pope Benedict drew upon a theological heritage closely allied to the journal *Communio* and its sympathizers. Archbishop Jorge Mario Bergoglio never belonged to a school of theology even though he schooled himself deeply in selected academic concerns and in the theological work of disparate ecclesial sources, not the least of which were his profound immersion in Ignatian spirituality, his respect for Lucio Gera, and his fervent belief in the continental vision of the Latin American church, including the guidance in this regard provided by the *Consejo Episcopal Latinoamericano* (CELAM).

We should not be surprised that the process of translating the theology of the people into the context of the US church has been fraught with difficulty. Few people truly understand its origins, motives, or original contexts. The books and articles now available in English by experts such as Austen Ivereigh, Juan Carlos Scannone, Massimo Borghesi, Emilce Cuda, Thomas Rourke, and Rafael Luciani help a great deal in avoiding the polemics and getting to the heart of the

---

[2] The case of Pope Benedict is different. As prefect of the Congregation for the Doctrine of the Faith, he visited the bioethics conference in Dallas annually and developed a high regard for the practice of bioethics in the United States prior to assuming the office of pope.

vision of Pope Francis.[3] The abiding polarizations nonetheless threaten to make it impossible to get a clear vision of Pope Francis's pontificate. I hope in this chapter to contribute not only to a learning process but also to a healing process. In that spirit, I will offer a reading of the theology of the people from and for the Catholic Church of the United States as well for the sake of the common good of our society and our world.

My reading is not without its own limitations and probably blind spots. My reading consciously avoids looking in any comprehensive way at the details of pastoral implementation that have provoked rival parties within the Catholic Church but underscores at the same time the extremely close connection between doctrine and pastoral practice that has been articulated by the pope in a systematic way. My reading is consciously Latino without ignoring the significance of Pope Francis for non-Latino/as in the US. Finally, my reading takes its point of departure from the pope's US visit but tries to place that visit in a broader, more global context of apostolic voyages in both North America and Latin America.

The argument I will develop in defense of a North American theology of the people proceeds in three steps. First, I will glean certain principles regarding the church in *América* on the basis of apostolic visits to the Americas that took place between 2015 and 2017. These principles will serve as the basis for thinking about an inculturation of the Argentine vision on our land and among our people. Second, I will try to address one of the most neuralgic and confusing points in the interpretation of the thought of Pope Francis: "What does he mean by 'people'?" Who are the "people" whose faith guides the theology of the people? There are important pre-understandings of that critical word and concept that need to be clarified. Third, given

---

[3] Austen Ivereigh, *The Great Reformer: Francis and the Making of a Radical Pope* (New York: Henry Holt, 2014); Juan Carlos Scannone, SJ, *La Teología del Pueblo*, and "Pope Francis and the Theology of the People," *Theological Studies* 77 (2016): 118–35; Massimo Borghesi, *The Mind of Pope Francis: Jorge Mario Bergoglio's Intellectual Journey* (Collegeville, MN: Liturgical Press, 2018); Emilce Cuda, *Para Leer a Francisco: Teología, Ética, y Política* (Buenos Aires: Manantial, 2016); Thomas R. Rourke, *The Roots of Pope Francis's Social and Political Thought: From Argentina to the Vatican* (Lanham, MD: Rowman & Littlefield, 2016); and Rafael Luciani, *Pope Francis and the Theology of the People* (Maryknoll, NY: Orbis, 2017).

that he has been hailed as the first Latino pope and given the current demographics of US Catholicism, I will attempt to answer the question, "What is the precise connection between the pope's *teología del pueblo* and Latino/a theology?" In this way, I hope that my essay contributes to a palpable and Catholic sense of unity in diversity in the church that transcends the present climate of animosities and suspicions.

Tears, Dreams, and a Samaritan Church

During the years 2015–2019, Pope Francis visited Paraguay, Ecuador, Peru, Cuba, the United States, Mexico, Colombia, and Panama (for World Youth Day 2019). These were not his only visits to the Americas during his pontificate, and we already know for certain that there will be more in the future. But I would like to reflect upon his significance for the church in the United States in the light of some of these particular apostolic journeys. All are examples of the theology of the people in action. Three themes join these visits and help to bring to light the distinctiveness of the theology of the people as it applies to our present concerns. The first concerns the stark juxtaposition of tears and dreams. The second theme is the reality of migration and the border. The third is the Samaritan church. All three of these themes were articulated during the pope's visit to the US, but they come into focus more clearly if we examine them in this broader context.

His first journey to the Americas in 2015 was to Bolivia, one of the poorest and most indigenous countries in these two continents. In fact, on July 9th, 2015, in Santa Cruz de la Sierra, Bolivia, the Holy Father participated in the Second World Meeting of Popular Movements, having already participated in the first meeting in Rome itself. The whole initiative was developed by Pope Francis to deal with the economy of exclusion and inequality (EG 53–54). Since Bolivia the group has had a Third Meeting in Rome and a Regional Meeting in Modesto, California that took place in 2017. The popular movements are one significant context for analyzing the theology of the people. In Bolivia, he said:

> The Bible tells us that God hears the cry of his people, and I wish
> to join my voice to yours in calling for the three "L's" for all our

brothers and sisters: land, lodging and labor [in Spanish, the three t's: *tierra, techo, y trabajo*]. I said it and I repeat it: these are sacred rights. It is important, it is well worth fighting for them. May the cry of the excluded be heard in Latin America and throughout the world.[4]

The sacred right to "land, labor, and lodging" has become a refrain of this pope. The pope is interested in a discerning analysis of global systems. He believes that the global system that imposes the mentality of profit at any price to be the "invisible thread" joining every form of exclusion. In this way, he links the problem of social exclusion to the destruction of nature. In general, the pope is trying to implement the method of "see, judge, act" enshrined by John XXIII in *Mater et Magistra* 236 for the sake of creating greater participation of the peoples of the world in political, economic, social, and cultural systems. He is adamant about the need to act defiantly. We cannot sit on the sidelines of history and watch the forces of consumerism destroy the human community and the environment. The global engagement with the *movimientos populares* (peoples' movements) in Bolivia thus sets the stage for the pope's entrance into the church of the Americas and lies in the background of any application of a theology of the people to the Americas, including to the plight of the people in the US.

Pope Francis's first wish was to come into the United States by crossing the Mexican border.[5] That turned out not to be possible, but he did still come from the South, namely, from Cuba. His linking of the two continents is not a new idea. In *Ecclesia in America*, Pope John Paul II said that trinitarian communion has as its fruit social solidarity.[6]

---

[4] Pope Francis, "Address of the Holy Father: Apostolic Journey of His Holiness Pope Francis to Ecuador, Bolivia and Paraguay (July 5–13, 2015), Participation at the Second World Meeting of Popular Movements," https://w2.vatican.va/content /francesco/en/speeches/2015/july/documents/papa-francesco_20150709_bolivia -movimenti-popolari.html.

[5] He offered this insight in an interview with a Mexican journalist. For an English translation of this interview, see Valentina Alazraki, "Two Years into His Pontificate: An Interview with a Mexican Media Company *Televisa*," *L'Osservatore Romano* 14, April 3, 2015.

[6] Pope John Paul II, *Ecclesia in America* 52: "Solidarity is thus the fruit of the communion which is grounded in the mystery of the triune God, and in the Son of God who took flesh and died for all. It is expressed in Christian love which seeks the good of others, especially of those most in need." See also Peter J. Casarella, "Solidarity as

Pope Francis literally inscribed solidarity into the journey by bringing the fruits of his trip to Cuba (and his earlier behind-the-scenes efforts to help with the thaw in US–Cuban relations) to the White House. In other words, a bond with the itinerant people of all the Americas and a renewed linking of the destiny of North and South America both contribute to Pope Francis's vision for the US.[7]

The first theme I would highlight for a new *Ecclesia in America* that actually starts from the South is the joining of tears and dreams. Why focus on tears and dreams? You cannot dream of a better future without shedding tears. There are too many faults of one's own and tangible injustices that cause us grief to avoid tears. Dreams without tears are not going to be realized. Tears without realizable dreams are oppressive, if not suicidal. This connection between tears and dreams was already made by Lucio Gera when in 1957 he wrote a pair of articles in a famous pastoral journal promulgated by Catholic Action. He chose as his title: "*Sunt lacrymae rerum.*"[8] There are tears that belong to the order of things, he said, citing Virgil. Gera taught the Argentines about the fruitfulness of acknowledging how tears are embedded in the order of creation.[9] Gera did not think that the shedding of tears before the senselessness of violence was futile or of merely therapeutic value. After all, Matthew 5:4 tells us: "Blessed are those who mourn, / for they will be comforted." For the Argentine school, the shedding of tears is not the indication that the people have been given an opiate in order to still their sense of justice. On the contrary, the shedding of tears is a cry for the establishment of new structures that stand in solidarity with God's tears. Luis Herrera, SJ, of Peru writes that the pope's theology of tears redresses the deliber-

---

the Fruit of Communion: *Ecclesia in America*, 'Post-Liberation Theology,' and the Earth," *Communio: International Catholic Review* 27 (Spring 2000): 98–123.

[7] This section of my chapter was inspired by reading Robert S. Pelton, CSC, "CELAM and the Emerging Reception of the 'Bridge Theology' of Pope Francis: From Marcos Gregorio McGrath to the Latin American Church Today," *Horizonte: Revista de Estudos de Teologia E Ciências da Religião* 16, no. 50 (2018): 454–81.

[8] Lucio Gera, "*Sunt lacrymae rerum* (Hay lágrimas en las cosas)," *Notas de pastoral jocista* (1957): 16–23.

[9] The article is reprinted and more readily available in Virginia R. Azcuy, Carlos María Galli, and Marcello González, eds., *Escritos Teológico-Pastorales de Lucio Gera*, vol. 1: *Del Preconcilio a la Conferencia de Puebla* (Buenos Aires: Ágape-Facultad de Teología, 2006), 113–19.

ate suppression of subversive memories by political authorities intent upon burying them: "The recovery in the public domain of memory runs contrary to the public political acts of silencing in order to bring to light what has been veiled, in order to bring the truth to light."[10]

"God weeps," said Pope Francis on September 27, 2015, in an unscheduled introduction to his address to the US bishops in Philadelphia that took place just after he prayed with victims of clerical sexual abuse. The divine weeping is for the victims of sexual abuse, a weeping that has only become more intense in the past few months. Francis maintains that the church weeps because God himself weeps. The well of tears collected by the church, from the church, and for the church is like the well of eternal life at which Jesus meets the Samaritan woman. Tears are the first sign that reconciliation with God and neighbor may be possible. At Ground Zero in New York City, the pope laid a white rose at the edge of one of the two massive waterfall pools where the names of those who died are inscribed. His words spoke to the meaning of flowing water at this memorial. He paints a vivid image of the flowing together of the waterfall pools and the tears of grief in which it is not clear if the pools catch the past tears or symbolize their uninterrupted flow in the present.

> Here grief is palpable. The water we see flowing towards that empty pit reminds us of all those lives which fell prey to those who think that destruction, tearing down, is the only way to settle conflicts. It is the silent cry of those who were victims of a mindset which knows only violence, hatred and revenge. A mindset which can only cause pain, suffering, destruction and tears. The flowing water is also a symbol of our tears. Tears at so much devastation and ruin, past and present. This is a place where we shed tears, we weep out of a sense of helplessness in the face of injustice, murder, and the failure to settle conflicts through dialogue. Here we mourn the wrongful and senseless loss of innocent lives because of the inability to find solutions which respect the common good. This flowing water reminds us

[10] Luis Herrera, SJ, "Whisper to Those in Despair: The Best Wine Is Yet to Come: Memory, Hope, and Resistance," in *The Search for God in América*, ed. Peter Casarella and Maria Clara Bingemer (volume forthcoming with The Catholic University of America Press).

of yesterday's tears, but also of all the tears still being shed today.[11]

Tears are used here in a figurative sense. "Tears" reflect internal and spiritual wounds that remain even after the water droplets have been wiped from our face.[12] In other words, they keep flowing even when we put on our game face. The task of the Christian is not to find a way past these tears but to align them to God's with the hope that God's liberating action of letting the tears flow will promote the common good in history.

Many tears have been shed over the years in Colombia, the native land of my own mother. In September 2017 Pope Francis went to Colombia to lend a hand to the bishops and pastors in the implementation of the new peace accords. The most memorable scene for me was his prayer before the mutilated black Christ of Bojayá. Having witnessed before his very eyes the tearful reconciliation of a victim of violence and a perpetrator of violence in Villavicencio, he prayed:

> O black Christ of Bojayá,
> who remind us of your passion and death;
> together with your arms and feet
> they have torn away your children
> who sought refuge in you.
>
> O black Christ of Bojayá,
> who look tenderly upon us
> and in whose face is serenity;
> your heart beats
> so that we may be received in your love.
>
> O black Christ of Bojayá,
> Grant us to commit ourselves to restoring your body.
> May we be your feet that go forth to encounter
> our brothers and sisters in need;
> your arms to embrace

[11] Pope Francis, "Address at the interreligious meeting held at the Ground Zero Memorial in New York," September 25, 2015, http://www.archivioradiovaticana.va /storico/2015/09/25/pope_francis'_address_at_ground_zero_memorial_in_new _york/en-1174651.

[12] Cf. E.M. Cioran, *Tears and Saints* (Chicago: University of Chicago Press, 1995).

those who have lost their dignity;
your hands to bless and console
those who weep alone.

Make us witnesses
to your love and infinite mercy.
Amen.[13]

The church's accompaniment of the peace process in Colombia is a searing image and a perfect example of how tears and dreams converge for the new *Ecclesia in America*.

Tears do not rule out dreams, but dreams are certainly difficult to achieve for the poor, the marginalized, and even those who suffer under a dysfunctional regime that has historically repressed the church. The dream of a better future was accordingly invoked before the youth of Cuba. There too the very notion of a dream for society was realistic and based more upon the social dimension of an authentically Christian hope than pious utopianism. In his meeting with Cuban youth at the Centro Cultural Padre Félix Varela, the pope cited (without a direct reference) the Guatemalan Nobel laureate Miguel Ángel Asturias. In his work "El Señor Presidente," Asturias spoke about a glass eye and another eye of truth: "those who see with their glass eye see because they dream. Those who see with their eye of flesh see because they are looking at the reality in front of them!" He alluded to the fact that the youth must dream with two eyes. Those who are not able to dream become entrapped in their selfhood. Using an Argentine expression, he warned them, "*¡No te arrugues!*" (Don't get wrinkled up!). The Catholic youth were urged to dream and share their dreams even if they did not conform to the expectations of their disgruntled peers or of the socialist government. They still have to keep abreast of the reality in front of them, especially if they hope to change that reality and work for a more just regime and society. The hope for a different future depends on the youth not being enervated and losing their desire to dream.

---

[13] Pope Francis, "Address of his Holiness Pope Francis, Reconciliation Liturgy, September 24, 2015: Apostolic Journey of His Holiness Pope Francis to Colombia (September 6–11, 2017)," https://w2.vatican.va/content/francesco/en/prayers/documents/papa-francesco_preghiere_20170908_colombia-bojaya.html.

We come now to the North American part of the equation. These words from Cuba were uttered just days before the pope arrived in the US and serve as a prologue to the new dream he invoked in the nation's capital. The address that Pope Francis gave to the United States Congress was in fact a meditation on and an act of dreaming. The fact that no previous pope had ever been invited to address this body is just one dimension of its uniqueness. Authentic appreciation and applause emanated from both sides of the aisle. But the most remarkable fact about the address was its manifold prophetic content. In the back of the Congress, an image of Moses can be clearly seen on the upper wall. The Pope was facing this image as he spoke and pointed to it during his address. He then recalled the figure of Moses as the one who receives guidance from God in formulating the laws of his people:

> Yours is a work which makes me reflect in two ways on the figure of Moses. On the one hand, the patriarch and lawgiver of the people of Israel symbolizes the need of peoples to keep alive their sense of unity by means of just legislation. On the other, the figure of Moses leads us directly to God and thus to the transcendent dignity of the human being. Moses provides us with a good synthesis of your work: you are asked to protect, by means of the law, the image and likeness fashioned by God on every human face.[14]

There is no genuine political vision unless lawmakers can see with Moses the transcendent dignity of the human person. At the heart of the speech was the echo of the words of Dr. Martin Luther King, Jr.: "I have a dream." For those around the globe inspired by King and committed to his legacy of civil and human rights, these words have a specific and enduring meaning. But the Argentine pope interwove the vision of King together with the visions of Abraham Lincoln, Dorothy Day, and Thomas Merton. Lincoln is an icon of the abolition

---

[14] Pope Francis, "Address of the Holy Father, Visit to the Joint Session of the United States Congress, September 24, 2015: Apostolic Journey of His Holiness Pope Francis to Cuba, to the United States of America and Visit to the United Nations Headquarters (19–28 September 2015)," https://w2.vatican.va/content/francesco/en/speeches/2015/september/documents/papa-francesco_20150924_usa-us-congress.html.

of slavery and "guardian of liberty" (the pope's phrase) for both political conservatives and liberals like the then president of the United States, Barack Obama. Lincoln symbolizes a North American dream of freedom in which solidarity and subsidiarity remain in balance. Day represents the Catholic personalism in a North American key that is close to the pope's own heart: "Her social activism, her passion for justice and for the cause of the oppressed, were inspired by the Gospel, her faith, and the example of the saints."[15] Out of his monastic solitude Merton taught US citizens "a capacity for dialogue and openness to God" that serves as a much needed antidote to the secular clarion calls for world peace. The dream that Pope Francis set before the Democrats and Republicans in the Congress was woven out of the fabric of this nation and its people. King's civic virtue was fused with Day's liturgical piety and radical acts of hospitality, Lincoln's republicanism, and Merton's contemplative insights into world order. The first pope ever in Congress, making his first trip to the United States, was an unexpected bard who fashioned a hope for the nation taken from the diverse aspirations of this people itself.

It is noteworthy that both sets of dreams are taken from the soil of the people and serve the deepest needs of the people. The contemplative stance of Merton is not directly relevant to Cubans, and the poetry of Asturias would not make much sense to pragmatically oriented youth in the US. In both cases the great lover of the Argentine epic poem *El Gaucho Martín Fierro* is entering into the naked public square not just to console or edify.[16] His goal is to forge a new discourse for political inclusion and participation that is grounded in the Christian doctrine of hope. He is not a legislator *manqué*; he is, rather, a grassroots Christian poet of public life. As such, Pope Francis is particularly interested in questions of social memory and time. Past, present, and future need to be brought together anew into a creative synthesis. Political ideologies by themselves cannot create such a hope. Artistry, dreams, and national aspirations are the stuff out of which this synthesis can be created and new directions for political work can be discovered.

---

[15] Francis, "Address of the Holy Father, Visit to the Joint Session of the United States Congress."

[16] Cf. Rourke, *Roots of Pope Francis's Social and Political Thought*, 146–47. He referenced this work in his address to the United Nations on September 15, 2015.

At its core the pope wove a story about four witnesses to mission and discipleship from this country: "Three sons and a daughter of this land, four individuals and four dreams: Lincoln, liberty; Martin Luther King, liberty in plurality and non-exclusion; Dorothy Day, social justice and the rights of persons; and Thomas Merton, the capacity for dialogue and openness to God. Four representatives of the American people."[17]

The configuration of these four offers a new way to rethink the witness of Catholicism in this country. As a configuration of the will of the people, only the first two would normally be considered as "political." In fact, the Argentine pope is expanding the definition of the political by including the radical Catholicism of Day and the monastic call for world peace of Merton. Lincoln's liberty and King's non-exclusion no longer appear like the partisan agendas to which we are too often accustomed. Instead there is the suggestion here of how the Catholic vision for national politics can be augmented and transformed as part of an overall plan of missionary discipleship.

Finally, the events in Philadelphia's Independence Mall were equally stimulating and filled with new dreams for the people of the United States. Here we saw the theology of gestures for which Pope Francis has become famous. He spoke on the steps of the Constitutional Convention about religious freedom using the same lectern that Abraham Lincoln used when he delivered the Gettysburg Address. His words were in Spanish, and they concerned the pressing issue of not allowing the federal government to violate the conscience of religious believers. He defined religious freedom in terms of concern for the Other. What struck me as quite brilliant was the linking of the theme of freedom with the *pueblo en marcha*. At the end of it, he noted that the inclusion of Latino Catholicism into the matrix of US culture is the final goal of exercising freedom. The US Constitution that was signed in the very building behind the pope protects and upholds the cultural and religious values of the Hispanic people of God.

In his trips to the Americas he not only spoke but listened to the bishops, to the laity, to the holy, faithful people of God, to the religious, to the popular movements, to political leaders, and to prisoners

---

[17] Francis, "Address of the Holy Father, Visit to the Joint Session of the United States Congress."

and victims of sexual abuse. The idea of a listening church in *Evangelii Gaudium* is taken from Paul VI's *Evangelii Nuntiandi* but is also minted with distinctively Bergoglian insights.[18] It is here that Pope Francis says that the preacher must lend *un oído al pueblo* ("an ear to the people") in order to discover what the faithful need to hear. Following Montini's pastoral insight, the listening is not restricted to the spiritual realm. The earlier discussion of hopes and dreams now meets its application in the realm of a theology of the Word and the reception of the Word in the life of the community. The preacher must enter into the entire web of life of the community to understand not only their mode of prayer but their loves, aspirations, and social engagements and despairs. Through this process of discerning in the light of the Word of God, the pastorally attuned preacher will be able to let God call upon his people by means of the proclaimed Word.

The second overarching theme is the ubiquity of the border in the life of a migrant. He spoke about this on the South Lawn of the White House in his greeting to President Barack Obama.[19]

> I am deeply grateful for your welcome in the name of all Americans. As the son of an immigrant family, I am happy to be a guest in this country, which was largely built by such families. I look forward to these days of encounter and dialogue, in which I hope to listen to, and share, many of the hopes and dreams of the American people.[20]

This son of immigrants introduced himself to the President of the United States and to this country by expressing his solidarity with the sons and daughters of immigrants that came here. He was making a point not only about his own identity but "American" identity. If the essence of being from the United States is linked to immigration, then a very different sense of nationhood and peoplehood emerges.

---

[18] He cites *Evangelii Nuntiandi* 53 and 33, as well as *Pastores Dabo Vobis* 10.

[19] For the full text of this ceremony, see "Remarks by President Obama and His Holiness Pope Francis at Arrival Ceremony," The White House: Office of the Press Secretary, September 23, 2015, https://www.whitehouse.gov/the-press-office/2015/09/23/remarks-president-obama-and-his-holiness-pope-francis-arrival-ceremony.

[20] Pope Francis, "Address of the Holy Father, Welcoming Ceremony, September 23, 2015," http://w2.vatican.va/content/francesco/en/speeches/2015/September/documents/papa-francesco_20150923_usa-benvenuto.html.

Mario Bergoglio, the pope's father, left the Piedmont region of Italy in 1929 because of a fear of being persecuted by the fascist Mussolini. Migration for Pope Francis is not, in the first instance, a social reality. The migrant is on a mission to bring the Word of God with himself or herself to a new land. It is clear from the canonization Mass on the steps of the Basilica of the Shrine of the Immaculate Conception in Washington, DC that Pope Francis sees Junípero Serra's mission to California as a form of missionary discipleship. I interpret the appeal to *"Siempre Adelante!"* in the canonization Mass as a direct appeal to the church today in the United States to place God first and challenge ourselves to greater inclusion and bolder witnessing to Christ among and outside of the people of God.

Then there is Mexico, the border that has haunted and defined US history for centuries. In 2016 Pope Francis traveled to Mexico and made a historic visit, the first one by any pope, to the US–Mexico border and prayed before a cross on the very border between Ciudad Juarez and El Paso. An event billed as "Two Nations, One Faith" took place during the Papal Visit in El Paso. About 28,000 people in El Paso's Sun Bowl erupted in cheers when Pope Francis talked to them during his televised Mass from Juárez, where another 200,000-plus people attended.[21] If it had not been so hot, even more might have attended. The pope in his homily from Mexico thanked his brothers and sisters in El Paso. There are reports that this liturgy was the largest "binational" Mass ever celebrated. The event included blessings for the people of Ciudad Juarez, the people of El Paso, and the refugees and others at a border levee near the Juárez Mass site. The Eucharist thus embraced not only two countries but also the pilgrims *en route* from one to the other.

The third and final clue to our transnational ecclesiology is the Samaritan church. It is a leitmotif that predates Francis. Already Paul VI in an address of December 7, 1965, in the last general session of the council said: "The old story of the Samaritan has been the model of the spirituality of the council."[22] As a cardinal in Argentina, the

---

[21] Cf. Vic Kolenc, "Sun Bowl's 28,000 Part of Papal Binational Mass," *El Paso Times*, February 17, 2016, http://www.elpasotimes.com/story/news/local/juarez/pope /2016/02/17/pope-francis-juarez-mexico-elpaso-sun-bowl-catholics/80393464/.

[22] Pope Paul VI, "Address of Pope Paul VI During the Last General Meeting of the Second Vatican Council, 7 December 1965," https://w2.vatican.va/content/paul-vi /en/speeches/1965/documents/hf_p-vi_spe_19651207_epilogo-concilio.html.

parable became for Bergoglio the authentic basis for constructing a model of Argentine nationhood.[23] On the eve of the canonization of Mother Teresa, Pope Francis spoke with the Workers of Mercy: "The world needs solidarity and a Samaritan Church."[24] In his general audience of April 27, 2016, his words are even more forceful: "What does it mean to ignore man's suffering? It means to ignore God! If I do not approach that man, or that woman, that child, that elderly man or elderly woman that is suffering, I do not come close to God."[25]

For Pope Francis there can be no question of reducing the reality of the church to a communal will to being a do-gooder. The church, according to his theology of the people, is an eruption of unbounded maternal love in the world, never just a compassionate Non-Governmental Organization (NGO). The image of the Samaritan as forged by Paul VI at the close of the Council and reiterated by Pope Francis is that of a church disposed to be at the service of those who are most in need.

To summarize, the church of Pope Francis in *América* is one that weeps and dreams, one that embraces and promotes the undocumented, and one that actualizes in an ecclesial way the spirituality of the good Samaritan. In the light of these three principles of Catholic existence, let us now turn to some of the specific issues that confront the church in the United States.

Who Are "the People?"

Populism as a political force is aligned today with forms of nationalism that are designed to stigmatize or exclude those on the margins. The pope's theology of the people is a radically inclusive form of engagement with political life, but he has still been accused of populism even as he constantly tries to differentiate his use of the term

---

[23] Rourke, *Roots of Pope Francis's Social and Political Thought*, 152–53.

[24] See also Pope Francis, papal bull, *Misericordiae Vultus*, https://w2.vatican.va /content/francesco/en/apost_letters/documents/papa-francesco_bolla_20150411 _misericordiae-vultus.html.

[25] Kathleen Naab, "Pope: Do We Know the Other Lesson From the Parable of the Good Samaritan?," *Zenit: The World Seen from Rome*, April 27, 2016, https://zenit .org/articles/pope-do-we-know-the-other-lesson-from-the-parable-of-the-good -samaritan/.

"people" from that of overt populists. The history of populism in Latin America is a long and varied one. In the United States, however, the matter is even more complicated. The exact relationship between "We, the people" and the Latin American and Latino/a concept of *pueblo* is hard to define. This terminological and theoretical problem is one of the most important challenges that need to be faced if the pope's vision is to be properly grasped. Furthermore, some pundits in North America are fearful of his alliance with popular movements, thinking that he must, as a result, have socialist tendencies in his political beliefs.

What, then, is the sociopolitical meaning of the term "people" in the pope's own lexicon? Before trying to answer this question, let us first consider the model of the polyhedron. The image of the polyhedron emerged early in the pontificate of Pope Francis. Even though it is presented as nothing more than a geometrical likeness, it contains a rich theological content. God establishes the polyhedron out of God's own love, and this mystery of God's love is present even as we are perplexed about how to relate wholes and parts in everyday life. As it says in 1 John 4:10: "In this is love: not that we have loved God, but that he loved us and sent his Son as expiation for our sins." This is the same verse that Pope Francis cited when he talks about *primereando* in *Evangelii Gaudium*.[26] This neologism drawn from the argot of Buenos Aires signifies the grace of God that goes before us. At least as subtle and mysterious as *gratia preveniens* in its classical articulation, this is the love of God that seeps into our lives before we are even aware of its presence. In his address to the College of Cardinals on March 15, 2013, just two days after his election to the see of Peter, he speaks to the brothers who elected him to this office of the Johannine image of the Paraclete, which is here presented as the harmonious force of unity in the midst of diversity:

---

[26] The full impact of this paragraph is evident only if one consults that Spanish text. "«*Primerear*»: *sepan disculpar este neologismo. La comunidad evangelizadora experimenta que el Señor tomó la iniciativa, la ha primereado en el amor* (cf. 1 Jn 4,10); *y, por eso, ella sabe adelantarse, tomar la iniciativa sin miedo, salir al encuentro, buscar a los lejanos y llegar a los cruces de los caminos para invitar a los excluidos. Vive un deseo inagotable de brindar misericordia, fruto de haber experimentado la infinita misericordia del Padre y su fuerza difusiva. ¡Atrevámonos un poco más a primerear!*" (EG 24).

He, the Paraclete, is the ultimate source of every initiative and manifestation of faith. It is a curious thing: it makes me think of this. The Paraclete creates all the differences among the Churches, almost as if he were an Apostle of Babel. But on the other hand, it is he who creates unity from these differences, not in "equality," but in harmony. I remember the Father of the Church who described him thus: "Ipse harmonia est." The Paraclete, who gives different charisms to each of us, unites us in this community of the Church, that worships the Father, the Son, and Him, the Holy Spirit.[27]

The true harmony that is not equality is the same image as the polyhedral unity that is not spherical. The community of cardinals and the community of the church that worships the Holy Trinity will be united by this Spirit of witnessing to a unity that is both identifiably Christian and reverberating beyond the confines of the church. In any case, a new Babel is the situation in which we find ourselves, and the Spirit is the apostle sent by Christ who makes a new Pentecost out of this Babel.[28]

The polyhedron appears in the section of *Evangelii Gaudium* dedicated to the common good and undergirds the principle of unity as greater than the sum of its parts. The principle of unity accompanies three other key Bergoglian insights: (1) time is greater than space, (2) unity prevails over conflict, and (3) reality is more important than ideas.[29] The polyhedron preserves unity and identity in a deracinated world that tends toward ever greater homogeneity: "The global need not stifle, nor the particular prove barren" (EG 217–37). It is a mode of intercultural fruitfulness and fundamentally about how one's roots not only are preserved but actually enhance the unity of the human

---

[27] Pope Francis, "Address of the Holy Father Pope Francis, Audience with the College of Cardinals, March 15, 2013," https://w2.vatican.va/content/francesco/en/speeches/2013/march/documents/papa-francesco_20130315_cardinali.html.

[28] On the new Babel, see George Steiner, *After Babel*, 3rd ed. (Oxford: Oxford University Press, 1998). The ecumenical and interreligious significance of a new Pentecost is explored in a fruitful manner by the Bulgarian Pentecostal theologian Daniela C. Augustine, *Pentecost, Hospitality, and Transfiguration: Towards a Spirit-Inspired Vision of Social Transformation* (Cleveland, TN: CPT Press, 2012).

[29] According to *El Jesuita*, Bergoglio speaks openly about the fact that this section of *Evangelii Gaudium* is taken verbatim from his unfinished thesis on Romano Guardini, a theme explored best by Borghesi, *Mind of Pope Francis*.

family in this new situation in which we find ourselves today. Instead of merely "tolerating" different cultures and identities, the present remaining task is to highlight difference for the sake of unity. In the specific case of polyhedral unity, Pope Francis accentuates the convergence of the pastoral and the political, the inclusion of the poor and their culture, and the search for a contributory element from those "people whose conduct may seem questionable on account of their errors" (EG 235).[30] Accordingly, the polyhedron is not derived from a worldly politics or from a merely supernatural realm. The polyhedron arises from a faith-filled vision of reality and history that seeks greater inclusion of those at the margins and the promotion of the common good in the midst of real strife and individualizing fragmentation.

Polyhedral unity sheds light on the meaning of "people" because the role of the "people" in the transformation in society is in fact polyhedral as opposed to spherical. In fact, the pope shuns the interpretation of the term "people" in church documents and in his own writing as referring to only one specific socioeconomic class. Emilce Cuda notes that one cannot assimilate his use of this antithesis between people and antipeople (*pueblo y antipueblo*) into the Marxist dialectic of a struggle between the proletariat and the owners of the means of production.[31] Cuda maintains that the Latin American political ethics favored by Bergoglio "de-structures" the values of the aggressor not for the sake of a class struggle but in search of a new synthesis and a new semantics.[32] It is not just a preference for an irenic resolution and the avoidance of physical and moral violence, although the language of peace is central to the new vocabulary of Pope Francis. Through Juan Carlos Scannone she highlights that a hermeneutics of culture based upon the priority of otherness and difference can contribute to the fostering of a "pluriform harmony"

---

[30] The English translation on the Vatican website leaves the false impression that those who commit errors are dubious characters. In fact, those who commit errors include the clergy and other persons of high standing in the institutional church. I am translating here from the Spanish: "*Aun las personas que puedan ser cuestionadas por sus errores, tienen algo que aportar que no debe perderse.*"

[31] Cuda, *Para leer a Francisco*, 174–83. Cuda has the deepest grasp of the complexity and fruitfulness of political theory in Argentine Catholicism today. Here she is developing how the cultural hermeneutics of the Jesuit philosopher Juan Carlos Scannone dovetails with the pope's theology of the people.

[32] Cuda, *Para leer a Francisco*, 177.

that respects religious liberty and simultaneously unmasks the ideological armaments of social oppression. Culture is not extracted from socioeconomic structures or processes as a neutral field of play in politics, but culture is also not reduced to the determinism of either the Marxist dialectic or the radical empiricism of some social scientists. Culture is born of an encounter of diverse peoples, and its fruitful existence is inexorably tied to an avoidance of false, hegemonic totalities.

The Bergoglian usage needs to be placed in a wider context. In Europe equivalent terms like *das Volk* and *il popolo* have become linked to totalitarian regimes of the past. This language seldom meets with acclaim, except by those who seek to pursue the dubious populism described above. Bergoglio is not using the word "people" in the right-wing European sense. Likewise, the word *pueblo* has a rich set of connotations in Spanish that are not evident with the English word. Some political analysts in Latin America do use the word *pueblo* to refer to the masses or even to a specific rung of the social ladder, such as the proletariat or working class. Bergoglio is very aware of this connotation and takes great pains not to limit his usage to this particular meaning. The term "people" and the term "masses" are carefully distinguished in the Bergoglian vocabulary. The very idea of a theology of the people is not intended to imbue a static group with privileges that they do not already have in their possession. People, on the contrary, "assumes a collective capable of generating its own historical processes."[33] The poor in the theology of the people are protagonists with their own unique wisdom, culture, and social agenda.[34] They are also called upon to be self-critical of their

---

[33] Víctor Manuel Fernández, *The Francis Project: Where He Wants to Take the Church*, trans. Sean O'Neill (New York: Paulist Press, 2016), 75.

[34] Austen Ivereigh writes: "Who were *el pueblo*? The word was used at the time by demagogues and ideologues—not least Marxists—as an abstract absolute. But for the La Plata school it had a much richer, deeper, and more specific connotation, drawn from the people-of-God ecclesiology of *Lumen Gentium*. For the COEPAL theologians, *el pueblo* meant the distinctive hybrid culture of Latin America born of the twin experiences of racial and cultural *mestizaje* on the one hand, and the evangelization of America on the other. Through baptism, the ancient Indian peoples and the mestizos became a new people (*Pueblo Nuevo*) with an awareness of their common dignity, and their equal participation in the common good." See Austen Ivereigh, "The Pope and the *Patria Grande*: How Francis is promoting Latin America's Continental Destiny," in *The Search for God in America*, ed. Maria Clara Bingemer and Peter Casarella (volume forthcoming with The Catholic University of America Press).

shortcomings, open to the insights of others, and forgers of a destiny that serves the common good of all classes and includes new bearers of wisdom and culture in an inclusive society.

The theology of the people in the US must therefore promote the popular wisdom of the people, including their public display of a devotional life (that is, *Via Crucis*) in the context of a society with strong but not univocal commitments to the idea of a civil society. This fusion has no real equivalent in North American civil religion and alienates many of my fellow Catholics in my country because its religious roots stand at odds with both the Puritan and the Jeffersonian strand in US religious history. As a secular language of independence, its initial defenders were José de San Martín and Simón Bolívar. Later figures such as the Dominican preacher Bartolomé de las Casas found a religious and truly popular idiom for forging a language of independence. For our purposes, the specific contribution of Bergoglio's contemporary Methol Ferré on the idea of being and defending *un pueblo fiel* cannot go unmentioned.[35] In Methol Ferré, Bergoglio found a fellow traveler who shared his deep trust in the sense of faith and common wisdom among the faithful people of God of the Southern Cone and in their instantiation of Vatican II's new vision of *mestizo* catholicity. In a certain sense, this is true of all popes and what they bring to the see of Peter, but here you have the additional element of a theology of the people with universal ramifications. Austen Ivereigh writes:

> Just as St John Paul II saw his pontificate as a providential means of facilitating the liberation of Eastern Europe from the Soviet yoke, Francis sees his as a God-given opportunity to further the emancipation of Latin America from the various colonialisms that have held the continent back from realizing its God-given potential. The Miami Strait [between the Cuba of exiles in Miami and the island nation of Cuba] and the Mexican-American border are to this pontificate what the Berlin Wall was to John Paul II's.[36]

---

[35] I am very indebted in all these questions to Ivereigh, "The Pope and the *Patria Grande*." On the general influence of Ferré, one should consult the introduction to Alver Metalli and Methol Ferré, *El Papa y El Filósofo* (Buenos Aires: Biblios, 2013), 19–34, and the other literature cited by Ivereigh.

[36] Ivereigh, "The Pope and the *Patria Grande*," 4.

In fact, the universality of this vision taken from the Southern Cone for all of Latin America and beyond cannot be taken for granted. In the 1970s and 1980s Ferré and Bergoglio both seemed to think that there was a confluence of a "Catholic resurgence" with the call of Paul VI and John Paul II for a new evangelization.[37] The theologians from the Southern Cone (Gera, Tello, Ferré, and the Chilean Schönstatt priest Joaquín Alliende) appeared too nationalist to the other liberation theologians in Latin America, and the other liberation theologians appeared too abstract ("reality prevails over the idea") to the theologians of the people from the Southern Cone. In this reading of the "signs of the times," the countries of the Southern Cone had a very special role to play and, in fact, their sometimes despised "theology of the people" began at this time to have an impact on the agenda of CELAM. Bergoglio once offered a simple and direct synthesis of this vision in what was originally an impromptu remark made to an Argentine rabbi:

> One issue that typifies our history is the capacity for *mestizaje* that we witnessed in Argentina. This shows a certain degree of universality and a respect for the identity of the other. I believe that in Latin America—[especially in Argentina] along with Uruguay, the south of Brazil, and part of Chile—*mestizaje* in the good and rich sense of the term became recognizable. I like to see where the encounter of cultures, as opposed to a fusion, prevailed. I like it when diverse collectivities appear in the celebrations (*en las fiestas*). For this reason, the government agreed to the organization of a Bicentennial, making room for all the collectivities and showing off our multi-facetedness.[38]

[37] Ivereigh, 13: "Noting how the experience of the US and postwar Europe showed that the future lay in 'continent-states,' Methol argued that the *Patria Grande* could be reborn from Perón's frustrated 'ABC' idea of a tariff-free zone between Argentina, Brazil and Chile outlined in a speech the Argentine leader gave in November 1953. In the same essay, Methol gave strong support to the formation of Mercosur following the Asunción Treaty of 1991, seeing it as similar to the Franco-German coal and steel agreement that paved the way to the European Union. For Methol, the Argentine-Brazilian nexus was key, for it allowed the *Patria Grande* to move beyond the exclusively Spanish-American vision of San Martín and Bolívar (Brazil was an empire until 1898). For Methol, this represented the recovery of an historical precedent, the 60 years (1580–1640) in which the Iberian Peninsula was united under one king, Philip II."

[38] Jorge Mario Bergoglio and Abraham Skorka, *Sobre el Cielo y la Tierra* (Buenos Aires: Sudamericana, 2010), 150–51. Translation my own.

What is most particular to a regional grasp of identity therefore becomes a hermeneutical key for the vision of the pontificate as a whole. By including Brazil and the new consciousness of the indigenous peoples in present-day Latin America in their synthesis, the new sense of identity was a new whole that overcame the narrow binomial between Spain and New Spain in the periods of colonialism and independence. The "whole" of the *Patria Grande* in the revisionist La Plata school of thought guided by Ferré reflected an unprecedented and to this day largely unfinished *"new mestizaje."*

What about the relationship between the sense of popular unity in the Argentine theology of the people and cultural integration?[39] One distinctive feature of the Argentine theology of the people was to seek an integration of popular piety and the theology of culture such that the pastoral orientations of theology truly reflected a new *mestizaje* of culture.[40] This, too, is a topic that was addressed in many contexts by the provincial, the churchman, and the archbishop. One important element has been overlooked in most of the English-speaking literature. On February 20, 2006, the archbishop of Buenos Aires wrote a brief prologue to Amelia Podetti's posthumously published commentary on the introduction to Hegel's groundbreaking work, *The Phenomenology of Spirit*. The words reflect a deep devotion to the philosophical career and intellectual witness of Podetti, a fellow traveler in Peronist politics, and her assiduous preparation for her influential seminars.[41] These words reveal surprisingly little by way of evaluation of Hegel's speculative thought. Cardinal Bergoglio notes that a renaissance of German philosophy was underway in Argentina and that Podetti held both Hegel and Augustine in high regard as two necessary poles in the history of philosophy. He also

---

[39] Fernández, *The Francis Project*, 79–81.

[40] On this point, there are unmistakable similarities between the theology of Pope Francis and the theology of the late Virgilio Elizondo. See, for example, his *The Future Is Mestizo: Life Where Cultures Meet* (Bloomington, IN: Meyer-Stone, 1988).

[41] Massimo Borghesi captured this testimony: "Influyó en mí el pensamiento de Amelia Podetti, decana de Filosofía de la Universidad, especialista en Hegel, que falleció joven. De ella tomé la intuición de las 'periferias.' Ella trabajaba mucho en eso. Uno de sus hermanos sigue publicando sus escritos y apuntes. Leyendo a Methol Ferré y a Podetti tomé algunas cosas de la dialéctica, en una forma antihegeliana, porque ella era especialista en Hegel pero no era hegeliana." Cf. Massimo Borghesi, "Amelia Podetti: La mujer que inspire a Bergoglio," *Aleteia*, November 24, 2017, https://es.aleteia.org/2017/11/24/amelia-podetti-la-mujer-que-inspiro-a-bergoglio/.

notes that Podetti herself engaged the Hegelian notion of "universal history" in a fairly critical manner, claiming that the heritage of Argentine sources still needed to be plumbed and that the "planetarization" (her words) of philosophy was still in process. He wanted to take the Hegelian idea of universal history to the peripheries in the same way that the church needed to go to the peripheries. He concludes, however, with a fascinating word about the philosophical setting and aspirations of Argentina in the Latin American context:

> I hope that the re-reading and dialogue with a classic of the history of philosophy, brought about from a distant shore of the West, continues to bear fruit in our universities and in all those places in which we have to re-affirm our passionate vocation for the mastery of philosophy. We are after all inheritors of a magnificent tradition in this regard, starting with the prophetic moment in which Alonso de Veracruz and Vasco de Quiroga in Mexico, or José de Acosta in Peru were moved to think for America, from America and as Americans (a América, desde América, y como americanos).[42]

Podetti's still nascent but prematurely ended project is lauded on its own terms and for its own worth. At the same time the archbishop and future protagonist at the Fifth General Conference of CELAM in Aparecida thinks about what the Argentine reception of a speculative genius who prematurely envisioned a totalizing history from Germany might mean for a new trajectory of Latin American thought. This "Americanizing" of the flawed Hegelian project of a universal history thus spurs a culture of encounter in which Latin Americans can reclaim their own view of universal history. In a typically Argentine manner, the parochialism of the local will be called into question through this global expansion of thought. Yet, the starting point in Argentina is suddenly a starting point for a new reflection, an insight Hegel did not imagine. Just as Methol Ferré advocated the transformation of Latin American culture from being a recipient to a source, the archbishop advocates the completion of an already underway project of generating a universal form of encounter for "multipolar cultures" in Latin America derived from the philosophically fertile

---

[42] Amelia Podetti, *Comentario a la Introducción a la Fenomenología del Espíritu* (Buenos Aires: Biblos, 2006), 13.

ground in and near the La Plata river basin. In other words, from Podetti's and Bergoglio's own unique location in time and space, an indigenous, postcolonial, and polyhedral history of philosophy might be possible that questions the fragmentation of Euro-American post-modernism as well as the false hegemony of Hegel's myopic vision of modernity.

In the context of the United States, "the people" in a theology of the people is not a class, an ethnicity, or a race. It refers to the faithful ones chosen by God to bring about a new unity in the church and in society that is polyhedral as opposed to spherical. This means that the individualism and consumerism of US culture will be challenged in a forceful way. It always means that the church must be at the vanguard of showing our fellow citizens what it means to accompany those who are most in need and at the margins of society. It is not a liberal or a conservative project. If it has any antecedent in US history that can be cited, it would probably be the vision of the church advocated by Dorothy Day (a witness that the pope cited before the Congress) and Peter Maurin.

The First Latino Pope?

The pope's emphasis on the people of God resonates with Latino/a Catholics. We are the people on the move, according to the Second National Hispanic Encuentro from 1977. The *Encuentros* began in the 1970s and continued through the year 2000.[43] The planning process for the Fifth Encuentro was blessed by Pope Francis during his trip to the US. The *Encuentros* have always been a process of listening for the US Catholic bishops and aided significantly in the process of forming diocesan and regional offices as well as a National Plan for Hispanic Ministry. Without using the language of missionary discipleship, it is clear that the spirit of the *Encuentros* is very close to the spirit of Pope Francis. In both cases the emphasis is placed on

---

[43] The history and ecclesiology of the *Encuentros* is a question that is only now beginning to be addressed. See, for example, Luis A. Tampe, SJ, *Encuentro Nacional Hispano de Pastoral (1972–1985): An Historical and Ecclesiological Analysis*, PhD diss., Catholic University of America, 2014, and Mario J. Paredes, *The History of the National Encuentros: Hispanic Americans in the One Catholic Church* (New York/Mahwah, NJ: Paulist Press, 2015).

mission and personal encounter. The *Encuentros* might be the closest that the US Catholic Church has ever come in recent history to living out a theology of the people.

At the core of *Evangelii Gaudium* and the *Encuentros* is the notion of the church as the People of God. *Pueblo de Dios*, people of God, has a particular meaning among Latino/as. *Lumen Gentium* 9 emphasized that the new people of God is called by the same God who calls Israel. The Latino/a people of God are heirs to this new covenant, one that serves as a universal sign for a new humanity.[44] I would like to underscore three distinctively Latino/a elements to the notion of the church as a new people of God: belongingness, its sociocentric nature, and the culture of encounter. The sense of belonging in *el pueblo de Dios* derives from the peculiarity of the Spanish word *pueblo*, which refers both to one's hometown and to the community to which one belongs. This is very different from the experience of the North, in which one commonly differentiates between one's ethnicity and one's place of origin: "I am Italian-American, *but* I was born in Connecticut." Latinos too often make this kind of differentiation but have a sense of belonging that trades on the ambiguity in the word *pueblo*. The physicality and spatiality of *pueblo* is clearer; it is not just a social construct. We see this dynamic at play in the account of the *Nican Mopohua*, in which *la Morenita* promises Juan Diego an *eremita*, a new dwelling place in which the indigenous can worship God and have a home. We see this as well in the practice of place *altarcitos* in the home and in the deep sense of *compadrazgo* that indwells Hispanic families. Being a people is as palpable as having a home. One senses a loss of home when one is separated from one's people, and a loss of peoplehood when one is separated from one's home. Reinforcing one's identity as a people is thus a form of homecoming. This is a very important dynamic in a world such as ours that is beset by many forms of socioeconomic and spiritual homelessness. Latino/as find themselves in a culture and economy that cherishes mobility and clearly devalues being rooted in just one place.

---

[44] See, in particular, Gary Riebe-Estrella, SVD, "Pueblo and Church," in *From the Heart of Our People*, Orlando O. Espín and Miguel H. Díaz, eds. (Maryknoll, NY: Orbis, 1999), 172–88. This is the most sustained reflection on the theme, although I do not agree with the opposition that the author draws between mere existence as a *pueblo* and the form of the institutional church.

Second, Latino theologians such as Gary Riebe-Estrella and Roberto Goizueta emphasize the sociocentric nature of the Latino *pueblo* and contrast it to the egocentrism of North American culture.[45] The theologians differ as to whether the dominant leitmotif for understanding the Latino peoplehood is that of the family or of community. The festivities of the life of the extended family and the politics of community organizing blend together and remain intertwined in the Hispanic *pueblo de Dios*. César Chavez, for example, was a dedicated *Guadalupano*. In any case, there does seem to be a clear contrast between Latino communitarianism and the rampant individualism of US culture. Latinos are not the only ones making sacrifices, and not all Latinos are open to making sacrifices for the good of the greater whole. There is still a cultural link in *el pueblo* that remains a countercultural witness in a society that advances workers based upon the ethic of the solitary agent and promotes the social life of "bowling alone."[46] Efforts by Latino/a theologians to harness the symbolic resources of popular religion are directed not only to the spiritual benefits of these practices but also to the intrinsic countercultural value of their public witness.[47]

Cultura de encuentro is a term that Pope Francis mentions in *Evangelii Gaudium* and elsewhere.[48] Virgilio Elizondo's thought parallels that of Pope Francis in this respect. What are the origins of Elizondo's thought? Elizondo first wrote his dissertation with the title *métissage*, showing the influence of cultural theorist Jacques Audinet.[49] His academic path in the early 1980s focused on Christology, and his most enduring work to this day remains *The Galilean Journey*, which he first published in 1983.[50] His insights into the Galilean identity of

[45] In addition to the chapter by Riebe-Estrella cited above, see Roberto Goizueta, *Caminemos con Jesús: Toward a Hispanic/Latino Theology of Accompaniment* (Maryknoll, NY: Orbis, 1995).

[46] Robert D. Putnam, *Bowling Alone: The Collapse and Revival of the American Community* (New York: Simon & Schuster, 2000).

[47] See, for example, Peter J. Casarella, "The Painted Word," *The Journal of Hispanic/Latino Theology* 6 (November 1998): 18–42.

[48] *Evangelii Gaudium* 7, 75, 78, 87–88, 91, 120, 171, and especially 220, 229, 237.

[49] Virgilio Elizondo, *Métissage, violence culturelle, annonce de l'évangile* (Paris: Institut Catholique, 1978).

[50] Virgilio Elizondo, *The Galilean Journey: The Mexican-American Promise* (Maryknoll, NY: Orbis, 1983; 2nd ed., 2000).

Jesus provide the groundwork for his later development as well as a blueprint for Latino/a theology as such. Interestingly, they also seemed to be echoed in some of the recent homilies and addresses of Pope Francis.[51] Elizondo gives a new twist to the biblical motif of "Galilee of the Gentiles."[52] He links this to his own experiences, but it is not so important, in my opinion, that Galilee historically may have represented the same social type as the working class, ethnically mixed, and oppressed Mexican people to whom Elizondo belongs.[53] Galilee is now the existential mix of cultural unity in difference.

In 1993 Elizondo introduced the US theologians assembled in San Antonio for the annual meeting of the Catholic Theological Society of America to the conquered people of the Southwest and to the pastoral needs that were still only barely being acknowledged in the US Catholic Church. The threefold conquest that he preached presented Catholic theology with a pastoral dilemma previously unimagined. First, the indigenous were conquered by the Spanish, who depreciated their Amerindian cosmovision. Second, the United States came and conquered their land. He refers to this expansion of manifest destiny as the work of "the WASP colonizers of the Northern United States."[54] Today, however, the challenge lies with a very different sort of incursion, namely, that of religious fundamentalists who exploit the indifference of a church shepherded by the children of European immigrants to its own *mestizo* faithful. The needs of the people are great, and Catholic theology must face up to this problem that threatens its very identity.

Pope Francis has been a great blessing to Latino Catholics and to the development of a Latino/a theology based upon an accompaniment of the Latino/a people of God. This does not mean that the pontificate of Pope Francis removes the tears that remain for those involved in Hispanic ministry. A Pew Research Center Report of 2014 is sobering. It shows that the future will hold great challenges for

---

[51] See, for example, his reference to an "existential Galilee" in the sermon that he preached in the Vatican Basilica on the Easter Vigil in 2014.

[52] Isa 9:1-2 and Matt 4:15-16.

[53] Cf. Michael E. Lee, "Galilean Journey Revisited: *Mestizaje*, Anti-Judaism, and the Dynamics of Exclusion," *Theological Studies* 70 (2009): 377–400.

[54] Lee, 395.

both Latino/a Catholics and the US Catholic Church.[55] The growth in the number of Hispanics in the US Catholic Church depends mainly on the influx of new immigrants. But the exiting of Hispanic Catholics to Pentecostal groups and even to the category of "none" continues. As a result, well over half of all young Catholics are Hispanic, but fewer than half of Hispanics under age thirty are Catholic. Outreach to the youth such as that done by the Instituto Fe y Vida in Stockton, California is crucial. This theme was also central to the Fifth Encuentro. Of the three thousand Hispanic participants, one-third were drawn from a pool of young adult Catholics. The young adult presence at the Fifth Encuentro is not a bad model for thinking about how the *teología del pueblo* is transforming and can continue to transform the Catholic Church in the US.

Conclusion

We live in the midst of a polarized Catholicism.[56] The current strife about the letter published by Archbishop Carlo Maria Viganò is only the latest round of that form of polarization that plagues us. To address this problem, I would like to recall some remarks that the young Bergoglio made when he was thinking about the unity of the church.

In 1987, he published *Reflexiones espirituales*, and in 1990 he discussed the union of souls in the collected essays, *Reflexiones en esperanza*. The latter collection contains the essay, "And you must conform yourself to this hope . . . Some reflections with regard to the union of souls," a reflection that recapitulates the spiritual principles of polyhedrism.[57] The idea of a union of souls refers to a phrase in the *Constitution* of the Society that describes the ideal state of provinces and local communities and includes all the individuals that were sent on a mission. In other words, Bergoglio was extrapolating from a fundamental experience of what it means to be a Jesuit to a general

[55] Pew Research Center, "The Shifting Religious Identity of Latinos in the United States," Pew report of May 7, 2014, http://www.pewforum.org/2014/05/07/the -shifting-religious-identity-of-latinos-in-the-united-states/.

[56] See Mary Ellen Konieczny, Charles C. Camosy, and Tricia C. Bruce, eds., *Polarization in the US Catholic Church: Naming the Wounds, Beginning to Heal* (Collegeville, MN: Liturgical Press, 2016).

[57] Jorge Mario Bergoglio, "Y conforme a esta esperanza," in *Reflexiones en esperanza* (Buenos Aires: Universidad de San Salvador, 1992), 221–51. The original publication of the essay is given as CIS, Vol. XX, Roma, 1990, 63–64, pp. 121–42.

Christian spirituality. The essay purports to be nothing more than an interpretation of the particular passages of the *Constitution* that deal with this reality. However, with the hindsight offered by *Evangelii Gaudium*, it appears to reveal a much broader vision. He states that the principle of seeking the union of souls is not only an administrative ideal but the concrete experience that derives from the earliest period of the Society. In this sense, he is seeking to uncover the notion of missionary discipleship as an apostolic reality in the foundation of the congregation itself. He describes the Ignatian conception of the union of souls in terms that are strikingly similar to polyhedric unity: it is a method that focuses on "the antinomy (*la contraposición*) 'unity-diversity' that is recognized by the *Constitution* when it speaks about this topic."[58] He also notes that it is this very principle that allowed the individual Jesuits physically dispersed throughout the world on their missionary assignments still to maintain a palpable sense of unity.[59] The particular feature of this writing that makes it count as a forerunner of the later reflections on the unity in diversity of the missionary church is the dynamic quality with which he invests the theological virtues of faith, hope, and charity:

> In the mind of St. Ignatius, *diversity* is an essential element of the *unio animorum*. The principal and foundation of this union of souls is the hope in God (hope that gives order, that orders in an ascending fashion), and the principal bond is the love that descends (that gives order, orders, in a descending form and as an efficient cause). As such, the *formalitas definitiva* ("explanatory pattern") that gives unity to the members of the Company and that conforms that into one body is loving hope.[60]

[58] Bergoglio, "Y conforme a esta esperanza," 222.

[59] Bergoglio, 223. The parallel between the early Ignatian vision and Pope Francis's call for a church as an ecclesial reality united for the sake of missionary discipleship is uncanny. For example, he writes: "*La dispersión apostólica (nacida de la misión y sostenida por la oración y el celo de las almas) dará consistencia a la pertenencia al cuerpo y este pertenecer al cuerpo—a su vez—posibilitará la dispersión apostólica. . . . Y ésta es la intuición fundamental de la unidad del cuerpo de la Compañía en relación a su aumento y conservación*" (225).

[60] Bergoglio, 232. While these theological virtues are not singled out in this essay, the parallel to Bergoglio's treatment of them here deserves to be compared to the pastoral approach to faith, hope, and charity developed by Rafael Tello. See, above all, Enrique Bianchi Ciro, *Pobres en este mundo, ricos en la fe (Sant 2,5): La fe de los pobres de América Latina según Rafael Tello* (Buenos Aires: Agape, 2012).

It is typical of Ignatian spirituality to speak simultaneously of the perspectives descending from above and ascending from below. This is the compatibilism of the divine initiative with human freedom that characterizes the theological anthropology of *The Spiritual Exercises*. But two additional features of this Ignatian spirituality point forward to the pope's theology. First, the dynamic perspective of the union of souls is, in the first instance, a discovery of order in the form of an *interior* unity in diversity that must precede any facilitation by the Superior General or any Jesuit of exterior unity in diversity.[61] This is deeply Ignatian but also speaks to the strong emphasis on the personal encounter with Christ in *Evangelii Gaudium*. Second, he speaks about the enactment of this unity in the dynamic relationship between consolation and desolation in order to underscore again the point about not fleeing from difficulties and challenges. Moreover, the union of souls has as its goal the forming of one body. Belonging to the one body (that is, the principle of *pertenencia* or "sensing that one belongs" to the corporate body in *Evangelii Gaudium*) must, as a foundational principle, be concretized in terms of one's specific "place, time, and accompanying persons."[62] This is the corollary of concreteness, that is, seeking the *reality* of a *unio animorum* that precedes the idea of such unity. Without sacrificing the generality of first principles to a mere ethics of the situation, Bergoglio clearly accentuates the historical meaning of this unity in specific places, times, and contexts.[63] If contextual theology can be Ignatian and principled in an Ignatian way, then the building blocks for such a contextual theology are undeniably present in this comprehensive essay from 1990. In sum, the Ignatian phrase "union of souls" therefore speaks to a very specific method of finding unity in diversity that is strikingly similar to the kind of multipolar catholicity that Pope Francis promotes in *Evangelii Gaudium* and elsewhere.

Multipolar catholicity is not a recipe for resolving conflicts in the church. It is the starting point for advocating a culture of encounter.

---

[61] Bergoglio, "Y conforme a esta esperanza," 235. He cites a then relatively recent work of the prolific personalist and Jesuit philosopher Ismael Quiles Sánchez (1906–1993) on the ontic and ethical determination of the human person as a being in dialogue (cf. 244, n. 53).

[62] Bergoglio, "Y conforme a esta esperanza," 248.

[63] Cf. Bergoglio, "Y conforme a esta esperanza," 249, n. 56.

It is a way to allow us to share tears and dreams. The innovation of Pope Francis is to see that this sharing is an ecclesial process and not just a therapeutic one. He speaks loud and clear about the need to conceive of the church as a "field hospital."[64] When he talks about the church as a "field hospital," he is offering a way for us to overcome our current polarization by attending first to those most in need and only in a second stage to work out our conflicts that are mainly ideological and not truly doctrinal. It will require considerable humility on both sides of this conflict to enter into the field hospital and attend to the wounds of those who are truly in need. But if the Jesuits were able to bring the Gospel of Christ to the far ends of the earth using a method drawn from these principles, then the Catholics of the United States could probably do well to learn from a Jesuit pope drawn from the ends of the earth.

[64] William T. Cavanaugh, *Field Hospital: The Church's Engagement with a Wounded World* (Grand Rapids, MI: Eerdmans, 2016).

Contributors

Bishop Robert Barron is an acclaimed author, speaker, and theologian. He is the founder of the global media ministry *Word on Fire*, which reaches millions of people by utilizing the tools of new media to draw people into or back to the Catholic faith. He is the creator and host of *Catholicism*, a groundbreaking, award-winning documentary series about the Catholic faith. Bishop Barron received a master's degree in philosophy from the Catholic University of America in 1982 and a doctorate in sacred theology from the Institut Catholique de Paris in 1992. He was ordained a priest in 1986 in the Archdiocese of Chicago, and then appointed to the theological faculty of Mundelein Seminary in 1992. He served as the rector-president of Mundelein Seminary University of St. Mary of the Lake (2012–15). On July 21, 2015, Pope Francis appointed Bishop Barron to be auxiliary bishop of the Archdiocese of Los Angeles. He was ordained bishop on September 8, 2015.

Massimo Borghesi is professor of moral philosophy at the Department of Philosophy, Social Sciences, Humanities and Education at the University of Perugia. He was professor of history of moral philosophy at the Faculty of the University of Lecce (1992–96). He taught aesthetics, ethics, and philosophical theology at the Pontifical Theological Faculty of St. Bonaventure in Rome (1981–2007) where he held the Bonaventuriana Chair (2000–2002). He taught philosophy and religion at the Pontifical Urban University (2008–17). He is a member of the advisory and editorial boards of several publishers and journals (*Studium*, *Atlantide*, and *Humanitas*). He was a member of the editorial board of the quarterly magazine *Il Nuovo Areopago* (1993–2002) and collaborator of the international magazine *30Giorni* (1984–2012).

Rocco Buttiglione is an Italian politician and philosopher. He studied law at the Universities of Turin and Rome, where in 1970 he obtained a degree with a thesis on the history of political doctrines. He belongs to the first group of disciples and friends of don Luigi Giussani who created the movement *Comunione e Liberazione* (Communion and Liberation). Since 1994 he has served in the Chamber of Deputies in the Italian Parliament, has been a member of the European Parliament since 1999, and was minister of European affairs (2001–5) and minister for Culture (2005–6). His main intellectual concerns have been philosophy, social ethics, economics, and politics. He has been the director of the St. John Paul II Chair at the Pontifical Lateran University in Rome, and has held professorships at the International Academy of Philosophy in Liechtenstein, at Saint Pius V University in Rome, and at the University of Urbino. He is currently professor at the IFES (Instituto de Filosofia Edith Stein) in Granada (Spain). He has been a member of the Pontifical Commission Justice and Peace and is a member of the Pontifical Academy of Social Sciences. He has published twelve books, including *Risposte amichevoli ai critici di Amoris Laetitia* (Friendly Answers to Critics of *Amoris Laetitia*), more than 130 essays (on philosophy and cultural topics), and several hundred articles in the national and international press.

Guzmán Carriquiry Lecour, a native of Uruguay and an attorney, received a doctorate of law and social sciences at the University of the Republic, in Montevideo. He has served the Holy See since 1977 when he was appointed bureau chief of the Pontifical Council for the Laity by Pope Paul VI. In 1991 Pope John Paul II appointed him undersecretary of the Pontifical Council for the Laity, the first layperson chosen as undersecretary of a Vatican dicastery, a position reconfirmed by Pope Benedict XVI in 2009. In 2011 Pope Benedict appointed him secretary of the Pontifical Commission for Latin America, the first layperson to serve in that role. He has numerous publications to his credit, including *Una apuesta por America Latina* (A Wager for Latin America; 2003) and *El bicentenario de la Independencia de los Paises latino-americanos; ayer y hoy* (The Bicentennial of the Independence of the Countries of Latin America: Yesterday and Today; 2011), both prefaced by Jorge Mario Bergoglio, whom Carriquiry has known since he was the provincial head of the Argentine Jesuits. He has been a visiting professor at various Italian pontifical universities and those of other European and Latin American countries. He has received several honors, including that of Knight Grand Cross of the Order of St. Gregory the Great.

Peter J. Casarella is associate professor of theology at the University of Notre Dame and the director of Latin American North American Church Concerns (LANACC). He holds a PhD in religious studies from Yale University, with a specialization in the philosophy of religion. His field of study is systematic theology and his research interests include Latino/a theology, medieval Christian thought (especially Bonaventure, Nicholas of Cusa), and theological aesthetics. He is author of, most recently, *Word as Bread: Language and Theology in Nicholas of Cusa* (2017). He has published sixty essays in scholarly journals on a variety of topics. He has edited, or coedited, *Cuerpo de Cristo: The Hispanic Presence in the U.S. Catholic Church* (with Raúl Gómez, SDS; 1998); *Christian Spirituality and the Culture of Modernity: The Thought of Louis Dupré* (1998); *Cusanus: The Legacy of Learned Ignorance* (2006); and *Jesus Christ: The New Face of Social Progress*, a collection of essays on the social encyclical *Caritas in Veritate* (2015). He previously served as professor of Catholic studies and director of the Center for World Catholicism and Intercultural Theology (CWCIT) at DePaul University, held teaching and administrative positions at The Catholic University of America and the University of Dallas, and was a 2014–15 Luce Fellow in Theology. In 2005, Casarella served as president of the Academy of Catholic Hispanic Theologians in the US (ACHTUS), and he was the president of the Academy of Catholic Theologians in 2017.

Brian Yong Lee is assistant professor of Sacred Scripture at Sacred Heart Seminary and School of Theology. He received a master's degree in philosophy from Boston College, a master's degree in theological studies from Weston Jesuit School of Theology, and a PhD in Theology from the University of Notre Dame in 2017, with a dissertation entitled "Rereading the Body of Christ: Askesis, Community, and Stoicism in 1 Corinthians" being revised for publication. He recently received a Templeton grant (Engaging Science in Seminaries) to research forgiveness in early Christianity and is currently working on a monograph on the relationship between faith, grace, justice and forgiveness in early Christianity. His academic research focuses on situating the development of early Christian theology within the context of the formation of early Jewish identities in the Greco-Roman world. He has been a member of the Community of Sant'Egidio since 1999.

Rodrigo Guerra López, a native of Mexico, received a PhD in philosophy from the International Academy of Philosophy in Liechtenstein and has studied at the Catholic University of Eichstätt (Germany). He is president of the Center of Advanced Social Research, and professor at Universidad Iberoamericana, Universidad Panamericana, and Universidad Anahuac. He is the author of *Como un gran movimiento* (Mexico: Fundación Rafael Preciado Hernández, 2006); *Afirmar a la persona por sí misma. La dignidad como fundamento de los derechos de la persona* (Mexico: Comisión Nacional de los Derechos Humanos, 2003); and *Volver a la persona. El método filosófico de Karol Wojtyla* (Madrid: Caparrós, 2002). He has also edited five books and is the coauthor of thirty books mainly devoted to philosophical anthropology, bioethics, and social philosophy, including *Catholics and Politicians: An Identity in Tension*, prologue by Jorge M. Bergoglio, SJ (Buenos Aires: CELAM-Agape, 2006). He is a member of the Pontifical Academy for Life and the Pontifical Council of Justice and Peace.

Austen Ivereigh is a British writer, journalist, and commentator on Catholic and political affairs, and is a fellow in contemporary church history at Campion Hall, Oxford. He holds a DPhil in history and politics from Oxford University. Ivereigh is author of *The Great Reformer: Francis and the Making of a Radical Pope* (Henry Holt/Picador, 2014) and of the best-selling *How to Defend the Faith without Raising Your Voice: Civil Responses to Catholic Hot-Button Issues* (Our Sunday Visitor, 2012, 2015). He is founder-coordinator of Catholic Voices, a project now in more than twenty countries worldwide, and writes regularly for *Crux*, *Commonweal*, and *America* magazines among others. He served as deputy editor of the Catholic weekly *The Tablet*, worked as public affairs director for the late archbishop of Westminster, Cardinal Cormac Murphy-O'Connor, and served as director of the London-based immigration campaign "Strangers into Citizens," based on Catholic social teaching. His volume on Pope Francis's reform efforts is entitled *Wounded Shepherd: Pope Francis's Struggle to Convert the Catholic Church* (Henry Holt, 2019).

Fr. Thomas L. Knoebel has been a priest of the Archdiocese of Milwaukee since 1969. He earned his doctorate in systematic theology from Fordham University. He has served as faculty at Saint Francis Seminary-School of Pastoral Ministry, St. Francis (1973–80), and for the past thirty years, beginning in 1981, Fr. Knoebel has served at Sacred Heart School of Theology as professor of systematic theology, director of spiritual formation (1988–94), academic dean (1994–2005), twice interim rector (1992–93, 2007), vice rector and vice president for external affairs (2005–13), and president-rector (2017–19). He published the first English translations of *De Ecclesiasticis Officiis* by St. Isidore, archbishop of Seville, in 2008; and of St. Isidore's *Sententiae*, in 2018; both published by the Paulist Press patristics series Ancient Christian Writers. Fr. Knoebel was appointed to the Editorial Advisory Board for the Ancient Christian Writers series in 2009. He was installed by Archbishop of Toledo, Spain, Francisco Alvarez Martinez as an honorary member of the Illustrious and Most Ancient Brotherhood of Mozarab Knights and Ladies of Our Lady of Hope of the Imperial City of Toledo, Spain, and the Mozarab community of Spain. He is a member of the Royal Academy of Fine Arts and Historical Sciences of Toledo, Spain, installed in the Aula of the Royal Academy in Toledo on October 4, 2009, and is one of only nine members who live in the United States.

Archbishop Christophe Pierre, a native of Rennes, France, was appointed as apostolic nuncio of the United States of America by Pope Francis on April 12, 2016. He was parochial vicar of the St. Peter and St. Paul Parish in Colombes, Diocese of Nanterre, France (1970–73). His service in the Diplomatic Corps of the Holy See began on March 5, 1977, with an appointment to the pontifical representation in New Zealand and the Islands of the Pacific Ocean (1977–81). Subsequently he served in Mozambique (1981), in Zimbabwe (1982–86), in Cuba (1986–89), in Brazil (1989–91), and at the Permanent Mission of the Holy See to the United Nations in Geneva, Switzerland (1991–95). He was elected titular archbishop of Gunela on July 12, 1995, and received the Episcopal Consecration on September 24, 1995, in Saint-Malo, France. Archbishop Christophe Pierre was appointed apostolic nuncio to Haiti (1995–99), to Uganda (1999–2007), and to Mexico (2007–16). Archbishop Pierre speaks French, English, Italian, Spanish, and Portuguese. He has a master's degree in sacred theology (Paris,

1971) and a doctorate in canon law from the Pontifical Lateran University, Rome (1973–77).

Susan K. Wood, SCL, a Sister of Charity of Leavenworth, Kansas, is academic dean and professor at Regis College in Toronto. She received her doctorate from Marquette University in 1986 and was professor of systematic theology at Marquette from 2005 to 2019. Her research interests have focused on the theology of ordained ministry, the ecclesial dimensions of sacramental theology, and the theology of Henri de Lubac. Very active in ecumenical work, she currently serves on the US Lutheran-Roman Catholic dialogue, the North American Roman Catholic-Orthodox Theological Consultation, and the International Lutheran-Catholic Dialogue. She coauthored a book on Catholic-Lutheran relations with Timothy Wengert, marking the 500th anniversary of the Reformation, *A Shared Spiritual Journey, Lutherans and Catholics Travel Toward Unity* (Paulist), and three other books. She is the editor of *Ordering the Baptismal Priesthood* (Liturgical Press, 2003) and coeditor, with Alberto Garcia, of *Critical Issues in Ecclesiology: Essays in Honor of Carl E. Braaten* (Eerdmans, 2011). She is an associate editor of *Pro Ecclesia* and serves on the editorial advisory board of the journal *Ecclesiology*. Wood is a past president of the Catholic Theological Society of America.

Bibliography

Alazraki, Valentina. "Two Years into His Pontificate: An Interview with a Mexican Media Company *Televisa*." *L'Osservatore Romano* 14, April 3, 2015.

Alessandri, Hernan. *Il futuro di Puebla*. Milan: Jaca Book, 1981.

Anzorena, Oscar. *Tiempo de Violencia y Utopía: 1966–1976*. Buenos Aires: Editorial Contrapunto, 1988.

Aquinas, Saint Thomas. *Summa Theologica*. Translated by the Fathers of the English Dominican Province. New York: Benziger Brothers, 1911–25.

Arendt, Hannah. *The Origins of Totalitarianism*. San Diego: Harcourt, 1968.

Arrupe, Pedro, SJ. "Letter on Inculturation, to the Whole Society." In *Other Apostolates Today*, vol. 3, *Selected Letters and Addresses*, edited by Jerome Aizala, SJ, 171–81. St. Louis: Institute of Jesuit Sources, 1981.

Augustine, Daniela C. *Pentecost, Hospitality, and Transfiguration: Towards a Spirit-Inspired Vision of Social Transformation*. Cleveland, TN: CPT Press, 2012.

Augustine, Saint, and Henry Chadwick. *Confessions*. Oxford: Oxford University Press, 2009.

Aumont, Michèle. *Philosophie sociopolitique de Gaston Fessard, S.J., «Pax nostra.»* Paris: Cerf, 2004.

———. *Ignace de Loyola et Gaston Fessard: l'un par l'autre*. Paris: L'Harmattan, 2006.

Azcuy, Virginia R., Jose C. Caamaño, and Carlos M. Galli, eds. *La eclesiología del Concilio Vaticano II: Memoria, reforma y profecía*. Buenos Aires: Agapé-Facultad de Teología, 2015.

Baronetto, Luis Miguel. *Vida y Martirio de Mons. Angelelli, Obispo de la Iglesia Católica*. Córdoba: Ediciones Tiempo Latinoamericano, 1996.

Bauman, Zygmunt. *Liquid Modernity*. Cambridge, UK: Polity Press, 2000.

Benedict XVI, Pope. "Message to the Participants of the International Convention on the Occasion of the Centenary of the Birth of the Swiss Theologian Hans Urs von Balthasar." October 6, 2005. https://w2. vatican.va/content/benedict-xvi/en/messages/pont-messages/2005/documents/hf_ben-xvi_mes_20051006_von-balthasar.html.

———. *Deus Caritas Est*. Encyclical Letter. December 25, 2005. http://w2 .vatican.va/content/benedict-xvi/en/encyclicals/documents/hf_ben -xvi_enc_20051225_deus-caritas-est.html.

———. "Homily, Mass before the Shrine of Meryem Ana Evì." Ephesus, November 29, 2006. http://w2.vatican.va/content/benedict-xvi/en /homilies/2006/documents/hf_ben-xvi_hom_20061129_ephesus.html.

———. "Homily at Mass for the Opening of the Fifth General Conference of the Latin American and Caribbean Bishops." Aparecida, May 13, 2007. http://w2.vatican.va/content/benedict-xvi/en/homilies/2007 /documents/hf_ben-xvi_hom_20070513_conference-brazil.html.

———. "Opening Address to the Fifth General Conference of the Bishops of Latin America." Shrine of Aparecida, May 13, 2007. http://w2 .vatican.va/content/benedict-xvi/en/speeches/2007/may/documents /hf_ben-xvi_spe_20070513_conference-aparecida.html.

———. "Address after screening the film 'Art and Faith—*Via Pulchritudinis.*'" October 25, 2012. http://w2.vatican.va/content/benedict-xvi/en /speeches/2012/october/documents/hf_ben-xvi_spe_20121025_arte -fede.html.

Benjamin, Walter. *The Origin of German Tragic Drama*. London: Verso, 1998.

Bergoglio, Jorge Mario. *"Condurre nelle grandi e nelle piccole circostanze." Boletín de Espiritualidad* 73 (October 1981).

———. *Meditaciones para religiosos*. Buenos Aires: Diego de Torres, 1982.

———. "La Acusación de sí mismo." Pp. 118–25 in *Reflexiones espirituales sobre la vida apostólica*. 1987. Reprint, Bilbao: Mensajero, 2013.

———. "Prologue." In *Las Cartas de la Tribulació*, by Lorenzo Ricci, SJ, and Juan Roothaan, SJ. Buenos Aires: Diego de Torres, 1988.

———. "En el solo poner la esperanza." Pp. 253–69 in *Reflexiones en esperanza*. 1992. Reprint, Madrid: Romana, 2013.

———. "Silencio y Palabra." Pp. 115–53 in *Reflexiones en esperanza*. 1992. Reprint, Madrid: Romana, 2013.

———. "Y conforme a esta esperanza." Pp. 221–51 in *Reflexiones en esperanza*. 1992. Reprint, Madrid: Romana, 2013. Originally published in *CIS*, Vol. XX, Roma, 1990, 63–64, pp. 121–42.

———. *Reflexiones en esperanza*. Buenos Aires: Universidad de San Salvador, 1992. Reprint, Madrid: Romana, 2013.

———. "Presentation of Luigi Giussani, *El atractivo de Jesucristo*." Buenos Aires, April 27, 2001. http://archivio.traces-cl.com/Giu2001/argent.htm.

———. "Prologue." In *La verdad los hará libres: Congreso internacional sobre la Encíclica* Veritatis splendor, edited by Carlos Alberto Scarponi, 19–36. Buenos Aires: Paulinas, 2005.

———. "Mensaje a las comunidades educativas." April 23, 2008. http://www.arzbaires.org.ar/inicio/homilias/homilias2008.htm#educacion.

———. "Propuesta de Aparecida para la Pastoral de la Iglesia en Argentina." Message to the meeting of Sociedad Argentina de Liturgia. June 15, 2009. http://www.arzbaires.org.ar/inicio/homilias/homilias2009.htm#Propuesta_de_Aparecida_para_la_Pastoral_de_la_Iglesia_en_Argentina.

———. *Nosotros como ciudadanos, nosotros como pueblo: Hacia un bicentenario en justicia y solidaridad 2010–2016*. Buenos Aires: Claretiana, 2011.

———. "Dios en la ciudad: Palabras iniciales en el Primer Congreso Regional de Pastoral Urbana." In *Dios en la ciudad*, edited by Jorge Eduardo Scheinig, 9–22. Buenos Aires: San Pablo, 2012.

———. "Message to the Cardinals in the General Congregations prior to the Conclave." March 9, 2013. https://www.telegraph.co.uk/news/2017/03/17/popes-handwritten-notes-2013-speech-cardinals-now-published/.

———. *Noi come cittadini noi come popolo. Verso un bicentenario in giustizia e solidarietà 2010–2016*. Milan: Jaca Book, 2013. Italian translation of *Nosotros como ciudadanos*.

———. *Chi sono i gesuiti: Storia della Compagnia di Gesù*. Bologna: EMI, 2014.

———. "Criteri di azione apostolica." In *Pastorale Sociale*, edited by Marco Gallo, Italian translation by A. Taroni. Milan: Jaca Book, 2015. Originally published in *Boletín de Espiritualidad de la Compañia de Jesús*, January 1980.

———. "Discorso di aperture alla Congregazione pronvicial." In *Pastorale Sociale*, edited by Marco Gallo, Italian translation by A. Taroni. Milan: Jaca Book, 2015.

————. *"Fede e giustizia nell'apostolato dei gesuiti."* In *Pastorale Sociale*, edited by Marco Gallo, Italian translation by A. Taroni. Milan: Jaca Book, 2015.

————. *"Necessità di un'antropologia politica: Un problema pastorale."* Originally published in *Stromata*, January–June 1989. In *Pastorale sociale*, edited by Marco Gallo, Italian translation by A. Taroni. Milan: Jaca Book, 2015.

————. *"Servizio della fede e promozione della giustizia."* Originally published in *Stromata*, January–June 1988. In *Pastorale sociale*, edited by Marco Gallo, Italian translation by A. Taroni. Milan: Jaca Book, 2015.

————. *"Una istituzione che vive il suo charisma: Discorso di apertura della Congregazione provincial"* (San Miguel, Buenos Aires, February 18, 1974). In *Pastorale sociale*, edited by Marco Gallo, Italian translation by A. Taroni, 234–37. Milan: Jaca Book, 2015.

————. *"Farsi custodi dell'eredità"* (June 1981). In *Nel Cuore di Ogni Padre: Alle Radici Della mia Spiritualità*, by Pope Francis, 13–34. Milan: Rizzoli, 2016.

————. *Nei tuoi occhi è la mia parola: Omelie e discorsi di Buenos Aires 1999–2013*. Edited by Antonio Spadaro, SJ. Translated by Giuseppe Romano. Milan: Rizzoli, 2016.

————. *"El mensaje de Aparecida a los presbíteros."* In *En tus ojos está mi palabra: Homilías y discursos de Buenos Aires, 1999–2013*, edited by Antonio Spadaro, SJ, 797–806. Madrid: Claretianas, 2018.

————. *"La misión de los discípulos al servicio de la Vida Plena."* In *En tus ojos está mi palabra: Homilías y discursos de Buenos Aires, 1999–2013*, edited by Antonio Spadaro, SJ, 852–59. Madrid: Claretianas, 2018.

————. *"La verdad que más brilla es la verdad de la misericordia."* In *En tus ojos está mi palabra: Homilías y discursos de Buenos Aires, 1999–2013*, edited by Antonio Spadaro, SJ, 1013–16. Madrid: Claretianas, 2018.

————. *"Volver a las raíces de la fe: la misión como propuesta y desafío."* In *En tus ojos está mi palabra: Homilías y discursos de Buenos Aires, 1999–2013*, edited by Antonio Spadaro, SJ, 745–54. Madrid: Claretianas, 2018.

Bergoglio, Jorge Mario, and Abraham Skorka. *Sobre el Cielo y la Tierra*. Buenos Aires: Sudamericana, 2010. Translated into English as *On Heaven and Earth* (London: Bloomsbury, 2013).

Bergson, Henri. *Creative Evolution*. Translated by Arthur Mitchell. 1911. Reprint, New York: Dover, 1998.

Bernanos, Georges. "Frère Martin." *Esprit* 19, no. 183 (October 1951): 433–45.

Bianchi, Enrique Ciro. *Pobres en este mundo, ricos en la fe (Sant 2,5): La fe de los pobres en América Latina, según Rafael Tello*. Buenos Aires: Agape, 2012.

Biehl, Andrés and Patricio Velasco, eds. *Pedro Morandé: Textos sociológicos escogidos*. Santiago: Ediciones Universidad Católica de Chile, 2017.

Boasso, Fernando. *¿Qué es la Pastoral Popular?* Buenos Aires: Patria Grande, 1974.

Borges, Jorge Luis. "El otro, el mismo." P. 5 in *Obras Completas*. Barcelona: Círculo de Lectores/Emecé, 1995.

Borghesi, Massimo. *Romano Guardini: Dialettica e antropologia*. Rome: Studium, 1990.

———. *L'era dello Spirito: Secolarizzazione ed escatologia moderna*. Rome: Studium, 2008.

———. "Amelia Podetti: La mujer que inspire a Bergoglio." *Aleteia*, November 24, 2017. https://es.aleteia.org/2017/11/24/amelia-podetti-la-mujer-que-inspiro-a-bergoglio/.

———. *Jorge Mario Bergoglio: Una Biografia Intellettuale. Dialectica e Mistica*. Milan: Jaca Book, 2017.

———. *Hegel: La cristologia idealista*. Rome: Studium, 2018.

———. "How Francis Thinks." *Il blog di Massimo Borghesi* (blog). February 9, 2018. https://www.massimoborghesi.com/how-francis-thinks-il-the-tablet-dedica-la-copertina-al-volume-sul-pensiero-del-papa/.

———. *Romano Guardini: Antinomia della vita conoscenza affettiva*. Milan: Jaca Book, 2018.

———. *The Mind of Pope Francis: Jorge Mario Bergoglio's Intellectual Journey*. Translated by Barry Hudock. Collegeville, MN: Liturgical Press, 2018.

Braun, Harald E. and Jesús Pérez-Magallón, eds. *The Transatlantic Hispanic Baroque: Complex Identities in the Atlantic World*. Farnham: Ashgate, 2014.

Brunstetter, Daniel R. "Sepúlveda, Las Casas and the Other: Exploring the Tension between Moral Universalism and Alterity." *Review of Politics* 72, no. 3 (2010): 409–35.

Buttiglione, Rocco. *Karol Wojtyła: The Thought of the Man Who Became John Paul II*. Translated by Paolo Guietti and Francesca Murphy. Grand Rapids, MI: Eerdmans, 1997.

———. *Il pensiero dell'uomo che divenne Giovanni Paolo II*. Milan: Mondadori, 1998.

————. "The Joy of Love and the Consternation of Theologians." *L'Osservatore Romano*, July 19, 2016. http://www.osservatoreromano.va/en/news /joy-love-and-consternation-theologians.

————. "*Amoris Laetitia.* Risposte ai critici." *Lateranum* 83 (2017): 191–239.

————. "Elementos para interpretar el Papado latinoamericano: A partir de algunas reflexiones de Alberto Methol-Ferré." *Humanitas* 22, no. 86 (Spring 2017): 66–79. http://www.humanitasreview.com/16-anthropology -culture/20-elements-for-interpreting-the-latin-american-papacy.

————. *Risposte amichevoli ai critici di* Amoris Laetitia. Milan: Ares, 2017.

Casarella, Peter J. "The Painted Word." *The Journal of Hispanic/Latino Theology* 6 (November 1998): 18–42.

————. "Solidarity as the Fruit of Communion: *Ecclesia in America*, 'Post-Liberation Theology,' and the Earth." *Communio: International Catholic Review* 27 (Spring 2000): 98–123.

Catholic Church. *Catechism of the Catholic Church*. 2nd ed. Vatican: Libreria Editrice Vaticana, 2012.

Cavanaugh, William T. *Field Hospital: The Church's Engagement with a Wounded World*. Grand Rapids, MI: Eerdmans, 2016.

Cioran, E.M. (Emil Mihai). *Tears and Saints*. Chicago: University of Chicago Press, 1995.

Conferencia del Episcopado Mexicano. *Carta pastoral del encuentro con Jesucristo a la solidaridad con todos: El encuentro con Jesucristo, camino de conversión, comunión, solidaridad y misión en México en el umbral del tercer milenio*. México: Conferencia del Episcopado Mexicano, 2000.

Conferencia Episcopal Argentina. *Declaración del Episcopado Argentino sobre la adaptación a la realidad actual del país de las Conclusiones de la II Conferencia General del Episcopado Latinoamericano (Medellín)* [Documento de San Miguel], 1969. http://www.familiasecnacional.org.ar/wp -content/uploads/2017/08/1969-ConclusionesMedellin.pdf.

Congregation for Divine Worship and the Discipline of the Sacraments. "Decree on the Celebration of the Blessed Virgin Mary Mother of the Church in the General Roman Calendar." February 11, 2018. http: //www.vatican.va/roman_curia/congregations/ccdds/documents /rc_con_ccdds_doc_20180211_decreto-mater-ecclesiae_en.html.

————. *Directory on Popular Piety and the Liturgy: Principles and Guidelines*. Vatican City, December 2001. http://www.vatican.va/roman_curia /congregations/ccdds/documents/rc_con_ccdds_doc_20020513_vers -direttorio_en.html.

Congregation for the Doctrine of the Faith. "Letter *Placuit Deo* to the Bishops of the Catholic Church on Certain Aspects of Christian Salvation." February 22, 2018. http://www.vatican.va/roman_curia/congregations /cfaith/documents/rc_con_cfaith_doc_20180222_placuit-deo_en .html.

Consejo Episcopal Latinoamericano [CELAM]. *Iglesia y religiosidad popular en América Latina: Ponencias y documento final.* Bogotá: CELAM, 1977.

———. *Religión y cultura: Perspectivas de la evangelización de la cultura desde Puebla.* Bogotá: CELAM, 1981.

———. *Globalización y nueva evangelización en América Latina y el Caribe. Reflexiones del CELAM 1999–2003,* no. 165. Bogotá: CELAM, 2003.

———. *Aparecida: Documento Conclusivo, V Conferencia General del Episcopado Latinoamericano y del Caribe.* Bogotá: CELAM, 2007. https://www .celam.org/aparecida/Espanol.pdf (original text). https://www.celam .org/aparecida/Ingles.pdf (English translation).

Cuda, Emilce. *Para Leer a Francisco: Teología, Ética, y Política.* Buenos Aires: Manantial, 2016.

Cullen, Carlos. *Reflexiones desde América.* Rosario: Fundación Ross, 1986.

Davies, Norman. *God's Playground: A History of Poland.* 2 vols. Oxford: Oxford University Press, 1981–83.

De Lubac, Henri. *The Church: Paradox and Mystery.* Translated by James R. Dunne. Staten Island: Alba House, 1969. Originally published as *Paradoxe et Mystère de L'Eglise* (Paris: Aubier-Montaigne, 1967). Translated into Italian as *Paradosso e mistero della chiesa* (Brescia: Queriniana, 1968).

———. *The Motherhood of the Church.* Translated by Sergia Englund. San Francisco: Ignatius Press, 1982. Originally published as *Les églises particulières dans l'Église universelle, suivi de La maternité de l'église, et d'une interview recueillie par G. Jarczyk* (Paris: Aubier-Montaigne, 1971).

———. "Particular Churches in the Universal Church." In *Motherhood of the Church,* translated by Sergia Englund, 171–335. San Francisco: Ignatius Press, 1982.

———. *De Lubac: A Theologian Speaks.* Los Angeles: Twin Circle Publishing Co., 1985.

———. *Paradoxes of Faith.* San Francisco: Ignatius Press, 1987.

———. *Catholicism: Christ and the Common Destiny of Man.* Translated by Lancelot C. Sheppard and Elizabeth Englund, OCD. San Francisco: Ignatius Press, 1988.

———. *At the Service of the Church: Henri de Lubac Reflects on the Circumstances That Occasioned His Writings*. San Francisco: Ignatius Press, 1993.

———. *The Splendor of the Church*. San Francisco: Ignatius Press, 1999. Originally published as *Méditation sur l'Ėglise* (Paris: Montaigne, 1953).

De Luca, Giuseppe. *Introduzione alla storia della pietà*. Roma: Edizioni di Storia e Letteratura, 1962.

Del Noce, Augusto. *Rosmini e la categoria filosofico-politica di Risorgimento* [unpublished]. http://www.cattedrarosmini.org and http://www.fondazioneaugustodelnoce.net.

Denaday, Juan Pedro. "Amelia Podetti: una trayectoria olvidada de las Cátedras Nacionales." *Nuevo Mundo, Mundos Nuevos*. August 29, 2013. http://journals.openedition.org/nuevomundo/65663.

Eagleson, John, and Philip J. Scharper, eds. *Puebla and Beyond: Documentation and Commentary*. Maryknoll, NY: Orbis, 1979.

Elizondo, Virgilio. *Métissage, violence culturelle, annonce de l'évangile*. Paris: Institut Catholique, 1978.

———. *The Galilean Journey: The Mexican-American Promise*. Maryknoll, NY: Orbis, 1983; 2nd ed., 2000.

Faggioli, Massimo. "A Wake-Up Call to Liberal Theologians: Academic Theology Needs the Church." *Commonweal*, May 18, 2018.

Fares, Diego, SJ. *Papa Francesco è come un bambù: alle radici della cultura dell'incontro*. Milan: Àncora–La Civiltà Cattolica, 2014.

———. *Papa Francisco. La cultura del encuentro*. Buenos Aires: Edhasa, 2014.

———. "Contro lo spirito del 'Accanimento.'" *La Civiltà Cattolica* 4029 (2018): 216–30. http://www.laciviltacattolica.it/articolo/contro-lo-spirito-di-accanimento/.

Fernández, Víctor Manuel. *The Francis Project: Where He Wants to Take the Church*. Translated by Sean O'Neill. New York: Paulist Press, 2016.

———, ed. *Hacia una cultura del encuentro: La propuesta del papa Francisco*. Buenos Aires: EDUCA, 2017.

Fessard, Gaston, SJ. *La Dialectique des Exercises Spirituels de Saint Ignace de Loyola*. 3 vols. Paris: Aubier, 1956–84.

———. *Le mystère de la société. Recherches sur le sens de l'histoire*. Edited by Michel Sales. Namur, Belgium: Culture et Vérité, 1997.

Feuerbach, Ludwig. *The Essence of Christianity*. Mineola, NY: Dover, 2008.

Fiorito, Miguel Ángel. "La Opción Personal de S. Ignacio." *Ciencia y Fe* 12 (1956): 23–56.

———. "Teoría y Práctica de G. Fessard." *Ciencia y Fe* 13 (1957): 333–52.

Francis, Pope. "Address of the Holy Father Pope Francis, Audience with the College of Cardinals, March 15, 2013." https://w2.vatican.va/content /francesco/en/speeches/2013/march/documents/papa-francesco _20130315_cardinali.html.

———. "Meeting with the International Press." Paul VI Audience Hall, March 16, 2013. http://w2.vatican.va/content/francesco/en/speeches /2013/march/documents/papa-francesco_20130316_rappresentanti -media.html.

———. "Address of the Holy Father Francis on the Vigil of Pentecost with the Ecclesial Movements." Saint Peter's Square, May 18, 2013. http://w2.vatican.va/content/francesco/en/speeches/2013/may /documents/papa-francesco_20130518_veglia-pentecoste.html.

———. "Profession of Faith with the Bishops of the Italian Episcopal Conference." Vatican Basilica, May 23, 2013. http://w2.vatican.va/content /francesco/en/homilies/2013/documents/papa-francesco_20130523 _omelia-professio-fidei-cei.html.

———. *Lumen Fidei*. Encyclical Letter. June 29, 2013. http://w2.vatican.va /content/francesco/en/encyclicals/documents/papa-francesco _20130629_enciclica-lumen-fidei.html

———. "Address of Pope Francis to Meeting with Brazil's Leaders of Society." Municipal Theatre, Rio de Janeiro, July 27, 2013. http://w2.vatican .va/content/francesco/en/speeches/2013/july/documents/papa -francesco_20130727_gmg-classe-dirigente-rio.html.

———. "Meeting with the Bishops of Brazil, Archbishop's House, Rio de Janeiro (Brazil)." July 27, 2013. http://w2.vatican.va/content/francesco /en/speeches/2013/july/documents/papa-francesco_20130727_gmg -episcopato-brasile.html.

———. "Lettera a chi non crede. Papa Francesco risponde al giornalista Eugenio Scalfari." *La Repubblica* (Rome), September 4, 2013. http://w2 .vatican.va/content/francesco/en/letters/2013/documents/papa -francesco_20130911_eugenio-scalfari.html.

———. "Address of Holy Father Francis to a Group of Recently Appointed Bishops." Clementine Hall, September 19, 2013. http://w2.vatican.va /content/francesco/en/speeches/2013/september/documents/papa -francesco_20130919_convegno-nuovi-vescovi.html.

———. *Evangelii Gaudium*. Apostolic Exhortation. November 24, 2013. http://w2.vatican.va/content/francesco/en/apost_exhortations /documents/papa-francesco_esortazione-ap_20131124_evangelii -gaudium.html.

————. "Never Be Afraid of Tenderness." Interview by Andrea Tornielli. *Vatican Insider—La Stampa* (Turin), December 14, 2013. http://www .lastampa.it/2013/12/14/esteri/never-be-afraid-of-tenderness -5BqUfVs9r7W1CJIMuHqNeI/pagina.html.

————."Presentation of Christmas Greetings to the Roman Curia." December 22, 2014. http://w2.vatican.va/content/francesco/en/speeches /2014/december/documents/papa-francesco_20141222_curia -romana.html.

————. *Misericordiae Vultus.* Papal Bull. April 11, 2015. https://w2.vatican .va/content/francesco/en/apost_letters/documents/papa-francesco _bolla_20150411_misericordiae-vultus.html.

————. *Laudato Si'.* Encyclical Letter. May 24, 2015. http://w2.vatican.va /content/francesco/en/encyclicals/documents/papa-francesco _20150524_enciclica-laudato-si.html.

————. "Address to the Second World Meeting of Popular Movements." Santa Cruz de la Sierra (Bolivia), July 9, 2015. http://w2.vatican.va /content/francesco/en/speeches/2015/july/documents/papa -francesco_20150709_bolivia-movimenti-popolari.html.

————. Homily. Campo grande, Ñu Guazú, Asunción (Paraguay). July 12, 2015. http://m.vatican.va/content/francesco/en/homilies/2015 /documents/papa-francesco_20150712_paraguay-omelia-nu-guazu .html.

————. "Video Message to Participants in an International Theological Congress Held at the Pontifical Catholic University of Argentina." Buenos Aires, September 1–2, 2015. http://w2.vatican.va/content/francesco /en/messages/pont-messages/2015/documents/papa-francesco _20150903_videomessaggio-teologia-buenos-aires.html.

————. "Address of the Holy Father, Welcoming Ceremony, September 23, 2015." http://w2.vatican.va/content/francesco/en/speeches/2015 /September/documents/papa-francesco_20150923_usa-benvenuto .html.

————. "Address of the Holy Father, Visit to the Joint Session of the United States Congress, September 24, 2015: Apostolic Journey of His Holiness Pope Francis to Cuba, to the United States of America and Visit to the United Nations Headquarters (19–28 September 2015)." https: //w2.vatican.va/content/francesco/en/speeches/2015/september /documents/papa-francesco_20150924_usa-us-congress.html.

————. "Address at the interreligious meeting held at the Ground Zero Memorial in New York." September 25, 2015. http://www

.archivioradiovaticana.va/storico/2015/09/25/pope_francis'_address
_at_ground_zero_memorial_in_new_york/en-1174651.

———. "Meeting with the Participants in the 5th Convention of the Italian Church." Florence, November 10, 2015. http://w2.vatican.va/content /francesco/en/speeches/2015/november/documents/papa-francesco _20151110_firenze-convegno-chiesa-italiana.html.

———. "Communication and Mercy: A Fruitful Encounter." January 24, 2016. http://w2.vatican.va/content/francesco/en/messages /communications/documents/papa-francesco_20160124_messaggio -comunicazioni-sociali.html.

———. "Letter to Cardinal Marc Ouellet." March 19, 2016. http://w2.vatican .va/content/francesco/en/letters/2016/documents/papa-francesco _20160319_pont-comm-america-latina.html.

———. *Amoris Laetitia*. Post-Synodal Apostolic Exhortation. March 19, 2016. http://w2.vatican.va/content/dam/francesco/pdf/apost_exhortations /documents/papa-francesco_esortazione-ap_20160319_amoris-laetitia _en.pdf.

———. "Address of his Holiness Pope Francis to the 36th General Congregation of the Society of Jesus." October 24, 2016. http://w2.vatican.va /content/francesco/en/speeches/2016/october/documents/papa -francesco_20161024_visita-compagnia-gesu.html.

———. "El peligro en tiempos de crisis es buscar un salvador que nos devuelva la identidad y nos defienda con muros." Interview by Antonio Caño and Pablo Orda. *El País* (Madrid), January 22, 2017. http://elpais.com/internacional/2017/01/21/actualidad/1485022162 _846725.html.

———. "Holy Mass for the Solemnity of Pentecost." Homily. June 4, 2017. http://press.vatican.va/content/salastampa/en/bollettino/pubblico /2017/06/04/170604a.html.

———. *Magnum Principium* (note on canon 838 of the Code of Canon Law). Apostolic Letter in the form of *Motu Proprio*. September 3, 2017. https: //press.vatican.va/content/salastampa/en/bollettino/pubblico /2017/09/09/170909a.html.

———. "Address of his Holiness Pope Francis, Reconciliation Liturgy, September 24, 2017: Apostolic Journey of His Holiness Pope Francis to Colombia (September 6–11, 2017)." https://w2.vatican.va/content /francesco/en/prayers/documents/papa-francesco_preghiere _20170908_colombia-bojaya.html.

———. Morning homily in the "Domus Sanctae Marthae" chapel. December 14, 2017. *TV2000*. http://youtu.be/HgtlqQyP1t0.

———. "Meeting with Priests, Consecrated Men and Women and Seminarians, Address of his Holiness Pope Francis." Santiago Cathedral. January 16, 2018. http://w2.vatican.va/content/francesco/en/speeches/2018/january/documents/papa-francesco_20180116_cile-santiago-religiosi.html.

———. *Gaudete et Exsultate*. Apostolic Exhortation. March 19, 2018. http://w2.vatican.va/content/francesco/en/apost_exhortations/documents/papa-francesco_esortazione-ap_20180319_gaudete-et-exsultate.html.

———. "Letter Sent by the Holy Father to the Bishops of Chile Following the Report of Archbishop Charles J. Scicluna." April 11, 2018. https://w2.vatican.va/content/francesco/en/letters/2018/documents/papa-francesco_20180408_lettera-vescovi-cile.html.

———. Private letter of Pope Francis to Chile's bishops. May 15, 2018. http://www.t13.cl/noticia/nacional/la-transcripcion-completa-del-documento-reservado-papa-entrego-obispos-chilenos.

———. Homily. Chapel, Casa Santa Marta. *Memorial of the Blessed Virgin Mary, Mother of the Church*, May 21, 2018. https://www.vaticannews.va/en/pope-francis/mass-casa-santa-marta/2018-05/pope-francis-mass-santa-marta-mary-church-woman-mother.html.

———. "Al Pueblo de Dios que peregrina en Chile." Letter to Chilean Church. May 31, 2018. http://w2.vatican.va/content/francesco/es/letters/2018/documents/papa-francesco_20180531_lettera-popolodidio-cile.html.

———. "Letter of His Holiness to the People of God." August 20, 2018. http://w2.vatican.va/content/francesco/en/letters/2018/documents/papa-francesco_20180820_lettera-popolo-didio.html.

———. "Discours du Pape François aux prêtres du diocèse de Créteil (France)." October 1, 2018. http://w2.vatican.va/content/francesco/fr/speeches/2018/october/documents/papa-francesco_20181001_sacerdoti-creteil.html.

Francis, Pope, Antonio Spadaro, and Shaun Whiteside. *My Door Is Always Open: A Conversation on Faith, Hope and the Church in a Time of Change*. London: Bloomsbury Publishing, 2014.

Galli, Carlos M. "El 'retorno' del pueblo de Dios. Un concepto-símbolo de la eclesiología del Concilio a Francisco." In *La eclesiología del Concilio Vaticano II: Memoria, reforma y profecía*, edited by Virginia R. Azcuy, Jose C. Caamaño, and Carlos M. Galli, 405–72. Buenos Aires: Agapé-Facultad de Teología, 2015.

————. *Cristo, Maria, la Chiesa e i popoli: La mariologia di papa Francesco.* Rome: Libreria Editrice Vaticana, 2017.

Gera, Lucio. "*Sunt lacrymae rerum* (Hay lágrimas en las cosas)." *Notas de pastoral jocista* (1957): 16–23.

————. *Escritos Teológico-Pastorales de Lucio Gera.* Vol. 1, *Del Preconcilio a la Conferencia de Puebla (1956–1981).* Edited by Virginia R. Azcuy, Carlos M. Galli, and Marcelo González. Buenos Aires: Agapé-Facultad de Teología, 2006.

————. *Escritos Teológico-Pastorales de Lucio Gera.* Vol. 2, *De la Conferencia de Puebla a nuestros días.* Edited by Virginia R. Azcuy, Carlos M. Galli, and Marcelo González. Buenos Aires: Agapé-Facultad de Teología, 2007.

Gillis, Hugh. "Gaston Fessard and the Nature of Authority." *Interpretation* 16, no. 3 (Spring 1989): 445–64.

Giussani, Luigi. *He Is If He Changes: Notes from Conversations with Young People.* Supplement no. 7/8 to *30 Days*, 7–8. Rome: 30Giorni, 1994.

————. *Afecto y morada.* Translated by Carmen Giussani. Madrid: Encuentro, 2004. Originally published as *Affezione e dimora* (Milan: Biblioteca Universale Rizzoli, 2001).

————. "Io e i ciellini, la nostra fede in faccia al mondo." Interview by Gian Guido Vecchi. *Corriere della Sera* (Rome), October 15, 2004. http://www.corriere.it/Primo_Piano/Cronache/2005/02_Febbraio/22/corriere.shtml.

————. *Il Movimento di Comunione e Liberazione (1954–1986): Conversazioni con Robi Ronza.* Milan: Biblioteca Universale Rizzoli, 2014.

Goizueta, Roberto. *Caminemos con Jesús: Toward a Hispanic/Latino Theology of Accompaniment.* Maryknoll, NY: Orbis, 1995.

Guardini, Romano. *Das Wesen des Christentums.* Würzburg: Werkbund, 1938. Originally published as "Das Wesen des Christentums," *Die Schildgenossen* 9 (1929): 129–52. Translated into Spanish as *La esencia del cristianismo: Una ética para nuestro tiempo* (Madrid: Cristiandad, 2006).

————. *Power and Responsibility: A Course of Action for the New Age.* Translated by Elinor C. Briefs. Chicago: Henry Regenery, 1961. Originally published as *Die Macht* (Würzberg: Werkbund, 1951).

————. *The End of the Modern World: A Search for Orientation.* Wilmington, DE: ISI Books, 1998. First English edition, New York: Sheed and Ward, 1957. Originally published as *Das Ende der Neuzeit* (Basel: Hess, 1950).

————. *Der Gegensatz: Versuche zu einer Philosophie des Lebendig-Konkreten.* 4th ed. Mainz: Matthias-Grünewald, 1998. First German edition, Mainz: Matthias-Grünewald, 1925.

Guerra López, Rodrigo. *Volver a la persona. El método filosófico de Karol Wojtyla.* Madrid: Caparrós, 2002.

————. "The Relevance of Some Reflections by Karol Wojtyła for Understanding 'Amoris Laetitia': creative fidelity." *L'Osservatore Romano,* July 22, 2016. http://www.osservatoreromano.va/en/news/relevance -some-reflections-karol-wojtyla-understan.

————. "Aprender los unos de los otros." Chiesa Espresso On Line, *L'Espresso,* August 18, 2016. http://chiesa.espresso.repubblica.it/articolo/1351355 .html.

————. "Para comprender *Amoris Laetitia.*" *Medellín* 43, no. 168 (May–August 2017): 409–47.

————. "Cristianismo y cambio de época: Transformaciones educativas y culturales de la sociedad y de la Iglesia en América Latina" (forthcoming).

Guido, Ángel. *Fusión Hispano-indígena en la arquitectura colonial.* Rosario: La Casa del Libro, 1925.

Herrera, Luis, SJ. "Whisper to Those in Despair: The Best Wine Is Yet to Come: Memory, Hope, and Resistance." In *The Search for God in América,* edited by Peter Casarella and Maria Clara Bingemer. Volume forthcoming with The Catholic University of America Press.

Ignatius of Loyola, Saint. *The Spiritual Exercises of St. Ignatius.* Edited by John F. Thornton. Translated by Louis J. Puhl, SJ. New York: Random House, 2000.

Ivereigh, Austen. *Catholicism and Politics in Argentina, 1810–1960.* New York: St. Martin's Press, 1995.

————. *The Great Reformer: Francis and the Making of a Radical Pope.* New York: Henry Holt, 2014.

————. "The Papal Obsession with Getting Close and Concrete." *Crux,* January 23, 2017. http://cruxnow.com/analysis/2017/01/23/papal -obsession-getting-close-concrete/.

————. Review of Massimo Borghesi, *Jorge Mario Bergoglio: Una biografia intellettuale. Crux,* November 18, 2017. http://cruxnow.com/book -review/2017/11/18/new-book-looks-intellectual-history-francis -pope-polarity/.

———. "Discernment in a Time of Tribulation: Pope Francis and the Church in Chile." *Thinking Faith*, May 8, 2018. https://www.thinkingfaith.org /articles/discernment-time-tribulation-pope-francis-and-church-chile.

———. "A Time to Keep Silence." *Thinking Faith*, August 30, 2018. https: //www.thinkingfaith.org/articles/time-keep-silence.

———. "The Pope and the *Patria Grande*: How Francis is promoting Latin America's Continental Destiny." In *The Search for God in America*, edited by Maria Clara Bingemer and Peter Casarella. Volume forthcoming with The Catholic University of America Press.

———. *Wounded Shepherd: Pope Francis's Struggle to Convert the Catholic Church*. New York: Henry Holt, 2019.

John Paul II, Pope. "Opening Address to the Puebla Conference." Puebla, Mexico, January 28, 1979. http://w2.vatican.va/content/john-paul-ii /en/speeches/1979/january/documents/hf_jp-ii_spe_19790128 _messico-puebla-episc-latam.html.

———. *Redemptor Hominis*. Encyclical Letter. March 4, 1979. http://w2 .vatican.va/content/john-paul-ii/en/encyclicals/documents/hf_jp-ii _enc_04031979_redemptor-hominis.html.

———. "Homily in Victory Square." Warsaw, June 2, 1979. http://w2.vatican .va/content/john-paul-ii/en/homilies/1979/documents/hf_jp-ii _hom_19790602_polonia-varsavia.html.

———. *Mulieris Dignitatem*. Apostolic Letter. August 15, 1988. http://w2 .vatican.va/content/john-paul-ii/en/apost_letters/1988/documents /hf_jp-ii_apl_19880815_mulieris-dignitatem.html.

———. *Christifideles Laici*. Post-Synodal Apostolic Exhortation. December 30, 1988. http://w2.vatican.va/content/john-paul-ii/en/apost_exhortations /documents/hf_jp-ii_exh_30121988_christifideles-laici.html.

———. *Redemptoris Missio*. Encyclical Letter. December 7, 1990. http://w2 .vatican.va/content/john-paul-ii/en/encyclicals/documents/hf_jp-ii _enc_07121990_redemptoris-missio.html.

———. *Centesimus Annus*. Encyclical Letter. May 1, 1991. https://w2.vatican .va/content/john-paul-ii/en/encyclicals/documents/hf_jp-ii_enc _01051991_centesimus-annus.html.

———. *Pastores Dabo Vobis*. Post-Synodal Apostolic Exhortation. March 25, 1992. http://w2.vatican.va/content/john-paul-ii/en/apost _exhortations/documents/hf_jp-ii_exh_25031992_pastores-dabo -vobis.html.

————. *Ecclesia in America*. Post-Synodal Apostolic Exhortation. January 22, 1999. http://w2.vatican.va/content/john-paul-ii/en/apost _exhortations/documents/hf_jp-ii_exh_22011999_ecclesia-in-america .html.

————. "Letter of His Holiness Pope John Paul II to Artists." April 4, 1999. http://w2.vatican.va/content/john-paul-ii/en/letters/1999/documents /hf_jp-ii_let_23041999_artists.html.

————. General Audience. April 14, 1999. https://w2.vatican.va/content /john-paul-ii/en/audiences/1999/documents/hf_jp-ii_aud_14041999 .html.

————. *Novo Millennio Ineunte*. Apostolic Letter. January 6, 2001. http://w2 .vatican.va/content/john-paul-ii/en/apost_letters/2001/documents /hf_jp-ii_apl_20010106_novo-millennio-ineunte.html.

Kasper, Walter. "The Unicity and Multiplicity of Aspects in the Eucharist." *Communio* 12 (1985): 115–38.

Keenan, James, SJ. "The Scandal of Mercy Excludes No One." *Thinking Faith*, December 4, 2015. https://www.thinkingfaith.org/articles/scandal -mercy-excludes-no-one.

Kolenc, Vic. "Sun Bowl's 28,000 Part of Papal Binational Mass." *El Paso Times*, February 17, 2016. http://www.elpasotimes.com/story/news/local /juarez/pope/2016/02/17/pope-francis-juarez-mexico-elpaso-sun -bowl-catholics/80393464/.

Konieczny, Mary Ellen, Charles C. Camosy, and Tricia C. Bruce, eds. *Polarization in the US Catholic Church: Naming the Wounds, Beginning to Heal*. Collegeville, MN: Liturgical Press, 2016.

Kusch, Rodolfo. *Geocultura del hombre americano*. Buenos Aires: Fernando García Cambeiro, 1976.

Lee, Michael E. "Galilean Journey Revisited: *Mestizaje*, Anti-Judaism, and the Dynamics of Exclusion." *Theological Studies* 70 (2009): 377–400.

Levy, Evonne, and Kenneth Mills, eds. *Lexicon of the Hispanic Baroque: Transatlantic Exchange and Transformation*. Austin: University of Texas Press, 2014.

Lezama Lima, José. *La curiosidad barroca: La expresión Americana*. Mexico: Fondo de Cultura Económica, 1993.

Louzeau, Frédéric. *L'anthropologie sociale du Père Gaston Fessard*. Paris: Presses Universitaires de France, 2009.

Luciani, Rafael. *Pope Francis and the Theology of the People*. Translated by Phillip Berryman. Maryknoll, NY: Orbis, 2017.

Maritain, Jacques. *Distinguer pour unir, ou, Les degrés du savoir*. Paris: Desclés, 1932.

Martí, Antonio. *La preceptiva retórica española en el Siglo de Oro*. Madrid: Gredos, 1972.

Matovina, Timothy. "Theologies of Guadalupe: From the Spanish Colonial Era to John Paul II." *Theological Studies* 70 (March 2009): 61–91.

Merecki, Jaroslaw. "Fidelity That Is Too Creative Becomes Infidelity," in Sandro Magister, "Second Challenge to L'Osservatore Romano. Merecki vs. Guerra López." Chiesa Espresso Online. *L'Espresso* (Rome), August 4, 2016. http://chiesa.espresso.repubblica.it/articolo/1351351bdc4.html?eng=y.

Merton, Thomas. *Conjectures of a Guilty Bystander*. New York: Image, 2014.

Methol Ferré, Alberto. *La dialectica hombre-naturaleza*. Montevideo: IEPAL, 1966.

———. *El Uruguay como problema: En la Cuenca del Plata entre Argentina y Brasil*. Montevideo: Diálogo, 1967.

———. "Marco histórico de la religiosidad popular." In *Iglesia y religiosidad popular en América Latina: Ponencias y documento final*, edited by CELAM, 47–56. Bogotá: CELAM, 1977.

———. "El resurgimiento católico latinoamericano." In *Religión y cultura: Perspectivas de la evangelización de la cultura desde Puebla*, edited by CELAM, 63–124. Bogotá: CELAM, 1981.

———. "La Chiesa, popolo fra i popoli." In *Il risorgimento cattolico latino-americano*, translated by P. di Pauli and C. Perfetti, 139–55. Bologna: CSEO, 1983.

———. "La Integración de América en el pensamiento de Peròn." [Unpublished paper; from the private papers of Alberto Methol Ferré]. http://www.metholferre.com/obras/conferencias/capitulos/detalle.php?id=7.

Methol Ferré, Alberto, and Alver Metalli. *El Papa y el filósofo*. Buenos Aires: Editorial Biblos, 2013.

Milia, Jorge. *Maestro Francesco: Gli allievi del Papa ricordano il loro professore*. Milan: Mondadori, 2014.

Morandé, Pedro. *Cultura y modernización en América Latina: Ensayo sociológico acerca de la crisis del desarrollismo y de su superación*. Santiago: Pontificia Universidad Católica de Chile, 1984.

———. *Iglesia y cultura en América Latina*. Lima: Paulinas, 1989.

————. "La formación del ethos barroco como núcleo de la identidad cultural iberoamericana." In *América Latina y la Doctrina Social de la Iglesia: Diálogo latinoamericano-alemán*, vol. 2, *Identidad cultural y modernización*, edited by Carlos M. Galli and Luis Scherz. Buenos Aires: Paulinas, 1992.

Naab, Kathleen. "Pope: Do We Know the Other Lesson From the Parable of the Good Samaritan?" *Zenit: The World Seen from Rome*, April 27, 2016. https://zenit.org/articles/pope-do-we-know-the-other-lesson-from -the-parable-of-the-good-samaritan/.

Neuhaus, Richard John. *American Babylon: Notes of a Christian Exile*. New York: Basic Books, 2009.

Nguyen-Hong, Giao. *Le Verbe dans l'histoire. La philosophie de l'historicité du Père Gaston Fessard*. Preface by J. Ladriere. Bibliothèque Des Archives De Philosophie; Nouv. Sér., 17. Paris: Beauchesne, 1974.

Nichols, Aidan. *The Thought of Benedict XVI: An Introduction to the Theology of Joseph Ratzinger*. New York: Burnes & Oates, 2005.

————. *Rome and the Eastern Churches: A Study in Schism*. 2nd ed. San Francisco: Ignatius Press, 2010.

Paredes, Mario J. *The History of the National Encuentros: Hispanic Americans in the One Catholic Church*. New York/Mahwah, NJ: Paulist Press, 2015.

Paul VI, Pope. *Ecclesiam Suam*. Encyclical Letter. August 6, 1964. http://w2 .vatican.va/content/paul-vi/en/encyclicals/documents/hf_p-vi_enc _06081964_ecclesiam.html.

————. "Address of Pope Paul VI During the Last General Meeting of the Second Vatican Council, 7 December 1965." https://w2.vatican.va /content/paul-vi/en/speeches/1965/documents/hf_p-vi_spe _19651207_epilogo-concilio.html.

————. *Evangelii Nuntiandi*. Apostolic Exhortation. December 8, 1975. http: //w2.vatican.va/content/paul-vi/en/apost_exhortations/documents /hf_p-vi_exh_19751208_evangelii-nuntiandi.html.

Pelton, Robert S., CSC. "CELAM and the Emerging Reception of the 'Bridge Theology' of Pope Francis: From Marcos Gregorio McGrath to the Latin American Church Today." *Horizonte: Revista de Estudos de Teologia E Ciências da Religião* 16, no. 50 (2018): 454–81.

Petrache, Ana. *Gaston Fessard, un chrétien de rite dialectique?* Paris: Les Éditions du Cerf, 2017.

Pew Research Center. "The Shifting Religious Identity of Latinos in the United States." May 7, 2014. http://www.pewforum.org/2014/05/07 /the-shifting-religious-identity-of-latinos-in-the-united-states/.

————. "The Future of World Religions: Population Growth Projections 2010–2050." April 2, 2015. http://www.pewforum.org/2015/04/02 /religious-projections-2010-2050/.

————. "News Use Across Social Media Platforms 2017." September 2017. http://www.journalism.org/wpcontent/uploads/sites/8/2017/09 /PJ_17.08.23_socialMediaUpdate_FINAL.pdf.

Podetti, Amelia. *La irrupción de América en la historia*. Buenos Aires: Centro de Investigaciones Culturales, 1981.

————. *Comentario a la Introducción a la Fenomenología del Espíritu*. Introduction by Jorge Mario Bergoglio. Buenos Aires: Editorial Biblos, 2007.

Putnam, Robert D. *Bowling Alone: The Collapse and Revival of the American Community*. New York: Simon & Schuster, 2000.

Rahner, Hugo. "Die Grabschrift des Loyola." *Stimmen der Zeit* (1947): 321–39.

Ratzinger, Joseph. "The Current Situation of Faith and Theology: Meeting with the Doctrinal Commissions of Latin America." Guadalajara, Mexico, May 7, 1996. http://www.vatican.va/roman_curia /congregations/cfaith/incontri/rc_con_cfaith_19960507_guadalajara -ratzinger_en.html.

————. "Funeral Homily for Msgr. Luigi Giussani." *Communio* 31, no. 4 (Winter 2004): 685–87.

————. "Presentation of the Book *The Power and the Grace*." *30Days* 5 (2005). http://www.30giorni.it/articoli_id_8926_l3.htm.

————. "The Ecclesiology of the Second Vatican Council." In *Church, Ecumenism, and Politics: New Endeavors in Ecclesiology*, translated by Michael J. Miller et al., 3–62. San Francisco: Ignatius Press, 2008.

Reyes Alcaide, Hernan. *Papa Francisco: Latinoamérica*. Buenos Aires: Planeta, 2017.

Riccardi, Andrea. *La sorpresa di papa Francesco*. Milan: Mondadori, 2013.

Riebe-Estrella, Gary, SVD. "Pueblo and Church." Pp. 172–88 in *From the Heart of Our People*, edited by Orlando O. Espín and Miguel H. Díaz. Maryknoll, NY: Orbis, 1999.

Rourke, Thomas R. *The Roots of Pope Francis's Social and Political Thought: From Argentina to the Vatican*. Lanham, MD: Rowman & Littlefield, 2016.

Rowland, Tracey. *Ratzinger's Faith: The Theology of Pope Benedict XVI*. Oxford: Oxford University Press, 2008.

Sales, Michel. *Gaston Fessard, 1897–1978: genèse d'une pensée; suivi d'un résumé du «Mystère de la société» par Gaston Fessard.* Brussels: Culture et vérité, 1997.

Saranyana, Josep-Ignasi. *Teología en América Latina.* Vol. 3, *El siglo de las teologías latinoamericanistas (1899–2001).* Madrid: Iberoamericana-Vervuert, 2002.

Savorana, Alberto. *The Life of Luigi Giussani.* Translated by Mariangela Sullivan and Christopher Bacich. Montreal: McGill-Queen's University Press, 2018.

Scannone, Juan Carlos, SJ. "Lucio Gera: un teólogo 'dal' popolo." *Civiltà Cattolica* 3954 (March 2015): 539–50.

———. "Pope Francis and the Theology of the People." *Theological Studies* 77 (2016): 118–35.

———. *La teología del pueblo: Raíces teológicas del papa Francisco.* Maliaño: Sal Terrae, 2017.

Schlumpf, Heidi. "At 'Authentic Reform,' Conservative Catholics Rally to 'Fix' Church Failures." *National Catholic Reporter*, October 5, 2018. http://www.ncronline.org/news/accountability/authentic-reform -conservative-catholics-rally-fix-church-failures.

Second Vatican Council. *Lumen Gentium.* Dogmatic Constitution on the Church. November 21, 1964. http://www.vatican.va/archive/hist _councils/ii_vatican_council/documents/vat-ii_const_19641121 _lumen-gentium_en.html.

Serra-Coetanea, Dominique. *Le défi actuel du Bien commun dans la doctrine sociale de l'Église. Études à partir de l'approche de Gaston Fessard S.J.* Zurich: LIT, 2016.

Spadaro, Antonio, SJ. "Intervista a Papa Francesco." *La Civiltà Cattolica* 3918 (September 19, 2013): 449–77. English translation published as "A Big Heart Open to God," *America*, September 19, 2013. https://www .americamagazine.org/faith/2013/09/30/big-heart-open-god -interview-pope-francis.

———. "L'amicizia è questione di un momento." Foreword to *Papa Francesco è come un bambù: alle radici della cultura dell'incontro,* by Diego Fares, SJ, 8–17. Milan: Àncora–La Civiltà Cattolica, 2014.

———. "Le orme di un pastore: una conversazione con Papa Francesco." Introduction to *Nei tuoi occhi è la mia parola: Omelie e discorsi di Buenos Aires 1999–2013,* by Jorge Mario Bergoglio, v–xix. Milan: Rizzoli, 2016.

————. "Grace Is Not an Ideology: Pope Francis' Private Conversation with Some Colombian Jesuits." *La Civiltà Cattolica*, September 28, 2017. http://laciviltacattolica.com/grace-is-not-an-ideology-a-private -conversation-with-some-colombian-jesuits/.

Steiner, George. *After Babel*. 3rd ed. Oxford: Oxford University Press, 1998.

Tagore, Rabindranath. *Gitanjali*. London: Macmillan, 1918.

Tampe, Luis A., SJ. *Encuentro Nacional Hispano de Pastoral (1972–1985): An Historical and Ecclesiological Analysis*. PhD diss., Catholic University of America, 2014.

Tanner, Kathryn. "Theology and Cultural Contest in the University." In *Religious Studies, Theology, and the University: Conflicting Maps, Changing Terrain*, edited by Linell E. Cady and Delwin Brown, 199–212. Albany, NY: SUNY Press, 2002.

Tarruella, Alejandro C. *Guardia de Hierro: De Perón a Bergoglio*. Buenos Aires: Punto de Encuentro, 2016.

Theobald, Christoph, SJ. *Urgences pastorales: comprendre, partager, réformer*. Paris: Bayard, 2017.

Toso, Mario, and José Paradiso, "Preface." In *Noi come cittadini, noi come popolo* [Italian translation of Bergoglio, *Nosotros como ciudadanos*], by Jorge Mario Bergoglio, 7–17. Milan: Jaca, 2013.

Vatican Secretary of State. *Annuario Pontificio (2017)*. Vatican City: Libreria Editrice Vaticana, 2017.

Vitale, Dario. "Il Papa sottolinea il ruolo dei laici per superare il clericalismo: Interview with Dario Vitale." By Andrea Tornielli. *Vatican Insider*, April 29, 2016. http://www.lastampa.it/2016/04/29/vaticaninsider /il-papa-sottolinea-il-ruolo-dei-laici-per-superare-il-clericalismo -yHbS2KESAr93tsC8ChYGGL/pagina.html.

Von Balthasar, Hans Urs. *A Theological Anthropology*. New York: Sheed and Ward, 1967. Originally published as *Das Ganze im Fragment: Aspekte der Geschichtstheologie* (Einsiedeln: Benziger, 1963). Translated into Spanish as *El todo en el fragmento* (Madrid: Encuentro, 2008).

————. *The Office of Peter and the Structure of the Church*. San Francisco: Ignatius, 1986. Originally published as *Der Antirömische Affekt* (Freiburg im Breisgau: Herder, 1974).

————. *Theo-Drama: Theological Dramatic Theory*, vol. 3, *Dramatis Personae: Persons in Christ*. Translated by Graham Harrison. San Francisco: Ignatius, 1992.

————. *Theo-Logic*, vol. 1, *The Truth of the World*. San Francisco: Ignatius, 2001. Originally published as *Wahrheit*, vol. 1, *Wahrheit der Welt* (Einsiedeln: Benziger, 1947), which was incorporated into his *Theologik* series as *Theologik*, vol. 1, *Wahrheit der Welt* (Einsiedeln: Johannes, 1985). Translated into Spanish as *La esencia de la verdad*. Buenos Aires: Sudamericana, 1955.

————. *The Glory of the Lord: A Theological Aesthetics*, vol. 1, *Seeing the Form*, 2nd ed. Translated by Erasmo Leiva-Merikakis. San Francisco: Ignatius, 2009. Originally published as *Herrlichkeit eine theologische Ästhetik*, vol. 1, *Schau der Gestalt* (Einsiedeln: Johannes, 1961). Translated into Spanish as *Gloria I* (Madrid: Encuentro, 1985).

White, Christopher. "Wealthy Catholics to Target Cardinals with 'Red Hat Report.'" *Crux*, October 1, 2018. http://cruxnow.com/church-in-the -usa/2018/10/01/wealthy-catholics-to-target-cardinals-with-red-hat -report/.

White House Office of the Press Secretary, The. "Remarks by President Obama and His Holiness Pope Francis at Arrival Ceremony." September 23, 2015. https://www.whitehouse.gov/the-press-office/2015/09/23 /remarks-president-obama-and-his-holiness-pope-francis-arrival -ceremony.

Wojtyła, Karol. *Amour et responsabilité. Étude de morale sexuelle*. Preface by Henri de Lubac. Paris: Societé d'Editions Internationales, 1965.

————. *The Acting Person*. Translated by Andrezej Potocki. Dordrecht: D. Reidel, 1979. Originally published as *Osoba i czyn*. Krakow: Pol. Tow. Teologiczne, 1969. Translated into Italian as *Persona e Atto. Testo polacco a fronte*. Edited by Giovanni Reale and Tadeusz Styczen. Milan: Bompiani, 2001.

Index